AZURE MASTERY

Azure Mastery

FROM NOVICE TO EXPERT

Dr. Hesham Mohamed Elsherif

ELDONUSA Publishing

Contents

1

ABOUT THE AUTHOR

Azure Mastery
From Novice to
Your Comprehensive Guide to Mastering Cloud Computing with
Microsoft Azure
By
Dr. Hesham Mohamed Elsherif

An expert in Empirical research methodology, Dr. Elsherif special-
izes particularly in the Qualitative approach and Action research. This
specialization has not only strengthened his research endeavors but has

also allowed him to contribute invaluable insights and advancements in these areas.

Over the years, Dr. Elsherif has made significant contributions to the academic world not only as a professional researcher but also as an Adjunct Professor. This multifaceted role in the educational landscape has further solidified his reputation as a thought leader and pioneer.

Furthermore, Dr. Elsherif's expertise isn't confined to one region. He has served as a consultant to numerous educational institutions on an international scale, sharing best practices, innovative strategies, and his deep insights into the ever-evolving realms of management and technology.

Combining a passion for education with an unparalleled depth of knowledge, Dr. Elsherif continues to inspire, educate, and lead in both the library and academic communities.

2

PREFACE

Welcome to "Azure Mastery: From Novice to Expert: Your Comprehensive Guide to Mastering Cloud Computing with Microsoft Azure," a journey designed to transform you from an Azure enthusiast into a skilled cloud computing expert. This book is the culmination of years of experience, learning, and passion for Azure cloud services. It aims to equip you with the knowledge and skills necessary to navigate, utilize, and excel in the Azure environment.

Why Azure?

In the world of cloud computing, Microsoft Azure has emerged as a leader, offering a wide range of services that cater to various IT needs—from simple web app hosting to complex machine learning algorithms and everything in between. Azure's scalability, security, and flexibility make it an excellent choice for businesses and individuals alike, driving an increasing demand for Azure-literate professionals in the job market.

Who Should Read This Book?

This book is crafted for anyone passionate about cloud computing, regardless of their current level of expertise. Whether you are a student stepping into the world of IT, a developer looking to expand your cloud computing skills, an IT professional aiming to transition to cloud services, or even a decision-maker seeking to understand the potential of Azure for your business, this book is for you.

What You Will Learn

"Azure Mastery: From Novice to Expert" is structured to take you through a comprehensive learning path, starting from the fundamental concepts of cloud computing to the advanced features and best practices of Azure. Here's what you can expect to learn:

- The basics of cloud computing and how Azure fits into the cloud ecosystem.
- Step-by-step guidance on setting up your Azure account and managing resources.
- In-depth exploration of Azure services, including computing, storage, and networking.
- Practical insights into managing Azure with the Azure Portal, PowerShell, and CLI.
- Key security principles, including securing your Azure environment and data compliance.
- Developing and deploying applications in Azure, utilizing databases, serverless computing, and more.
- Advanced topics, such as Azure DevOps, architecture best practices, data analytics, and AI.
- Real-world case studies to demonstrate the application of Azure solutions in various scenarios.
- Preparation for Azure certifications to validate your skills and enhance your career prospects.

How This Book Is Organized

The book is divided into four parts, each building on the knowledge gained in the previous one. We begin with the basics, gradually move to practical applications and development, then to advanced topics and real-world scenarios, and finally, we guide you through preparing for Azure certifications.

Your Journey Ahead

Embarking on this journey will not only enhance your technical skills but also open up new opportunities in your career. Cloud computing is a field that continues to evolve, and with Azure at the forefront, mastering it will ensure you are well-equipped for the future.

We invite you to dive into the pages that follow with an open mind and a keen desire to learn. "Azure Mastery: From Novice to Expert" is not just a book but a companion on your journey to becoming an Azure expert.

Let the journey begin!!

3

WHO SHOULD READ THIS BOOK?

"Azure Mastery: From Novice to Expert: Your Comprehensive Guide to Mastering Cloud Computing with Microsoft Azure" is meticulously designed to cater to a wide audience, ranging from beginners with no prior knowledge of Azure to seasoned professionals looking to deepen their expertise. Whether you're embarking on a new career, seeking to upgrade your skills, or exploring the vast opportunities Azure cloud services offer, this guide is tailored for you. Below, we outline specific groups who will find this book particularly beneficial:

Beginners in Cloud Computing

If cloud computing seems like uncharted territory, this book is your compass. It starts with the fundamentals, making it perfect for readers with little to no background in cloud technology. You'll learn the basics of cloud services, the architecture of cloud computing, and gradually move to more complex concepts, all while being supported with practical examples.

IT Professionals and Developers

For IT professionals and developers looking to transition into cloud services or enhance their cloud computing skills, this book offers a deep dive into Azure's services and best practices. It covers everything from virtual machines and web services to AI and machine learning capabilities within Azure, providing you with the skills needed to design, deploy, and manage Azure solutions effectively.

Students and Educators

Students pursuing a degree in IT or computer science, as well as educators teaching cloud computing courses, will find this book an invaluable resource. It not only covers the theoretical aspects of Azure cloud computing but also includes practical exercises and real-world case studies that bring the concepts to life.

Decision Makers and Business Leaders

Understanding the capabilities and benefits of Azure can empower decision-makers to make informed choices about their IT infrastructure. This book demystifies cloud computing for non-technical readers, providing insights into how Azure can be leveraged to drive business innovation, agility, and digital transformation.

Azure Certification Aspirants

If you're aiming to achieve Azure certification, this book serves as a comprehensive study guide. It aligns with the core objectives of the Azure certification exams, offering detailed explanations, practical scenarios, and tips to help you prepare and succeed in earning your certification.

Tech Enthusiasts and Hobbyists

Even if you're exploring Azure out of personal interest or as a hobby, this book offers a structured way to learn and experiment with cloud computing. The step-by-step guides and project-based learning approach make it engaging for anyone keen on understanding the cloud's potential.

Professionals Seeking Career Advancement

For those in the tech industry looking to advance their careers, mastering Azure can open doors to new opportunities. With the demand for cloud computing skills on the rise, this book provides the knowledge and tools needed to position yourself as a valuable asset in the job market.

"Azure Mastery: From Novice to Expert" is not just a book; it's a roadmap to unlocking the full potential of Microsoft Azure. It's designed to grow with you, providing deeper insights and more complex scenarios as your skills develop. No matter where you are in your professional journey, this guide aims to elevate your understanding of cloud computing and equip you with the skills to master Azure.

Dr. Hesham Mohamed Elsherif

4

WHY THIS BOOK IS ESSENTIAL READING?

Bridging the Gap Between Theory and Practice

"Azure Mastery: From Novice to Expert" is not just another textbook on cloud computing; it is a practical guide that bridges the gap between theoretical knowledge and real-world application. This book provides a comprehensive look into Microsoft Azure, one of the leading cloud platforms, making it essential reading for anyone looking to deepen their understanding of cloud computing and how to apply it using Azure. Through detailed explanations, practical examples, and real-world case studies, this book ensures that readers not only learn the concepts but also understand how to apply them in their daily work.

Comprehensive Coverage

From the foundational principles of cloud computing to the intricacies of Azure's services, this book covers it all. Whether you're interested in virtual machines, web apps, databases, AI, or IoT, "Azure Mastery" provides detailed insights into each aspect. The breadth and depth of topics make this book an invaluable resource for learners at all levels, ensuring that even experienced professionals will find new insights and techniques.

Up-to-Date and Future-Ready

In the rapidly evolving field of cloud computing, staying current is crucial. "Azure Mastery: From Novice to Expert" is crafted with the latest developments and best practices in Azure and cloud computing. The book not only covers the current landscape but also looks ahead, preparing readers for future trends and technologies. This forward-thinking approach ensures that you remain relevant in the field.

Hands-On Learning

One of the core strengths of this book is its emphasis on hands-on learning. Through guided tutorials, practical exercises, and access to online labs, readers can apply what they learn in real-time. This hands-on approach solidifies understanding and builds confidence, making complex concepts more accessible and enjoyable to learn.

Preparing for Certifications

For those looking to validate their skills and advance their careers, "Azure Mastery" serves as an excellent resource for preparing for Azure certifications. The book aligns with the objectives of key Azure certification exams, providing readers with the knowledge and practice needed to succeed. Certification can open doors to new job opportunities, promotions, and professional recognition.

For the Curious and Ambitious

"Azure Mastery: From Novice to Expert" is more than just a guide to Azure; it's a testament to the power of curiosity and ambition in the tech world. It encourages readers to explore, experiment, and excel. By the end of this book, you won't just be proficient in Azure; you'll be empowered to innovate and lead in the cloud computing space.

A Community of Learners

Finally, this book offers more than knowledge—it offers entry into a community. Through online forums, webinars, and group discussions, readers can connect with peers, share insights, and find support. This community aspect enriches the learning experience, making "Azure Mastery" not just a book but a journey shared with like-minded individuals passionate about cloud computing.

In a landscape dominated by technology, understanding cloud computing is not just an advantage; it's a necessity. "Azure Mastery: From Novice to Expert" is the key to unlocking that understanding, making it essential reading for anyone looking to make their mark in the world of cloud computing with Microsoft Azure.

Happy Reading!!!!

Dr. Hesham Mohamed Elsherif

5

Chapter 1: Understanding Cloud Computing

Part I: Introduction to Azure

Cloud computing has revolutionized the way we think about IT infrastructure and software delivery, offering a more flexible, scalable, and cost-effective alternative to traditional on-premises solutions. At its core, cloud computing is the delivery of computing services—including servers, storage, databases, networking, software, analytics, and intelligence—over the Internet ("the cloud") to offer faster innovation, flexible resources, and economies of scale.

The Evolution of Cloud Computing

To appreciate the significance of cloud computing, it's important to understand its evolution. Traditionally, businesses and individuals would host their own hardware and software, requiring significant upfront investment and ongoing maintenance. As the internet became more robust and reliable, the possibility of hosting these services remotely became viable, leading to the birth of cloud computing. This paradigm shift has enabled users to access and manage their resources online, with providers taking care of the backend complexities.

Key Characteristics of Cloud Computing

Cloud computing is defined by several key characteristics that differentiate it from traditional hosting:

On-demand self-service:

Users can provision computing resources such as processing power and storage without requiring human interaction with the service provider.

One of the defining characteristics of cloud computing is on-demand self-service, a feature that fundamentally changes how resources are consumed and managed in the IT landscape. This characteristic allows users to automatically provision computing resources, such as server time and network storage, as needed without requiring human interaction with the service provider. This self-service capability underpins the flexibility, scalability, and efficiency that make cloud computing so appealing.

The Essence of On-demand Self-service

At its core, on-demand self-service enables users to access computing resources and services anytime and anywhere, provided they have an internet connection. This means that businesses and developers can launch new applications, scale existing ones, or allocate additional storage on the fly, without the need to wait for approval or assistance from the cloud provider's personnel. This autonomy is pivotal in accelerating development cycles, improving responsiveness to business needs, and enhancing the overall agility of organizations.

How On-demand Self-service Works

On-demand self-service in cloud computing typically involves a web-based dashboard or API through which users can manage their resources. This interface allows users to:

Provision Resources: Users can create, configure, and deploy instances of virtual machines, databases, storage, and more within minutes.

Scale Resources: Based on the demand, users can scale resources up or down, ensuring optimal performance and cost efficiency.

Monitor and Manage: Users have the tools to monitor the performance and health of their resources, manage configurations, and troubleshoot issues as they arise.

Automate: Advanced users can automate common tasks such as backups, scaling, and deployments through scripting and cloud management tools.

Benefits of On-demand Self-service

Speed and Agility: Enables rapid deployment of resources, helping organizations to quickly respond to opportunities and challenges.

Cost Efficiency: Pay-per-use pricing models mean organizations only pay for what they use, reducing wasted resources and overhead.

Reduced Dependency: Minimizes reliance on IT staff for resource provisioning, allowing them to focus on more strategic tasks.

Empowerment and Innovation: Developers and business units can experiment and innovate more freely, testing new ideas without lengthy procurement processes.

Challenges and Considerations

While on-demand self-service offers numerous advantages, it also presents challenges that organizations need to manage:

Governance and Control: Ensuring proper oversight and management of resources to avoid sprawl and maintain compliance.

Cost Management: While pay-per-use models offer cost efficiency, unmonitored resource consumption can lead to unexpected expenses.

Security and Privacy: Self-service access increases the potential for misconfigured services, which can expose vulnerabilities.

On-demand self-service is a cornerstone of cloud computing, offering unprecedented flexibility and control over computing resources. It empowers users to manage their IT needs efficiently, fostering innovation and agility within organizations. However, realizing its full benefits requires careful management of governance, cost, and security. As we delve deeper into cloud computing and specifically Azure, understanding and leveraging on-demand self-service will be key to maximizing the potential of the cloud environment.

Broad network access:

Services are available over the network and accessed through standard mechanisms that promote use by heterogeneous thin or thick client platforms (e.g., mobile phones, tablets, laptops, and workstations).

Broad network access is a fundamental characteristic of cloud computing that ensures services are accessible over the network through standard mechanisms. This feature supports a wide array of devices, including mobile phones, tablets, laptops, and workstations, enabling users to access computing resources and applications from anywhere, at any time. This accessibility is crucial for the modern, mobile, and interconnected world, where businesses and individuals expect to remain productive and connected regardless of location.

The Principle of Broad Network Access

Broad network access is designed to ensure that cloud services and resources are readily available over the Internet or a private network, using protocols that maintain the security and integrity of data transmission. This universal access principle means that resources hosted in the cloud are not confined to a single device or location; instead, they can be accessed and used across various platforms and devices, fostering flexibility and mobility.

Implementing Broad Network Access

Cloud providers implement broad network access through highly available and scalable infrastructures that are optimized for access over public and private networks. This involves:

Support for Multiple Devices: Cloud services are designed to be device-agnostic, offering interfaces and experiences optimized for desktops, laptops, tablets, and smartphones.

Use of Standard Protocols: Cloud services use standard Internet protocols (HTTP, HTTPS, SMTP, FTP, etc.) and web services standards (SOAP, REST, etc.), ensuring interoperability and ease of access across different platforms and devices.

Secure Access Controls: Despite the broad availability, security is a top priority, with encryption, authentication, and access controls in place to protect data and resources from unauthorized access.

Benefits of Broad Network Access

Flexibility and Mobility: Users can access services and data from anywhere, enabling remote work, real-time collaboration, and continuous productivity.

Device Independence: The ability to use cloud services from any device enhances user experiences and satisfaction, catering to the diverse preferences and working styles of users.

Cost Efficiency: Organizations can reduce investments in physical infrastructure and device-specific applications, as cloud services can be accessed through standard, commonly available devices.

Challenges and Considerations

While broad network access provides significant advantages, it also introduces challenges that need to be addressed:

Bandwidth and Connectivity: Adequate bandwidth and reliable Internet connectivity are crucial for accessing cloud services, which can be a limitation in areas with poor infrastructure.

Security and Privacy: The wide accessibility of cloud services necessitates robust security measures to protect against cyber threats and ensure data privacy.

Performance Optimization: Ensuring consistent performance across different devices and network conditions requires careful optimization and testing by cloud providers.

Broad network access is a key characteristic that distinguishes cloud computing from traditional computing models, offering unprecedented flexibility and connectivity. It enables a seamless, device-agnostic user experience, empowering users to access and utilize cloud resources from anywhere in the world. However, leveraging this advantage effectively requires careful consideration of connectivity, security, and performance issues. As cloud computing continues to evolve, broad network access will remain a critical feature, facilitating the ongoing shift towards more mobile, flexible, and accessible computing solutions.

Resource pooling:

The provider's computing resources are pooled to serve multiple consumers using a multi-tenant model, with different physical and virtual resources dynamically assigned and reassigned according to consumer demand.

Resource pooling is a fundamental characteristic of cloud computing that enables providers to serve multiple customers (tenants) from the same physical resources, using a multi-tenant model. This approach maximizes efficiency by dynamically allocating and reallocating resources based on demand, without the tenants needing to manage or control the underlying technology infrastructure. Resource pooling allows for cost savings, scalability, and flexibility, making it a cornerstone of cloud computing's value proposition.

The Concept of Resource Pooling

At the heart of resource pooling is the idea that physical and virtual resources (such as storage, processing power, memory, and network bandwidth) are pooled by the cloud provider to serve multiple customers. These resources are dynamically assigned and reassigned according to customer demand. The process is largely transparent to the user, who sees only the abstracted capabilities (e.g., storage space or processing power) they're using, not the complex mechanisms managing those resources behind the scenes.

How Resource Pooling Works

Dynamic Allocation: Cloud systems automatically control and optimize resource use, dynamically assigning resources to customers as needed. This is done through sophisticated algorithms and management software that monitor demand in real time.

Multi-tenancy: Multiple customers share the same infrastructure and applications, with each tenant's data and configurations kept isolated and secure. This model is similar to an apartment building, where many tenants live in separate units but share the same underlying structure.

Scalability and Elasticity: Resource pooling supports rapid scaling of resources to accommodate spikes in demand, ensuring that services remain responsive and available without requiring customers to over-provision resources.

Benefits of Resource Pooling

Cost Efficiency: By aggregating demand and sharing resources among multiple users, cloud providers achieve high levels of utilization and efficiency, translating into lower costs for customers.

Flexibility and Scalability: Customers can scale their usage up or down based on their needs, without worrying about physical hardware limitations.

Simplified Management: The cloud provider manages the pooled resources, relieving customers of the complexity of directly managing hardware and infrastructure.

Challenges and Considerations

Privacy and Security: Ensuring data isolation and security in a multi-tenant environment is critical. Cloud providers implement robust security measures to protect data, but customers should understand these measures and their responsibilities.

Performance: "Noisy neighbor" issues can arise when one tenant's heavy usage impacts the performance for others. Providers use sophisticated resource allocation strategies to mitigate this risk.

Compliance and Data Sovereignty: Sharing resources across multiple jurisdictions can raise compliance and data sovereignty issues. Customers need to ensure their cloud usage complies with relevant laws and regulations.

Resource pooling is a key feature that allows cloud computing to deliver its promise of efficiency, scalability, and flexibility. By abstracting the physical details of the infrastructure and dynamically allocating resources among multiple customers, cloud providers can offer scalable services that can be adjusted to meet changing demands. While resource pooling offers numerous advantages, it also requires careful consideration of security, performance, and compliance issues. Understanding how resource pooling works and how it benefits your organization is essential for leveraging the cloud effectively. This foundational knowledge sets the stage for deeper exploration into the specific services and capabilities offered by platforms like Microsoft Azure, which utilize resource pooling to provide a wide range of scalable, efficient cloud solutions.

Rapid elasticity:

Capabilities can be elastically provisioned and released, in some cases automatically, to scale rapidly outward and inward commensurate with demand.

Rapid elasticity is a defining characteristic of cloud computing that distinguishes it from traditional computing paradigms. It refers to the ability of cloud services to be quickly scaled up or down to match demand, ensuring that resources are efficiently utilized and that users only pay for what they need. This capability is essential for handling variable workloads, enabling businesses to respond swiftly to changes in demand without the cost and complexity of maintaining underutilized resources.

The Essence of Rapid Elasticity

Rapid elasticity allows cloud resources—such as computational power, storage, and bandwidth—to be elastically provisioned and released. This means that resources can be dynamically scaled to accommodate workload changes, often automatically, providing the illusion of infinite resources on demand. This characteristic is crucial for applications with unpredictable workloads or for businesses that experience seasonal fluctuations in demand.

How Rapid Elasticity Works

Automated Scaling: Cloud platforms typically offer auto-scaling features that automatically adjust resource levels based on real-time demand. This process involves monitoring resource usage and automatically scaling resources up or down to maintain optimal performance and cost efficiency.

On-demand Provisioning: Users can manually scale resources through cloud management interfaces, allowing for quick adjustments to meet sudden changes in demand.

Resource Metering: Cloud platforms measure the use of resources to enable pay-per-use pricing models. This ensures that users pay only for the resources they consume, which is facilitated by the rapid elasticity of the cloud.

Benefits of Rapid Elasticity

Cost Efficiency: Organizations can optimize their spending on IT resources by scaling services to match demand, avoiding the need to over-provision resources "just in case."

Agility and Competitive Advantage: Businesses can quickly respond to opportunities and challenges without the delays associated with traditional IT provisioning, providing a competitive edge.

Improved User Experience: Rapid elasticity helps ensure that applications remain responsive under varying loads, enhancing the end-user experience.

Challenges and Considerations

While rapid elasticity offers significant advantages, there are also challenges and considerations that organizations need to address:

Capacity Planning: Although cloud resources can be scaled dynamically, effective capacity planning is still necessary to anticipate major demand spikes and to optimize the scaling strategy.

Cost Management: Without careful monitoring and management, the costs associated with rapidly scaling resources can escalate unexpectedly.

Performance Optimization: As resources are added or removed, applications and services need to be designed to seamlessly handle such changes without degrading performance.

Rapid elasticity is a cornerstone of cloud computing, enabling resources to be scaled precisely and efficiently according to demand. This characteristic supports the dynamic nature of modern digital services and applications, where demand can fluctuate widely and unpredictably. By leveraging rapid elasticity, organizations can achieve significant cost savings, improve service levels, and maintain a competitive stance in the marketplace.

Understanding and effectively managing the elastic capabilities of cloud resources is crucial for maximizing the benefits of cloud computing. As we delve deeper into Microsoft Azure and other cloud platforms, appreciating the nuances of rapid elasticity will be key to designing scalable, resilient, and cost-effective solutions.

Measured service:

Cloud systems automatically control and optimize resource use by leveraging a metering capability at some level of abstraction appropriate to the type of service (e.g., storage, processing, bandwidth, and active user accounts).

Measured service is a fundamental characteristic of cloud computing that allows resources to be monitored, controlled, and reported, providing transparency for both the provider and the consumer. This pay-per-use model is integral to the cloud's cost-efficiency and scalability, ensuring users only pay for the resources they actually use, such as storage, processing, bandwidth, and active user accounts. Measured service transforms traditional IT financing from a capital expenditure (CapEx) model to an operational expenditure (OpEx) model, aligning costs directly with usage.

The Principle of Measured Service

The principle of measured service revolves around the ability of cloud systems to automatically monitor and measure the use of resources in real-time. This metering capability enables dynamic allocation of resources and provides detailed usage reports, helping users to optimize their cloud spending and resource utilization. By leveraging measured service, organizations can achieve significant cost savings and operational efficiencies.

Implementing Measured Service

Cloud providers implement measured service through advanced metering technologies that track the consumption of resources. These technologies allow for:

Granular Usage Metrics: Providers track the usage of each resource (CPU cycles, memory usage, data transfer, etc.) with high granularity, often in real-time.

Billing and Chargeback: Usage data is used to generate billing information, allowing for transparent chargeback to departments or customers based on their consumption.

Resource Optimization: Detailed usage statistics help users identify inefficient resource allocations, enabling them to adjust their consumption patterns to improve efficiency and reduce costs.

Benefits of Measured Service

Cost Transparency and Accountability: Users have clear visibility into their resource consumption and costs, promoting responsible usage and allowing for accurate budgeting and forecasting.

Flexibility and Scalability: The ability to pay for only what is used encourages experimentation and innovation, as there is no significant financial penalty for scaling resources up or down.

Optimized Resource Utilization: Real-time monitoring and reporting enable users to optimize their resource usage, eliminating waste and improving overall efficiency.

Challenges and Considerations

While measured service offers numerous advantages, it also presents challenges that organizations need to manage:

Complex Billing: The granularity of cloud billing can sometimes lead to complexity, making it difficult for users to predict and manage costs without proper tools and processes.

Resource Management: The dynamic nature of cloud resource allocation requires continuous monitoring and management to avoid unnecessary expenses.

Cost Control: Without careful management, the ease of provisioning resources can lead to "bill shock" if consumption is not closely monitored.

Measured service is a key characteristic that distinguishes cloud computing from traditional IT provisioning, offering a level of flexibility, scalability, and financial control that was previously unattainable. It empowers organizations to closely align their IT spending with business value, ensuring that they only pay for the resources they need when they need them. Understanding and effectively managing measured service is essential for maximizing the benefits of cloud computing. As part of the broader cloud computing model, measured service plays a critical role in enabling the efficient and cost-effective use of resources, making it a cornerstone of the value proposition offered by cloud platforms like Microsoft Azure.

Service Models

Cloud computing is often categorized into three primary service models, each offering different levels of control, flexibility, and management:

Infrastructure as a Service (IaaS):

Provides virtualized computing resources over the internet. Users manage the operating systems, storage, and deployed applications, and sometimes limited control of select networking components (e.g., host firewalls).

Infrastructure as a Service (IaaS) is one of the fundamental service models of cloud computing, providing virtualized computing resources over the internet. IaaS offers a highly scalable and automated compute infrastructure, granting users access to computing resources such as virtual machines (VMs), storage, networks, and operating systems. This model allows businesses to purchase resources on-demand and scale up or down as required, reducing the need for expensive and underutilized in-house hardware.

The Essence of IaaS

IaaS delivers a virtualized platform, abstracting the physical hardware (servers, network technology, storage, and data center space) and allowing users to deploy and run arbitrary software, including operating systems and applications. The service provider manages the infrastructure, while the user has control over operating systems, storage, deployed applications, and possibly limited control of select networking components (e.g., host firewalls).

Key Components of IaaS

Virtual Machines (VMs): Software emulations of physical computers, providing the compute environment.

Storage: Scalable storage solutions, including block storage for VMs, file storage for accessibility, and object storage for scalability.

Networking: Virtual networks and connectivity services that link VMs to each other and to the internet, providing secure access to the IaaS environment.

Management Tools: Automated and manual tools for managing, monitoring, and optimizing the cloud resources.

Benefits of IaaS

Flexibility and Scalability: Easily scalable resources to meet demand, with users paying only for what they use, facilitating both temporary spikes and long-term growth.

Cost-Effectiveness: Reduces the upfront cost of setting up and maintaining an on-premises data center, shifting capital expenditure (CapEx) to operational expenditure (OpEx).

Control and Customization: Users retain complete control over the software environment, allowing for customization based on specific needs.

Speed and Agility: Rapid deployment of resources shortens the time to market for applications and services.

Use Cases for IaaS

Web Hosting: Hosting websites on virtual servers that scale on demand, accommodating traffic spikes without the need for physical hardware.

Test and Development: Providing flexible, cost-effective environments for development, testing, and staging applications.

Storage, Backup, and Recovery: Addressing data storage needs with scalable solutions, while simplifying backup and recovery strategies.

Web Apps: Supporting web applications with scalable, on-demand resources to handle varying loads.

High-Performance Computing (HPC): Utilizing vast computing power on demand for complex computations like simulations and big data analytics.

Challenges and Considerations

Security: While providers ensure the security of the infrastructure, users are responsible for securing their software and data, necessitating a shared security model.

Management Complexity: The flexibility and control offered by IaaS can also introduce complexity in configuration, management, and monitoring.

Cost Management: Without careful monitoring and management, the cost of consumed resources can escalate quickly.

Infrastructure as a Service (IaaS) is a versatile and powerful model that enables businesses of all sizes to leverage sophisticated computing infrastructure without the significant capital investment traditionally required. It offers scalability, flexibility, and cost-efficiency, making it an ideal solution for a wide range of computing tasks from web hosting to high-performance computing. As organizations continue to embrace digital transformation, IaaS stands out as a critical component of an effective cloud computing strategy, providing the foundation upon which businesses can innovate and grow in the digital era.

Platform as a Service (PaaS):

Offers hardware and software tools over the internet, typically for application development. Users manage the applications and data, while the provider manages everything else.

Platform as a Service (PaaS) is one of the primary cloud computing service models, providing developers and IT professionals with a platform and environment to develop, host, and deploy applications. PaaS delivers a framework for developers that they can build upon and use to create customized applications. Unlike Infrastructure as a Service (IaaS), where the focus is on managing virtual machines, storage, and networking, PaaS provides a higher level of abstraction. It automates and manages infrastructure tasks, allowing developers to focus on the development and deployment of their applications without worrying about underlying hardware and software layers.

Core Components of PaaS

PaaS typically includes a suite of integrated development tools, libraries, and languages that developers can use to build applications quickly and efficiently. Key components often include:

Development Tools: Integrated development environments (IDEs), version control, compilation, testing, and debugging tools.

Middleware: Software that connects different applications or services for data exchange, such as web servers, content management systems, and messaging systems.

Operating Systems: Managed and maintained by the PaaS provider, offering a stable environment for application deployment.

Database Management: Managed database services that support various database types, ensuring scalability, data security, and backup.

Application Hosting: The infrastructure and systems necessary to host and run applications, ensuring they are accessible to users over the internet.

Advantages of PaaS

Reduced Development Time: By providing a pre-configured platform, PaaS significantly reduces the time and complexity involved in setting up environments, allowing developers to focus on coding.

Cost-Efficiency: PaaS follows a pay-as-you-go model, eliminating the need for significant upfront investment in hardware and software. Additionally, it reduces the cost associated with purchasing, managing, and upgrading hardware and software.

Scalability: Applications built on PaaS can easily scale resources up or down based on demand, without requiring changes to the application.

Multi-language and Multi-framework Support: PaaS platforms typically support multiple programming languages and frameworks, offering developers flexibility in choosing the best tools for their applications.

Considerations and Challenges

Vendor Lock-in: Developers may become dependent on specific services and tools provided by the PaaS platform, potentially making it difficult to migrate to another platform in the future.

Limited Control: While PaaS offers ease of use and efficiency, it provides less control over the underlying infrastructure compared to IaaS. This may not be suitable for applications requiring specific customizations or configurations.

Security Concerns: Since applications are hosted on shared infrastructure, there may be concerns about data security and privacy. It's crucial to evaluate the security measures and compliance certifications of the PaaS provider.

Popular PaaS Examples

Microsoft Azure App Service: Offers a fully managed platform for building, deploying, and scaling web apps and APIs quickly and efficiently.

Google App Engine: Allows developers to build highly scalable applications on a fully managed serverless platform.

Heroku: A cloud platform as a service supporting several programming languages, Heroku lets developers build, run, and scale applications in a similar manner across all languages.

Platform as a Service (PaaS) represents a significant evolution in cloud computing, providing developers with a powerful and flexible platform for application development and deployment. By abstracting much of the complexity associated with infrastructure management, PaaS enables organizations to focus on innovation and delivering value to their users. Whether developing new applications or scaling existing ones, PaaS offers a comprehensive, cost-effective, and scalable solution that aligns with the needs of modern software development.

Software as a Service (SaaS):

Delivers software applications over the internet, on a subscription basis. Users do not manage or control the underlying infrastructure but may have user-specific application configuration settings.

Software as a Service (SaaS) is a cloud computing service model that delivers software applications over the internet, on a subscription basis. SaaS eliminates the need for organizations to install and run applications on their own computers or in their data centers, which alleviates the expense of hardware acquisition, provisioning and maintenance, as well as software licensing, installation, and support. With SaaS, service providers host and maintain the servers, databases, and code that constitute an application.

Key Characteristics of SaaS

SaaS applications are accessible from any internet-enabled device, providing users with flexibility and mobility that traditional software models cannot match. This ease of access, combined with a subscription pricing model, makes SaaS a popular choice for businesses of all sizes. Key characteristics include:

Accessibility: SaaS applications are accessible from anywhere with an internet connection, typically through a web browser on various devices, enhancing user mobility.

Subscription Model: Users pay for SaaS applications on a subscription basis, which often includes maintenance, compliance, and security updates.

Multi-tenancy: A single instance of the application serves multiple customers. Each customer's data and configurations are kept separate, ensuring privacy and security.

Automatic Updates: Service providers manage software updates and patches, ensuring users always have access to the latest features without additional upgrade costs.

Advantages of SaaS

Lower Initial Costs: SaaS applications do not require large initial investments in hardware or software licenses, making it easier for businesses to adopt new technologies.

Scalability and Integration: SaaS solutions are scalable on demand, and they can be easily integrated with other SaaS offerings. Subscription plans typically offer different tiers to suit the size and scale of a business.

Outsourced IT Management: SaaS providers handle IT responsibilities and maintenance, such as software updates and security patching, reducing the burden on in-house IT staff.

Ease of Use and Deployment: SaaS applications are often user-friendly and can be deployed quickly, enabling businesses to accelerate their digital transformation efforts.

Considerations and Challenges

Data Security: Since data is stored on the service provider's servers, concerns about data security and privacy are paramount. Users must trust the provider to implement robust security measures.

Limited Control: Users have less control over the functionality and performance of a SaaS application compared to on-premises software. Customization options may be limited.

Internet Dependency: Accessing SaaS applications requires a reliable internet connection. Performance issues can arise from low bandwidth or high latency.

Vendor Lock-in: Migrating from one SaaS provider to another can be challenging, potentially leading to vendor lock-in. It's crucial to evaluate data portability options before committing to a SaaS product.

Popular SaaS Examples

Microsoft Office 365: Provides a suite of office applications, including Word, Excel, and PowerPoint, delivered over the internet with additional collaboration tools and cloud storage.

Salesforce: A comprehensive customer relationship management (CRM) solution that offers applications for sales, service, marketing, and more, all accessible via the cloud.

Google Workspace: A suite of productivity and collaboration tools that includes Gmail, Docs, Drive, Calendar, and more, designed for business use.

Software as a Service (SaaS) has emerged as a dominant model in cloud computing by offering a compelling alternative to traditional software delivery. It provides accessibility, cost savings, and flexibility, making it an attractive option for businesses looking to streamline operations and focus on their core competencies. As with any technology decision, businesses should weigh the benefits and challenges of SaaS to determine if it aligns with their operational needs and strategic goals. With the ongoing evolution of cloud services, SaaS continues to expand its offerings, providing solutions across a broad spectrum of industries and use cases.

Deployment Models

Cloud computing can be deployed using different models, each suited to specific needs:

Public cloud:

Services are delivered over the public internet and are available to anyone willing to pay for them. Azure, AWS, and Google Cloud are examples of public clouds.

The public cloud is one of the primary deployment models in cloud computing, characterized by services and infrastructure provided over the internet by third-party cloud service providers. This model offers vast pools of resources that are shared among multiple customers, known as a multi-tenant environment. Public cloud services are available to anyone willing to subscribe or use them, often through a pay-as-you-go pricing model. This approach to cloud computing has become popular due to its scalability, reliability, and cost-effectiveness.

Key Features of Public Cloud

Scalability and Elasticity: Public clouds can easily scale resources up or down based on user demand, offering significant flexibility for fluctuating workloads.

Cost-Effectiveness: Users pay only for the resources they consume, without the need for significant upfront investments in hardware or ongoing maintenance costs. This can lead to substantial cost savings, especially for small to medium-sized enterprises.

Simplicity and Speed of Deployment: Services in the public cloud can be rapidly deployed and managed, allowing businesses to bring applications to market quickly without the delays associated with setting up and maintaining physical infrastructure.

Reliability: Due to the vast network of servers distributed across various locations, public cloud services offer high levels of reliability. Data can be mirrored at multiple redund**Low Entry Barrier**: The public cloud model allows businesses of any size to access advanced computing capabilities without needing significant capital investment in physical hardware or IT staff.

Maintenance and Upgrades: Cloud service providers are responsible for maintaining, updating, and upgrading hardware and software, ensuring that users always have access to the latest technologies.

Global Reach: Public cloud services are delivered over the internet, enabling global access. This is particularly beneficial for organizations with a widespread workforce or customer base.

Considerations and Challenges

Security and Privacy: While public cloud providers implement robust security measures, sharing resources with other organizations can raise concerns about data security and privacy. It's crucial for users to understand the security controls and compliance certifications of their chosen provider.

Compliance and Data Sovereignty: Organizations subject to regulatory requirements must ensure that their use of public cloud services complies with relevant laws, including those related to data sovereignty and protection.

Performance Variability: In a public cloud, resources are shared among multiple users, which can lead to variable performance. Organizations with high-demand applications may need to consider hybrid or private cloud solutions for more consistent performance.

Popular Public Cloud Examples

Amazon Web Services (AWS): A leading provider of public cloud services, offering a broad set of global compute, storage, database, analytics, application, and deployment services.

Microsoft Azure: Provides a wide range of cloud services, including those for computing, analytics, storage, and networking. Users can pick and choose from these services to develop and scale new applications, or run existing applications in the public cloud.

Google Cloud Platform (GCP): Offers services in computing, storage, data analytics, and machine learning, among others, leveraging Google's extensive infrastructure.

The public cloud deployment model offers a flexible, scalable, and cost-effective solution for businesses and individuals looking to leverage cloud computing. By understanding the key features, advantages, and considerations associated with the public cloud, organizations can make informed decisions about how best to incorporate these services into their IT strategy. Whether used exclusively or as part of a hybrid approach, public cloud services continue to play a pivotal role in the digital transformation of businesses worldwide.

Private cloud:

The cloud infrastructure is exclusively used by a single organization. It can be managed by the organization or a third party and can exist on or off premises.

The private cloud is a cloud computing deployment model that provides a dedicated environment for a single organization. This model combines many of the benefits of cloud computing, such as scalability and efficiency, with greater control over security, compliance, and data sovereignty. Private clouds can be hosted on-premises, in a company's data center, or by third-party service providers. Unlike public clouds, which serve multiple organizations (tenants), a private cloud is used exclusively by one organization, offering a higher level of privacy and security.

Key Features of Private Cloud

Exclusivity: Resources in a private cloud are not shared with other organizations. The infrastructure and services are maintained on a private network, providing enhanced security and control.

Customization and Control: Organizations have the flexibility to customize the cloud environment according to their specific requirements, including hardware, software, and networking configurations.

Scalability: While dedicated to a single organization, private clouds still offer scalability. Resources can be scaled up or down as needed, albeit within the constraints of the deployed infrastructure.

Enhanced Security: The private cloud model offers improved security features, as resources are not shared with other tenants. Organizations can implement their security controls, policies, and compliance measures.

Advantages of Private Cloud

Improved Security and Compliance: For organizations with strict regulatory requirements or sensitive data, private clouds provide a secure environment where compliance standards can be easily managed and enforced.

Dedicated Resources: The absence of a "noisy neighbor" effect (where another user's behavior affects your performance) ensures stable and predictable performance.

Greater Control Over the Infrastructure: Organizations maintain complete control over their infrastructure, allowing for custom configurations and optimizations to meet specific business needs.

Considerations and Challenges

Higher Costs: Setting up and maintaining a private cloud requires significant investment in hardware, software, and expertise. The costs may be higher compared to public cloud services, especially for small to medium-sized organizations.

Complexity in Management: Operating a private cloud demands a high level of expertise. Organizations need to manage, update, and secure their infrastructure, which can be complex and resource-intensive.

Limited Scalability Compared to Public Cloud: While private clouds offer scalability, they are typically constrained by the physical capacity of the underlying infrastructure. Expanding capacity may involve additional capital expenditure.

Deployment Options for Private Cloud

On-premises Private Cloud: The organization hosts the private cloud in its data center. This approach offers the highest level of control and security but requires significant investment in infrastructure and management.

Hosted Private Cloud: A third-party provider hosts the private cloud. This model reduces the need for on-premises infrastructure but still provides the benefits of a private cloud, including exclusivity and control.

Virtual Private Cloud (VPC): Offered by public cloud providers, a VPC provides a segregated section of the public cloud where resources are isolated for use by a single organization, offering a balance between control and convenience.

Popular Private Cloud Examples

VMware vCloud Suite: Offers a comprehensive private cloud solution that integrates VMware's virtualization, management, and interface technologies.

Microsoft Azure Stack: Enables organizations to bring Azure services into their data center, creating a hybrid environment that allows for running applications in both private and public clouds.

OpenStack: An open-source platform for cloud computing, primarily deployed as an infrastructure-as-a-service (IaaS) solution, allowing for the creation of private clouds.

The private cloud deployment model offers organizations enhanced control, security, and customization of their cloud environment, making it an ideal choice for businesses with strict regulatory requirements, sensitive data, or specific performance needs. While it may come with higher upfront costs and complexity in management compared to public cloud solutions, the benefits of dedicated resources and improved security often justify the investment for certain organizations. As cloud computing continues to evolve, private clouds remain a critical component of many organizations' IT strategies, providing a tailored approach to cloud computing that public clouds cannot match.

Hybrid cloud:

A combination of public and private clouds, allowing data and applications to be shared between them. This provides businesses greater flexibility and more deployment options.

The hybrid cloud is a strategic deployment model that combines public cloud, private cloud, and on-premises resources, leveraging the best of what each environment has to offer. This model provides businesses with greater flexibility, more deployment options, and helps optimize existing infrastructure, security, and compliance. By allowing workloads to move between private and public clouds as computing needs and costs change, hybrid clouds give businesses greater flexibility and more data deployment options.

Key Features of Hybrid Cloud

Interoperability: Hybrid clouds are designed to enable seamless communication and interoperability between public and private cloud environments. This allows for the free movement of applications and data between different cloud models.

Flexibility and Scalability: Organizations can scale their on-premises infrastructure up to the public cloud for handling peak loads or specific tasks, providing a flexible and cost-effective solution for varying workloads.

Balance of Control: Hybrid cloud models allow organizations to maintain sensitive data or critical applications on-premises or in a private cloud for security and compliance, while also taking advantage of the public cloud's scalability and efficiency for less sensitive workloads.

Cost Optimization: By allowing organizations to use public cloud resources for spikes in demand, the hybrid cloud model can help optimize costs. Businesses can keep their regular, predictable workloads on-premises or in a private cloud, where it might be more cost-effective.

Advantages of Hybrid Cloud

Strategic Flexibility: Businesses are not locked into a single provider or platform; they can pick and choose which workloads to run in which cloud, based on performance, cost, and regulatory requirements.

Enhanced Security: Sensitive or critical data can be kept within a private cloud or on-premises environment, while still taking advantage of the computational power of the public cloud for other tasks.

Business Continuity and Resilience: The hybrid cloud offers diverse options for disaster recovery and business continuity planning by utilizing multiple platforms, thus minimizing the risk of downtime and data loss.

Innovation and Agility: Organizations can rapidly develop and deploy applications in a public cloud environment where resources are virtually unlimited and then scale those applications into a private cloud or on-premises environment as they become more critical and stable.

Considerations and Challenges

Complexity in Management: Managing a hybrid cloud environment can be complex, requiring a good understanding of both public and private cloud technologies and the ability to integrate and manage both effectively.

Compliance and Security: Ensuring data security and regulatory compliance across multiple environments can be challenging. Businesses must implement consistent security policies and practices across all platforms.

Networking Considerations: Robust networking is crucial for a hybrid cloud to ensure data and applications can move seamlessly between environments without latency or loss of functionality.

Implementation Strategies

Successful hybrid cloud implementation involves careful planning and execution:

Assessment and Planning: Evaluate current IT infrastructure, workloads, and business requirements to identify what should run where.

Integration and Interoperability: Use middleware, APIs, and management tools that support hybrid cloud environments to ensure smooth integration between public and private clouds.

Security and Compliance: Implement a unified security strategy that covers all parts of the hybrid cloud to protect data and ensure compliance with regulations.

Continuous Monitoring and Optimization: Regularly review performance, costs, and security posture to optimize the hybrid cloud environment continually.

Popular Hybrid Cloud Examples

AWS Outposts: Brings AWS services, infrastructure, and operating models to virtually any data center, co-location space, or on-premises facility for a truly consistent hybrid experience.

Azure Arc: Enables deployment of Azure services anywhere and extends Azure management to any infrastructure, providing a unified system for managing across environments.

Google Anthos: An open platform that lets you run an application anywhere—simply, flexibly, and securely. It bridges on-premises and public cloud environments, allowing businesses to modernize their applications faster.

The hybrid cloud deployment model represents a powerful and flexible approach to enterprise computing, enabling businesses to leverage the advantages of both public and private clouds while mitigating their limitations. By thoughtfully integrating various cloud services and on-premises resources, organizations can create a responsive, scalable, and cost-efficient IT environment that supports their strategic goals and adapts to their evolving needs. As cloud technologies continue to advance, the hybrid cloud model is poised to become an increasingly prevalent and strategic choice for businesses seeking to maximize their cloud investments.

Understanding these fundamentals of cloud computing is crucial as they form the basis for exploring and mastering Microsoft Azure. Azure builds upon these concepts, offering a comprehensive suite of services that leverage the power of cloud computing to meet the diverse needs of individuals and organizations. As we delve deeper into Azure, keep these principles in mind—they are the key to unlocking the full potential of the cloud.

Cloud Computing Service Models

Cloud computing service models define the level of control, management, and responsibility held by the cloud service provider versus the user. These models are essential for understanding the different ways in which cloud services can be utilized to support various business needs. The three primary service models are Infrastructure as a Service (IaaS), Platform as a Service (PaaS), and Software as a Service (SaaS). Each model offers distinct advantages and is suitable for different types of applications and business requirements.

Infrastructure as a Service (IaaS)

Definition and Key Features:

IaaS provides virtualized computing resources over the internet. It is the most flexible cloud computing model and allows for automated deployment of servers, processing power, storage, and networking.

Users manage the operating systems, applications, and middleware, while the cloud provider manages the infrastructure.

Advantages:

Flexibility and Scalability: IaaS allows businesses to scale up or down quickly as required, making it ideal for temporary, experimental, or changing workload needs.

Cost-Effectiveness: With a pay-as-you-go model, IaaS eliminates the upfront cost of setting up and maintaining an on-site data center, making it a cost-effective option for many businesses.

Control: Users retain full control of their applications, without having to manage the underlying hardware.

Use Cases:

Developing and testing applications.

Website hosting.

Storage, backup, and recovery.

Platform as a Service (PaaS)

Definition and Key Features: PaaS provides a platform allowing customers to develop, run, and manage applications without the complexity of building and maintaining the infrastructure typically associated with developing and launching an app. PaaS can include development tools, database management systems, business analytics services, and more.

Advantages:

Simplified Development: Developers can concentrate on building software without worrying about operating systems, software updates, storage, or infrastructure.

Cost-Effective Development and Deployment: PaaS includes infrastructure and development tools, reducing the cost of purchasing and managing separate licenses and underlying infrastructure.

Built-in Scalability: Applications built on PaaS can easily scale up or down based on demand, without the developer needing to manage the scaling process.

Use Cases:

Development framework for building software applications.

Analytics or business intelligence tools that provide data insights.

Additional services like workflow, directory, security, and scheduling.

Software as a Service (SaaS)

Definition and Key Features:

SaaS delivers software applications over the internet, on a subscription basis. It is managed from a central location, and users can access the software from any internet-enabled device. The cloud provider manages the infrastructure, operating systems, middleware, and data necessary to deliver the program, ensuring the software is available and secure.

Advantages:

Accessibility: SaaS applications can be accessed from anywhere, making it ideal for businesses with mobile workforces.

Cost Savings: SaaS can provide significant savings as it eliminates the need to purchase, install, maintain, and upgrade hardware and software.

Seamless Updates: Providers manage updates and patches, ensuring that users do not have to manage software updates.

Use Cases:

Email and collaboration tools.

Customer relationship management (CRM) software.

Human resources management software.

Understanding the distinct cloud computing service models is crucial for organizations to effectively leverage cloud technologies. Each model offers unique benefits and is designed to suit different business needs and technical requirements. By selecting the appropriate service model, organizations can achieve greater efficiency, agility, and cost savings, driving their digital transformation efforts forward. Whether it's the scalable and flexible infrastructure of IaaS, the development environment of PaaS, or the accessible and comprehensive software solutions of SaaS, cloud computing continues to offer a range of powerful tools for businesses navigating the challenges of the digital age.

Introduction to Microsoft Azure

Microsoft Azure is a comprehensive cloud computing service created by Microsoft for building, testing, deploying, and managing applications and services through Microsoft-managed data centers. As one of the leading cloud platforms, alongside Amazon Web Services (AWS) and Google Cloud Platform (GCP), Azure provides a wide range of cloud services, including those for computing, analytics, storage, and networking. Its integrated tools, pre-built templates, and managed services make it easier for developers and IT professionals to build and manage enterprise, mobile, web, and Internet of Things (IoT) applications.

Azure's Core Services and Features

Azure offers an extensive array of services that span various categories, including:

Compute:

Virtual Machines, Azure Kubernetes Service (AKS), and Azure Functions for processing and running applications.

Microsoft Azure's Compute services form the backbone of its cloud offering, enabling users to deploy and manage virtualized applications in the cloud efficiently. These services provide the computational power necessary for running applications, from simple web apps to complex machine learning algorithms. Azure's Compute options are designed to offer flexibility, scalability, and performance to meet the needs of different applications, workloads, and scenarios. Let's delve into the key Compute services offered by Azure:

Virtual Machines (VMs)

Azure Virtual Machines (VMs) are one of the most fundamental Compute services provided by Azure. They allow users to deploy and manage Windows and Linux virtual machines in the cloud. This service offers the flexibility of virtualization for a wide range of computing solutions, including development and testing environments, applications hosting, and data processing. VMs can be customized with a wide variety of sizes, operating systems, and configurations to suit any workload.

Scenarios: Ideal for migrating existing applications to the cloud, extending data center capacities, and running applications that require full control over the operating system and environment.

Azure Kubernetes Service (AKS)

Azure Kubernetes Service (AKS) simplifies deploying, managing, and scaling containerized applications using Kubernetes on Azure. AKS offers integrated continuous integration and continuous delivery (CI/CD) experiences, security and governance, designed to facilitate the management of containerized applications at scale.

Scenarios: Perfect for modern applications that require microservices architecture, need to scale quickly based on demand, and leverage open-source tools for orchestration.

Azure Functions

Azure Functions is a serverless compute service that enables users to run event-triggered code without explicitly provisioning or managing infrastructure. It allows developers to focus on writing code that reacts to events, such as changes in data, updates from web requests, and messages from other Azure services, without worrying about the underlying infrastructure.

Scenarios: Suited for tasks that need to run in response to events, automate small pieces of code in cloud environments, or build APIs and microservices in a serverless architecture.

Azure App Service

Azure App Service is a fully managed platform for building, deploying, and scaling web apps and APIs. It supports multiple languages, including .NET, .NET Core, Java, Ruby, Node.js, PHP, and Python. App Service makes it easy to integrate with Azure services and external resources, providing a powerful platform for building enterprise-grade web applications.

Scenarios: Ideal for web-based applications that require scalable, secure, and easy-to-manage platforms, including e-commerce solutions, content management systems, and SaaS applications.

Azure Virtual Desktop

Azure Virtual Desktop is a desktop and app virtualization service that runs on the cloud. It enables users to access a full Windows desktop or specific applications from anywhere, providing a scalable and secure virtual desktop infrastructure (VDI) solution.

Scenarios: Suitable for remote work solutions, providing access to desktop environments for contractors or employees on a variety of devices, and managing software development and testing environments.

Azure Batch

Azure Batch is a managed service for running large-scale parallel and high-performance computing (HPC) applications efficiently in the cloud. It automates the management, scheduling, and execution of batch processing jobs, making it easier to run large-scale applications that require massive computational resources.

Scenarios: Optimized for batch processing jobs, including rendering, simulation, and analysis workloads that require high-performance computing capabilities.

Azure's Compute services offer a comprehensive and versatile range of options that cater to different needs and scenarios in the cloud computing landscape. Whether it's through virtual machines, container orchestration, serverless functions, web hosting, virtual desktops, or batch processing, Azure provides the tools and infrastructure necessary for businesses to deploy and manage their applications with ease, efficiency, and scalability. By leveraging Azure's Compute services, organizations can achieve greater agility, operational flexibility, and cost-efficiency in their computing operations, driving innovation and growth in the digital era.

Storage:

Solutions like Azure Blob Storage and Azure Disk Storage provide scalable cloud storage for data of all types and sizes.

In the vast ecosystem of cloud computing, storage solutions are pivotal for managing and securing the exponentially growing data volumes of today's digital world. Microsoft Azure, a leading cloud service provider, offers a comprehensive and flexible range of storage solutions tailored to meet the diverse needs of its users. Azure's storage services are designed for high availability, security, and scalability, ensuring that data is accessible whenever and wherever it's needed while maintaining integrity and confidentiality.

Overview of Azure Storage Services

Azure provides a variety of storage services, each designed to address specific needs:

Azure Blob Storage: Azure Blob Storage is an object storage solution for the cloud. It allows you to store large amounts of unstructured data, such as text or binary data, which is ideal for serving images or documents directly to a browser, storing files for distributed access, streaming video and audio, writing to log files, and storing data for backup, restore, disaster recovery, and archiving.

Azure File Storage: Azure File Storage offers fully managed file shares in the cloud that are accessible via the industry-standard Server Message Block (SMB) protocol. This enables migration of legacy applications to Azure that rely on file share capabilities, simplifying cloud integration and enabling shared access from anywhere in the world.

Azure Queue Storage: Azure Queue Storage supports the management of asynchronous messaging between application components, whether they are running in the cloud, on desktops, on-premises, or on mobile devices. Queue Storage facilitates communication and message queuing for large workloads, improving application scalability and reliability.

Azure Table Storage: Azure Table Storage stores large amounts of structured, non-relational data. It's a NoSQL data store for semi-structured data, perfect for web applications, address books, device information, or any other datasets that don't require complex joins or transactions.

Azure Disk Storage: Azure Disk Storage provides high-performance, durable block storage for Azure Virtual Machines. With options including Ultra Disks, Premium SSDs, Standard SSDs, and Standard HDDs, it caters to scenarios ranging from high I/O-intensive workloads to cost-effective archival storage.

Key Features of Azure Storage

Global Availability and Scalability: Azure Storage provides a massively scalable object store for data objects, disk storage for Azure virtual machines (VMs), a file system service for the cloud, a messaging store for reliable messaging, and a NoSQL store. It is globally available, ensuring users can deploy their data replication and redundancy strategies effectively across multiple regions.

Security and Compliance: Azure Storage offers advanced security features, including encryption of data in transit and at rest, network isolation using private endpoints, access control for managing permissions, and comprehensive monitoring and logging. Compliance with various industry standards (such as ISO, HIPAA, and GDPR) ensures that data governance and privacy requirements are met.

Data Redundancy and Recovery: Azure Storage provides robust data protection options through its data replication capabilities. Data can be replicated locally within the same data center, across different regions, or even geo-redundantly to protect against regional outages. This ensures high availability and disaster recovery.

Integration and Compatibility: Azure Storage is designed to work seamlessly with other Azure services, like Azure Virtual Machines, Azure Functions, and Azure Kubernetes Service, enabling a wide range of application scenarios from simple websites to complex enterprise applications.

Azure's storage services offer scalable, secure, and cost-effective solutions to meet the demands of any application or workload. By leveraging Azure's global infrastructure and advanced features, organizations can ensure their data is stored efficiently, securely, and accessibly, enabling them to focus on innovation and growth while Azure manages the complexities of data storage and protection. Whether it's unstructured data in Blob Storage or structured data in Table Storage, Azure provides the flexibility and performance needed to drive today's data-intensive applications.

Networking:

Services such as Azure Virtual Network, Load Balancer, and VPN Gateway offer robust networking capabilities for enhanced connectivity and security.

Networking in cloud computing is a foundational element that ensures the seamless connectivity of resources, applications, and data across the cloud ecosystem. Microsoft Azure, as a frontrunner in the cloud services arena, offers a sophisticated suite of networking services designed to provide secure, reliable, and scalable networking solutions. Azure's networking services facilitate the creation of a highly available and flexible network infrastructure that can support the diverse and evolving needs of modern businesses, ranging from simple web applications to complex enterprise systems.

Overview of Azure Networking Services

Azure provides a comprehensive set of networking tools and services that allow users to implement a wide range of network configurations, including hybrid connections that integrate on-premises networks with the cloud. Key components of Azure's networking services include:

Azure Virtual Network (VNet): Azure VNet is the fundamental building block for your private network in Azure. It enables many types of Azure resources, such as Azure Virtual Machines (VM), to securely communicate with each other, the internet, and on-premises networks. VNet is similar to a traditional network that you'd operate in your own data center but brings with it the scalability, availability, and isolation benefits of the Azure infrastructure.

Azure Load Balancer: Azure Load Balancer delivers high availability and network performance to your applications. It is a Layer 4 (TCP, UDP) load balancer that can distribute incoming traffic among healthy service instances in cloud services or virtual machines defined in a load-balanced set.

Azure Application Gateway: Application Gateway is a web traffic load balancer that enables you to manage traffic to your web applications. Traditional load balancers operate at the transport layer (OSI layer 4 - TCP and UDP) and route traffic based on source IP address and port, to a destination IP address and port. In contrast, Application Gateway operates at the application layer (OSI layer 7) and routes traffic based on the content of the request.

Azure VPN Gateway: Azure VPN Gateway connects your on-premises networks to Azure through Site-to-Site VPNs in a similar way that you set up and connect to a remote branch office. It provides a secure and reliable connection between your on-premises network and your Azure virtual network.

Azure ExpressRoute: ExpressRoute lets you extend your on-premises networks into the Microsoft cloud over a private connection facilitated by a connectivity provider. With ExpressRoute, you can establish connections to Microsoft cloud services, such as Microsoft Azure, Microsoft 365, and Dynamics 365.

Azure DNS: Azure DNS provides hosting for DNS domains, offering name resolution using Microsoft Azure infrastructure. By hosting your domains in Azure, you can manage your DNS records using the same credentials, APIs, tools, and billing as your other Azure services.

Key Benefits of Azure Networking

Security and Isolation: Azure networking provides secure and isolated environments for your applications and data, leveraging advanced security features such as network security groups, application security groups, and encryption.

Global Reach and Scalability: With Azure's global infrastructure, networking services are available worldwide, allowing you to deploy your applications close to your users to ensure optimal performance. Scalability is a core feature, enabling you to easily adjust your network resources based on demand.

Integration and Automation: Azure networking services are deeply integrated with other Azure services, enabling a seamless and efficient cloud environment. Automation capabilities allow for the easy deployment, management, and scaling of network resources through Azure Resource Manager templates and Azure CLI.

Hybrid Cloud Capabilities: Azure offers strong hybrid cloud capabilities, including VPN Gateway and ExpressRoute, allowing for smooth integration and connectivity between on-premises networks and the Azure cloud. This is essential for businesses transitioning to the cloud or operating in a hybrid cloud environment.

Microsoft Azure's networking services provide the backbone for deploying and managing cloud-based applications and services, offering unparalleled flexibility, security, and scalability. By leveraging Azure's comprehensive suite of networking tools, businesses can create robust, high-performance networks that support their operational needs while benefiting from the agility and innovation that cloud computing offers. Whether you're establishing simple web applications or complex, distributed systems, Azure's networking services ensure that your network infrastructure is reliable, secure, and ready to meet the challenges of the digital age.

Databases:

Azure supports multiple database services, including Azure SQL Database, Azure Cosmos DB, and Azure Database for MySQL, providing scalable and secure database solutions.

In the realm of cloud computing, database services are crucial for storing, managing, and accessing data efficiently and securely. Microsoft Azure, as a key player in the cloud ecosystem, offers a wide array of database services that cater to the diverse needs of modern applications. These services not only support traditional relational databases but also embrace the flexibility and scalability of NoSQL options, providing developers and businesses with the tools they need to build scalable, high-performance applications.

Overview of Azure Database Services

Azure's database services are designed to offer high availability, security, and scalability. Here's a look at some of the primary database services provided by Azure:

Azure SQL Database: A fully managed relational database service based on SQL Server. Azure SQL Database is highly scalable, automated, and intelligent, offering built-in AI and security features. It supports a broad range of applications from simple web apps to complex data-driven solutions.

Azure Cosmos DB: A globally distributed, multi-model database service designed for high availability and low latency at global scale. It supports document, key-value, graph, and column-family data models, making it an ideal choice for developing applications that require support for diverse data structures.

Azure Database for MySQL: A fully managed database service that provides MySQL compatibility, enabling developers to leverage open-source tools and technologies. It offers built-in high availability, security, and scalability for running MySQL-based applications.

Azure Database for PostgreSQL: Similar to its MySQL offering, Azure provides a fully managed PostgreSQL database service. It's designed for developers who need to build and run PostgreSQL-based applications, providing scalability, security, and compliance features.

Azure Table Storage: A NoSQL key-value store for rapid development using massive semi-structured datasets. It's ideal for applications that require a scalable, durable, and highly available storage for their data.

Azure SQL Managed Instance: Bridges the gap between on-premises SQL Server and Azure SQL Database, providing a fully managed instance that supports SQL Server applications. It's compatible with the latest SQL Server features and offers a native virtual network (VNet) implementation.

Key Features of Azure's Database Services

Global Distribution and Scalability: Azure's database services are designed for global distribution, allowing developers to replicate data across multiple regions worldwide. This ensures low-latency access to data, regardless of where the users are located.

Built-in Intelligence and Security: Azure databases are equipped with advanced security features, including data encryption, threat detection, and network isolation. Additionally, services like Azure SQL Database leverage built-in intelligence to automate updates, performance tuning, and threat detection.

Flexible Deployment Options: Azure offers flexible deployment options, including fully managed platforms as a service (PaaS) and infrastructure as a service (IaaS) for hosting databases. This flexibility allows businesses to choose the best environment for their specific workload requirements.

Integration and Compatibility: Azure's database services seamlessly integrate with other Azure services, providing a comprehensive environment for developing, deploying, and managing applications. They also offer compatibility with popular frameworks and languages, enabling a smooth transition to the cloud for existing applications.

Azure's extensive portfolio of database services underscores its commitment to providing robust, scalable, and secure data storage solutions for the cloud ecosystem. Whether you're developing new applications or migrating existing databases to the cloud, Azure offers a range of options to suit any data storage requirement. With its global infrastructure, advanced security features, and built-in scalability, Azure empowers businesses to build data-driven solutions that are both powerful and efficient, making it an indispensable part of the modern cloud computing landscape.

AI and Machine Learning:

Tools like Azure Machine Learning and Azure Cognitive Services enable developers to incorporate intelligent features into their applications

In the rapidly evolving cloud ecosystem, artificial intelligence (AI) and machine learning (ML) have become pivotal in enabling businesses to derive insights from data, automate processes, and create intelligent applications. Microsoft Azure stands out as a leading platform offering a comprehensive suite of AI and ML services that cater to both seasoned data scientists and developers looking to infuse AI into their applications without deep machine learning expertise.

Azure AI and Machine Learning Services Overview

Azure provides an extensive array of AI and ML services designed to support various aspects of building intelligent solutions, from data preparation and model training to deployment and management. Key offerings include:

Azure Machine Learning: A cloud-based environment for training, deploying, automated ML, and managing ML models. It supports a wide range of ML algorithms, frameworks, and tools, enabling data scientists and developers to build, train, and track machine learning models. Azure Machine Learning facilitates end-to-end machine learning lifecycle management, making it easier to bring ML models into production with efficiency and scalability.

Azure Cognitive Services: A collection of pre-built AI services designed to enable applications to see, hear, speak, understand, and interpret user needs using natural methods of communication. These services include vision, speech, language, decision, and search APIs that developers can use to easily add AI capabilities to their applications without having deep data science knowledge.

Azure Bot Services: Tools for building, testing, deploying, and managing intelligent bots. By using Azure Bot Services, developers can create conversational interfaces for various scenarios like customer support, e-commerce, and content delivery, enhancing user experiences through natural language interactions.

Key Features of Azure's AI and Machine Learning Services

Scalability and Flexibility: Azure's AI and ML services are designed to scale automatically with demand, providing the flexibility to handle large datasets and complex models while managing costs effectively.

Integrated Development Environment: Azure offers integrated tools and environments, such as Azure Notebooks and Azure Databricks, that support collaborative development and simplify the process of building, training, and deploying machine learning models.

Comprehensive Security and Compliance: Azure ensures that AI and ML workloads are protected with industry-leading security practices, including encryption, access control, and compliance with global and industry-specific standards.

Extensive Ecosystem Support: Azure supports a wide range of open-source frameworks and languages, enabling developers and data scientists to use the tools and technologies they are familiar with. This support accelerates the development of AI and ML applications and facilitates innovation.

Azure's Place in AI and Machine Learning

Microsoft Azure is uniquely positioned in the cloud ecosystem to leverage its vast computing resources, advanced analytics capabilities, and robust security features to provide powerful AI and ML services. Azure democratizes AI and machine learning, offering accessible and efficient solutions for businesses of all sizes to innovate and solve complex problems. Whether it's through developing custom ML models with Azure Machine Learning or integrating intelligent features with Azure Cognitive Services, Azure provides the tools and infrastructure necessary for the next generation of AI-driven applications.

Azure's commitment to ethical AI and responsible machine learning practices further enhances its reputation, ensuring that AI technologies are developed and used in a manner that is transparent, secure, and aligned with societal values and norms.

Microsoft Azure's AI and Machine Learning services represent a cornerstone of its cloud ecosystem, empowering organizations to harness the power of AI and data science for competitive advantage. By providing scalable, secure, and easy-to-use tools and services, Azure enables businesses to accelerate their AI and machine learning initiatives, transforming how they operate, make decisions, and engage with customers. As AI and ML continue to evolve, Azure's commitment to innovation, security, and accessibility ensures it remains at the forefront of enabling intelligent cloud solutions.

Identity:

Azure Active Directory provides identity and access management, ensuring secure and seamless access to applications.

In the cloud ecosystem, managing identities and access is crucial for ensuring security and compliance across all services and resources. Microsoft Azure provides robust identity and access management (IAM) solutions through Azure Active Directory (Azure AD), a comprehensive identity platform designed to meet the security and scalability needs of modern organizations. Azure's identity services play a pivotal role in securing cloud environments, enabling seamless access management, and facilitating digital transformation.

Azure Identity Services Overview

At the heart of Azure's identity services is Azure Active Directory (Azure AD), which offers a rich set of capabilities:

Azure Active Directory (Azure AD): A cloud-based identity and access management service that helps employees sign in and access resources. It includes internal resources like apps on your corporate network and intranet, along with cloud services like Microsoft 365, Azure portal, and thousands of other SaaS applications. Azure AD is central to Azure's identity services, providing single sign-on (SSO), multi-factor authentication (MFA), and conditional access policies to protect users from cybersecurity threats.

Azure AD B2C (Business to Consumer): A customer identity access management solution capable of supporting millions of users. It allows organizations to customize and control how customers sign up, sign in, and manage their profiles when using applications. This service is tailored for external users, providing scalable, secure authentication for apps, websites, and mobile platforms.

Azure AD Domain Services: Provides managed domain services such as domain join, group policy, LDAP, and Kerberos/NTLM authentication that are fully compatible with Windows Server Active Directory. This enables organizations to lift and shift legacy directory-aware applications running on-premises to Azure, without having to worry about managing a domain controller.

Key Features of Azure's Identity Services

Comprehensive Security: Azure AD offers robust security features, including conditional access policies, MFA, and identity protection, which leverage AI to detect potential vulnerabilities and automated responses to identified threats.

Seamless Integration: Azure's identity services integrate seamlessly with other Azure services, Microsoft 365, and thousands of third-party SaaS applications, facilitating a unified and secure access management system across all enterprise resources.

Developer-Friendly Tools: Azure provides developers with APIs and tools to incorporate Azure AD's capabilities into their applications, enabling custom authentication experiences and secure API access.

Scalability and Reliability: Built on Microsoft's global network infrastructure, Azure AD ensures high availability and scalability to meet the demands of any organization, from small startups to global enterprises.

Azure's Place in Identity Management

Microsoft Azure, through Azure Active Directory, has established itself as a leader in cloud identity and access management. Azure AD's comprehensive suite of identity services empowers organizations to enhance security, improve user experiences, and embrace a mobile-first, cloud-first approach to business. In an era where cybersecurity threats are ever-evolving, the importance of robust IAM solutions cannot be overstated. Azure's identity services provide the foundation for secure and efficient management of digital identities, enabling businesses to leverage the full potential of cloud computing while ensuring that their data and resources remain protected.

Azure's commitment to security, compliance, and seamless integration positions it as an indispensable tool in the cloud ecosystem, particularly for organizations looking to modernize their IAM practices. As businesses continue to navigate the complexities of digital transformation, Azure's identity services offer a reliable and scalable solution for managing access to critical resources in the cloud and beyond.

Azure's identity services, spearheaded by Azure Active Directory, play a crucial role in the security and operational efficiency of cloud environments. By providing advanced authentication mechanisms, comprehensive access management, and seamless integration capabilities, Azure empowers organizations to protect their resources while facilitating easy access for legitimate users. As part of Microsoft Azure's extensive cloud ecosystem, Azure AD exemplifies the platform's commitment to delivering secure, scalable, and user-friendly cloud services, solidifying Azure's position as a leading cloud service provider in today's digital landscape.

Advantages of Microsoft Azure

Flexibility and Scalability:

Azure supports a broad spectrum of programming languages, frameworks, operating systems, databases, and devices, allowing developers to use the tools and technologies they are comfortable with. It also offers auto-scalability, which automatically adjusts resources based on demand.

One of the defining characteristics of cloud computing is the ability to scale resources on demand, providing flexibility that traditional IT infrastructures cannot match. Microsoft Azure, as a leading cloud service provider, embodies this principle by offering unparalleled flexibility and scalability to its users. These features are central to Azure's appeal and utility in the cloud ecosystem, allowing businesses of all sizes to adapt to changing demands without the need for significant upfront investment in physical hardware.

Flexibility in Computing Options

Microsoft Azure provides a wide range of computing services, from virtual machines (VMs) and Kubernetes services for container orchestration to serverless computing options like Azure Functions. This diversity in computing services ensures that organizations can select the optimal computing resources for their specific applications, whether they require control over the operating system and environment (as provided by VMs) or wish to focus solely on code execution without managing the underlying infrastructure (as offered by serverless computing).

Virtual Machines (VMs): Azure VMs offer the flexibility to deploy a wide variety of computing solutions with your choice of operating systems and workloads. It's ideal for applications that require isolation, custom configurations, or specific versions of operating systems and software.

Azure Kubernetes Service (AKS): For applications that benefit from containerization, AKS provides an integrated Kubernetes environment, simplifying deployment, management, and scaling of containerized applications.

Azure Functions: This serverless compute service enables developers to run event-triggered code without explicitly provisioning or managing infrastructure, allowing businesses to focus on innovation and reducing costs.

Scalability to Meet Demand

Azure's architecture is designed for high availability and scalability, supporting both vertical scaling (adding more power to your existing machines) and horizontal scaling (adding more machines to your pool). This ensures that applications can handle increases in traffic or data volume without degradation in performance.

Auto-scaling: Azure offers automatic scaling capabilities, allowing services to dynamically adjust the amount of resources based on current demand, ensuring performance and cost-efficiency. For instance, Azure App Service can automatically scale web app instances up or down based on load, and Azure SQL Database can adjust performance levels as needed.

Global Reach with Azure Regions: Microsoft Azure's infrastructure spans across more than 60 regions worldwide, more than any other cloud provider. This global presence enables businesses to deploy services and applications closer to their users, reducing latency and improving the user experience. Additionally, it allows for geo-redundant storage solutions, ensuring data durability and high availability across the globe.

The flexibility and scalability offered by Microsoft Azure stand out as some of its most compelling advantages. By providing a broad spectrum of computing resources that cater to different needs and offering the ability to scale these resources dynamically, Azure enables businesses to innovate quickly and respond to changes in demand efficiently. Whether it's a startup experiencing rapid growth or an established enterprise managing seasonal fluctuations, Azure's cloud computing services ensure that the infrastructure can adapt seamlessly, without the constraints of traditional IT environments. This adaptability not only optimizes performance and costs but also supports businesses in their growth and transformation initiatives, underscoring Azure's vital role in the cloud computing ecosystem.

Integrated Development Environment:

Azure seamlessly integrates with Visual Studio, the leading development tool for .NET applications, enhancing productivity and simplifying the development process.

One of the key advantages of Microsoft Azure that significantly enhances its standing in the cloud ecosystem is its integrated development environment (IDE). This feature streamlines the development process, from initial coding to deployment, making it easier for developers to build, test, and manage applications efficiently within the Azure platform. The integration of various development tools and services within Azure provides a cohesive and productive environment for developers working on cloud-native applications or migrating existing applications to the cloud.

Seamless Development and Deployment

Azure's IDE integration encompasses a range of tools and services designed to support the development lifecycle:

Visual Studio and Visual Studio Code: Azure deeply integrates with Visual Studio, Microsoft's flagship IDE, and Visual Studio Code, a popular open-source code editor. These tools offer advanced features for developing, debugging, and deploying applications directly to Azure. Developers can leverage Azure SDKs and extensions available within these IDEs to easily interact with Azure services, enhancing productivity and reducing the complexity of cloud development.

Azure DevOps Services: Formerly known as Visual Studio Team Services, Azure DevOps provides a suite of cloud services for collaborating on code development, including Git repositories, CI/CD pipelines, and Agile planning tools. Azure DevOps integrates seamlessly with Azure, enabling teams to automate the build, testing, and deployment of applications across multiple Azure services.

Azure PowerShell and Azure CLI: For developers who prefer to work within a command-line interface, Azure offers PowerShell and CLI tools for managing Azure resources. These tools allow for scripting and automating deployment and management tasks, providing flexibility and efficiency in handling cloud resources.

Enhanced Productivity with Pre-built Services

Azure App Service: A platform-as-a-service (PaaS) offering that allows developers to quickly build, deploy, and scale web applications and APIs. Azure App Service supports multiple languages and frameworks, such as .NET, Java, Node.js, and PHP, and integrates with Azure DevOps, GitHub, and Bitbucket for continuous deployment.

Azure Functions: Provides a serverless computing environment that enables developers to run code triggered by events without provisioning or managing servers. Integration with Azure DevOps and GitHub Actions supports automated deployment workflows for Azure Functions, further simplifying the development process.

Collaboration and Version Control

GitHub Integration: Microsoft's acquisition of GitHub, the world's leading software development platform, has further strengthened Azure's IDE capabilities. Azure and GitHub offer tight integration, enabling developers to easily deploy applications from GitHub to Azure, leverage GitHub Actions for Azure to automate workflows, and utilize Azure services directly from GitHub repositories.

The integrated development environment offered by Microsoft Azure represents a significant advantage for developers and organizations looking to leverage cloud computing. By providing powerful tools for coding, debugging, deployment, and collaboration, Azure empowers development teams to bring their applications to market faster and with higher quality. The seamless integration of Azure services with popular development tools and platforms underscores Microsoft's commitment to supporting developers' needs and enhancing productivity, making Azure a compelling choice for cloud development projects.

Hybrid Capabilities:

Azure provides extensive hybrid cloud capabilities, allowing businesses to integrate on-premises datacenters with the cloud, which is beneficial for organizations with existing investments in on-premises hardware or those with specific regulatory or data sovereignty requirements.

In the contemporary cloud computing landscape, hybrid capabilities represent a crucial advantage for businesses seeking the perfect balance between on-premises infrastructure and cloud services. Microsoft Azure stands at the forefront of this hybrid movement, offering robust solutions that allow for seamless integration between data centers and its cloud environment. Azure's hybrid capabilities facilitate a flexible, scalable, and secure IT infrastructure, empowering organizations to innovate without the constraints of physical location or resource limitations.

Azure's Comprehensive Hybrid Solutions

Azure's suite of hybrid services and tools is designed to support a variety of hybrid scenarios, from application development and data storage to security and management. Key components of Azure's hybrid offerings include:

Azure Arc: A groundbreaking service that extends Azure management and governance capabilities to any infrastructure, Azure Arc allows businesses to deploy Azure services anywhere—on-premises, in multi-cloud environments, or at the edge. This ensures a consistent and unified management layer across the entire IT estate, simplifying complex environments and enabling deployment of Azure data services and management across diverse landscapes.

Azure Stack: Azure Stack is a portfolio of products that extend Azure services and capabilities to your environment of choice—from the datacenter to edge locations and remote offices. With Azure Stack, organizations can run Azure applications using the same tools and APIs in a local, disconnected, or edge environment, bridging the gap between cloud and on-premises deployments.

Azure Hybrid Benefit: This cost-saving benefit allows customers to maximize the value of their existing on-premises Windows Server and SQL Server license investments when migrating to Azure. It provides significant savings on Azure Virtual Machines, Azure SQL Database managed instances, and Azure App Service plan rates.

Azure VPN Gateway and ExpressRoute: These services provide secure and reliable connectivity between on-premises networks and Azure through an internet-based VPN connection or a private connection facilitated by a connectivity provider. This ensures that organizations can securely extend their on-premises networks into the Azure cloud.

Advantages of Azure's Hybrid Capabilities

Flexibility and Innovation: Azure's hybrid solutions offer the flexibility to run applications where they perform best—whether in the cloud or on-premises. This enables businesses to innovate with the latest cloud technologies while retaining critical workloads in their own datacenters when necessary.

Cost Efficiency: By leveraging Azure Hybrid Benefit and integrating existing infrastructure with cloud services, organizations can significantly reduce costs associated with cloud migration and operation.

Seamless Integration and Consistency: Azure provides a consistent set of tools, APIs, and services across cloud and on-premises environments, simplifying development, deployment, and management. This consistency reduces complexity and training requirements for IT staff.

Security and Compliance: Azure's hybrid capabilities do not compromise on security or compliance. Organizations can extend Azure security features to their on-premises environments, ensuring unified security management and compliance across their hybrid estate.

Microsoft Azure's hybrid capabilities address the evolving needs of businesses navigating the complexities of digital transformation. By offering an extensive array of tools and services that bridge the gap between on-premises infrastructure and the cloud, Azure enables organizations to create a truly flexible, scalable, and secure IT environment. These hybrid capabilities not only allow businesses to leverage the full potential of cloud computing but also provide the freedom to maintain sensitive workloads on-premises, ensuring operational excellence and strategic agility in a competitive landscape.

Comprehensive Security:

Microsoft invests heavily in cybersecurity and has a robust framework for securing cloud infrastructure and services. Azure's security and compliance offerings are among the most comprehensive in the industry.

In the evolving landscape of cloud computing, security stands as a paramount concern for businesses transitioning to or operating in the cloud. Microsoft Azure addresses this critical need by embedding comprehensive security measures at the core of its services. Azure's multi-layered security approach is designed to protect data, applications, and infrastructure from potential threats, making it a cornerstone of Azure's value proposition in the cloud ecosystem.

Foundations of Azure's Security Architecture

Azure's security architecture is built on the principles of secure development, operational security, and threat mitigation. This comprehensive framework encompasses a range of tools, services, and practices:

Secure Development Lifecycle (SDL): Azure incorporates security at every phase of its development lifecycle, from initial design to deployment, ensuring that services are designed with security in mind from the ground up.

Physical Security: Azure data centers are physically secured with multiple layers of defense, including perimeter fencing, video surveillance, security personnel, and strict access controls.

Network Security: Azure provides robust network security mechanisms, including isolation, segmentation, and encryption. Services like Azure Firewall, Virtual Network, and ExpressRoute offer enhanced protection and private connectivity to Azure resources.

Identity and Access Management (IAM): Azure Active Directory (Azure AD) serves as the primary tool for managing identities, providing features such as Multi-Factor Authentication (MFA), conditional access policies, and role-based access control (RBAC) to ensure that only authorized users can access resources.

Data Security: Azure offers encryption in transit and at rest, along with a range of data protection services such as Azure Information Protection and Azure Key Vault, which manage encryption keys and other sensitive information securely.

Threat Protection and Monitoring: Azure Security Center and Azure Sentinel deliver advanced threat detection, providing real-time security alerts and automated threat response capabilities. These services leverage machine learning and global threat intelligence to identify and mitigate potential security threats.

Compliance and Certifications

Understanding the importance of regulatory compliance, Azure adheres to a comprehensive set of international and industry-specific standards, including GDPR, HIPAA, ISO 27001, and SOC 1, 2, and 3, among others. Azure's compliance offerings are designed to simplify the compliance process for organizations by providing detailed compliance documentation, blueprints, and tools that align with regulatory requirements.

Azure's Security Advantage

The depth and breadth of Azure's security features represent a significant advantage for businesses concerned about protecting their cloud environments. Azure's integrated security services empower organizations to:

Protect Against Evolving Threats: With its advanced analytics, machine learning capabilities, and global cybersecurity intelligence, Azure stays ahead of emerging threats, offering businesses proactive protection.

Ensure Data Privacy and Sovereignty: Azure's global infrastructure allows organizations to store data in specific regions, adhering to data sovereignty laws and regulations, while encryption services ensure data privacy.

Achieve and Maintain Compliance: Azure simplifies the process of meeting complex regulatory requirements, providing an extensive array of compliance certifications and tools that help businesses stay compliant in a cost-effective manner.

Microsoft Azure's comprehensive security measures are a testament to its commitment to providing a secure cloud computing environment. By integrating advanced security technologies and practices across its platform, Azure ensures that organizations can confidently move their operations to the cloud, knowing their data, applications, and infrastructure are protected against the full spectrum of cybersecurity threats. This robust security foundation, coupled with Azure's commitment to compliance and data protection, cements its place as a leader in the cloud ecosystem, offering businesses a secure and compliant path to cloud adoption and digital transformation.

Azure's Place in the Cloud Ecosystem

Microsoft Azure holds a significant place in the cloud computing ecosystem, catering to a wide range of customers from small businesses to global enterprises. Its growth has been driven by its strong enterprise background, comprehensive service offerings, and deep integration with Microsoft's software products. Azure is particularly well-regarded for its hybrid cloud solutions, enterprise-grade security, and its ability to support mission-critical applications.

Azure competes in the cloud market by continuously expanding its global infrastructure, launching new and innovative services, and forming partnerships that enhance its ecosystem. It is a key player in digital transformation initiatives across various industries, enabling businesses to leverage cloud technology to innovate, scale, and improve efficiency.

Azure's commitment to sustainability, with a pledge to be carbon negative by 2030, aligns with the increasing importance of environmental responsibility in technology infrastructure. This commitment further strengthens its position in the cloud ecosystem as businesses increasingly prioritize sustainability in their operations and cloud strategy.

Conclusion

Microsoft Azure's comprehensive suite of services, combined with its enterprise focus and global reach, positions it as a leading platform in the cloud computing ecosystem. Its continuous innovation, extensive support for various technologies, and strong commitment to security and sustainability make it a compelling choice for businesses embarking on their cloud journey. Whether for developing new applications, migrating existing ones, or deploying hybrid solutions, Azure offers the tools, infrastructure, and services to meet a wide range of cloud computing needs.

Chapter 2: Setting Up Your Azure Environment

Establishing your Microsoft Azure environment is the foundational step toward leveraging the expansive range of cloud services Azure has to offer, from computing power and storage solutions to artificial intelligence and Internet of Things (IoT) capabilities. This comprehensive guide outlines the essential steps to set up your Azure environment, ensuring a structured and secure approach to deploying and managing your cloud resources.

Step 1: Create an Azure Account

Sign Up:

The first step in harnessing the power of Microsoft Azure's cloud services is to create an Azure account. This initial phase is crucial as it lays the groundwork for accessing Azure's comprehensive suite of cloud computing resources, from virtual machines and web apps to databases and artificial intelligence services. Below is a detailed guide on signing up for an Azure account, ensuring you embark on your Azure journey smoothly.

Navigating to the Azure Sign Up Page

Visit Azure's Website: Start by navigating to the official Microsoft Azure website. Here, you'll find the option to start with a free account or see various pricing options.

Choose Your Account Type: Microsoft Azure offers different account types to cater to various needs, including individual developers, small businesses, and large enterprises. Most new users can benefit from starting with the Azure free account, which provides limited access to a range of services for 12 months, plus a set of services that are always free.

Starting with a Free Azure Account

Free Account Benefits: The Azure free account is an excellent way to explore what Azure has to offer without committing financially. It includes $200 in Azure credits for the first 30 days and limited access to a variety of Azure services for 12 months. Beyond this, certain services remain free indefinitely, within usage limits.

Eligibility: To sign up for a free Azure account, you need a Microsoft account, a phone number, and a credit card. The credit card is for identity verification purposes only, and you won't be charged unless you decide to upgrade to a pay-as-you-go account.

The Sign-Up Process

Microsoft Account: If you don't already have a Microsoft account (previously known as a Windows Live ID), you'll need to create one. This single account gives you access to all Microsoft services, including Azure, Outlook.com, Office Online, OneDrive, and more.

Verification: During the sign-up process, Microsoft will verify your identity through your phone number and credit card. This step is crucial for preventing fraud and ensuring that each user can benefit from the free account offer.

Azure Subscription: After verification, you'll be prompted to choose a subscription. For new users, the free subscription is typically the best choice. This step also involves agreeing to the Microsoft Azure subscription agreement, offer details, and privacy statement.

Azure Portal Access: Once the sign-up process is complete, you'll gain access to the Azure portal, a web-based user interface where you can create, manage, and monitor everything from simple web apps to complex cloud deployments.

Signing up for an Azure account is the gateway to exploring and utilizing the vast array of services offered by Microsoft Azure. By starting with a free account, individuals and businesses can experiment with Azure's capabilities without immediate investment, laying the foundation for future cloud-based solutions and innovations. As you become more familiar with Azure's offerings, you can easily transition to more comprehensive plans that suit your growing needs, all while benefiting from Azure's flexibility, scalability, and robust security features.

Subscription:

After navigating the initial sign-up process for Microsoft Azure, selecting the right subscription plan is a pivotal next step. A subscription in Azure acts as a logical container through which billing, management, and access to resources are governed. It's essential to understand the types of subscriptions available and how they align with your needs, whether for individual development projects, business operations, or enterprise-level deployments.

Understanding Azure Subscriptions

An Azure subscription is a contract with Microsoft to use Azure services, which allows you to provision resources within Azure. Each resource is associated with a subscription, and the subscription governs access permissions and billing for those resources. Here's what you need to know about managing and selecting subscriptions:

Types of Azure Subscriptions

Free Subscription: Ideal for new users to start experimenting with Azure services, offering $200 in Azure credits for the first 30 days and limited free access to certain services for 12 months, followed by access to a set of services that are free indefinitely.

Pay-As-You-Go (PAYG) Subscription: Suitable for individuals, small to medium businesses, or those running production workloads in Azure. This subscription offers the flexibility to pay only for the resources you consume without upfront costs.

Enterprise Agreement (EA) Subscription: Designed for large organizations that want to purchase cloud services under a volume licensing agreement. This type is beneficial for organizations that commit to a certain level of spending in exchange for discounted rates.

Student Subscription: Available for verified students and offers free access to certain Azure services without requiring a credit card for sign-up. This subscription aims to support learning and development in cloud computing skills.

Visual Studio Subscribers: For individuals with an active Visual Studio subscription, Azure offers monthly Azure credits that can be used towards any Azure service.

Selecting the Right Subscription

Assess Your Needs: Consider your project or organization's needs, including the types of resources you plan to deploy, estimated consumption, and budget. This assessment will guide you in selecting the most appropriate subscription type.

Understand Billing and Management: Each subscription has its billing terms and access management settings. For businesses and organizations, consider how you will manage costs and who will have administrative access to the Azure resources.

Consider Future Growth: While starting with a free or pay-as-you-go subscription might be suitable for initial experiments or small projects, think ahead about how your usage might scale. Azure allows you to change or add more subscriptions as your needs evolve.

Setting Up a Subscription

Azure Portal: Once you have an Azure account, you can add or modify subscriptions directly from the Azure portal. This flexibility allows you to adapt your subscriptions as your projects grow or change.

Cost Management Tools: Azure provides tools to help manage and monitor your spending, ensuring that you stay within budget.

These tools can alert you to unexpected increases in spending, helping prevent bill shock.

Choosing the right Azure subscription is crucial for effectively managing your cloud resources and controlling costs. By carefully assessing your needs and understanding the different subscription options available, you can select a subscription that best fits your project or organizational requirements. As your familiarity with Azure grows, you can adjust your subscriptions to match your evolving needs, taking full advantage of the scalability and flexibility that Azure offers.

Step 2: Set Up a Subscription and Resource Groups:

Manage Subscriptions:

Once you've created an Azure account, managing your subscriptions becomes a crucial next step in setting up your Azure environment effectively. Subscriptions in Azure serve as containers for billing, management, and access control for the resources you will deploy and use. Efficient management of these subscriptions is key to maintaining organizational structure, controlling costs, and ensuring proper access levels throughout your Azure environment.

Understanding Azure Subscription Management

Azure subscription management involves several critical aspects, including:

Access Control and Permissions: Each subscription can be associated with one or more Azure Active Directory (Azure AD) tenants, allowing you to define access controls and permissions for users and groups within your organization. This is crucial for maintaining security and ensuring that only authorized personnel can access or modify resources within a subscription.

Billing and Cost Management: Subscriptions are the boundary for billing; all usage of Azure resources within a subscription is billed together. Effective subscription management allows you to organize resources in a way that aligns with your budgeting and reporting requirements.

Resource Organization: Subscriptions provide a way to group and organize your Azure resources. You might choose to have separate subscriptions for different environments (e.g., development, testing, and production) or different departments within your organization.

Best Practices for Managing Azure Subscriptions

Use Multiple Subscriptions: For larger organizations or projects with distinct phases (development, testing, production), using multiple subscriptions can help isolate environments, simplify billing, and enhance security. This separation can prevent accidental changes or access to production resources and align cost tracking with organizational structures.

Implement Naming and Tagging Standards: Establish clear naming and tagging conventions for your subscriptions (and resources). This practice is vital for identifying the purpose, owner, environment, and any other relevant information about a subscription at a glance. Tags can also facilitate detailed cost analysis and governance.

Configure Access with Azure RBAC: Use Azure Role-Based Access Control (RBAC) to define who can do what within your subscriptions. RBAC allows you to assign roles that limit access and actions users can perform, such as read-only access or the ability to create and manage resources.

Monitor and Optimize Costs: Utilize Azure Cost Management and Billing tools to monitor usage and expenditures across your subscriptions. Set up alerts to notify you of unexpected increases in spending and take advantage of Azure Advisor recommendations to optimize costs.

How to Manage Subscriptions in Azure

Azure Portal: The Azure portal provides a user-friendly interface for managing your subscriptions. You can view all your subscriptions, change their properties, and configure settings such as access control and billing from within the portal.

Azure CLI and PowerShell: For those who prefer command-line tools, Azure CLI and PowerShell offer powerful options to manage subscriptions programmatically. These tools are especially useful for automating subscription management tasks in larger or more complex environments.

Azure Policy: Implement Azure Policy to enforce organizational standards and assess compliance across your subscriptions. Policies can ensure that resources are deployed with specific configurations, within certain regions, or tagged correctly.

Effective management of Azure subscriptions is foundational to setting up and maintaining a well-organized, secure, and cost-efficient Azure environment. By leveraging multiple subscriptions, implementing access controls with Azure RBAC, and adhering to naming and tagging standards, you can create a robust framework for your cloud resources. Utilizing Azure's tools for monitoring and optimization further enhances your ability to manage subscriptions effectively, ensuring that your Azure environment aligns with your organizational goals and requirements.

Create Resource Groups:

Once you have your Azure subscriptions in place, the next critical step in organizing your Azure environment is creating resource groups. Resource groups are fundamental constructs in Azure that provide a way to group your resources for easy or logical management. Understanding how to create and utilize resource groups effectively is essential for maintaining an organized, manageable, and secure Azure environment.

What Are Resource Groups?

A resource group in Azure is a container that holds related resources for an Azure solution. The resources can include virtual machines, storage accounts, web apps, databases, and more. Resource groups make it easier to manage and monitor resources, enforce policies, and calculate billing by grouping resources that share a lifecycle, permissions, and policies.

Why Use Resource Groups?

Simplified Resource Management: By organizing resources that share the same lifecycle into a resource group, you can deploy, update, and delete them as a single unit.

Access Control and Security: Resource groups work seamlessly with Azure Role-Based Access Control (RBAC) to provide precise access management for groups of resources, improving security and governance.

Cost Management and Billing: Resource groups allow for easier tracking and management of costs since you can view aggregated billing data for the group. It also facilitates applying tags for even more granular cost management.

Logical Grouping: Grouping resources that support a specific application, project, or service makes it easier to understand and manage your Azure environment.

Steps to Create a Resource Group

Log in to the Azure Portal: Start by logging into the Azure Portal with your Azure account credentials.

Navigate to Resource Groups: From the Azure Portal dashboard, select "Resource groups" from the sidebar or use the search bar to find the Resource Groups service.

Create a New Resource Group: Click on "Add" or "Create resource group" to start the creation process. You'll be prompted to fill in some details:

- **Subscription**: Select the subscription under which you want to create the resource group. This determines which billing account is used for the resources in the group.
- **Resource Group Name**: Enter a descriptive name for your resource group. It's crucial to follow a naming convention that reflects the resource group's purpose, environment, and any other relevant categorizations.

- **Region**: Choose the region where the resource group will be located. While the group itself is not tied to a specific location, some policies and resource placements can be region-specific.

Configure Access Control (IAM): Optionally, at this point, you can set up access control by assigning roles to users, groups, or service principals for the resource group.

Review and Create: Once all information is entered, review your settings and click "Create" to establish your new resource group.

Add Resources: With the resource group created, you can start adding resources to it. Each resource you create or move into the group will inherit the policies and permissions defined at the resource group level.

Best Practices for Using Resource Groups

Plan Resource Group Strategy: Before creating resource groups, plan how you'll organize resources. Consider grouping them by application, environment (prod, dev, test), department, or any other logical division that aligns with your organization's structure and billing practices.

Consistent Naming Convention: Adopt a consistent naming convention for resource groups and resources within them. This facilitates easier management, especially as your Azure environment grows.

Leverage Tags for Additional Organization: Beyond resource groups, use tags to categorize resources further based on criteria like project codes, owners, or operational hours.

Resource groups are a foundational aspect of setting up and managing your Azure environment efficiently. They not only aid in organizing and administering your cloud resources but also play a critical role in access control, cost management, and compliance. By thoughtfully planning your resource group strategy and adhering to best practices, you can ensure a well-structured and manageable Azure infrastructure.

Step 3: Configure Networks and Security:

Virtual Networks (VNet):

Configuring Virtual Networks (VNets) is a fundamental step in setting up your Azure environment, providing the backbone for your cloud network infrastructure. Azure Virtual Network (VNet) enables Azure resources like VMs, web apps, and databases to securely communicate with each other, the internet, and on-premises networks. Understanding how to configure VNets correctly is crucial for creating isolated, highly secure, and scalable networks within Azure.

What is Azure Virtual Network (VNet)?

Azure VNet is a representation of your own network in the cloud. It is a logical isolation of the Azure cloud dedicated to your subscription. You can fully control your network environment, including selecting your own private IP address range, creating subnets, and configuring route tables and network gateways. VNets facilitate a range of networking functions, including the connection between Azure resources, secure communications with the internet and on-premises networks, and the filtering and routing of network traffic.

Key Components of Azure VNet

IP Address Spaces: VNets are created with a specific IP address space, using public and private (RFC 1918) addresses. You define the IP address ranges, subnets, and related settings.

Subnets: Within a VNet, you can create one or more subnets to segment the VNet into one or more sub-networks. This allows you to group and isolate resources based on your security and operational requirements.

Route Tables: Route tables contain a set of rules (routes) that determine where network traffic from subnets or virtual network gateways is routed.

Network Security Groups (NSGs): NSGs are used to allow or deny network traffic to subnets or network interfaces (NIC) in a VNet. NSGs work by applying security rules that filter traffic by source and destination IP address, port, and protocol.

Steps to Configure a Virtual Network

Plan Your Network Architecture: Before creating a VNet, plan your network's structure, including the IP address range, how many subnets you require, and the security policies you'll need to enforce.

Create a Virtual Network:

- Navigate to the Azure Portal and select "Create a resource."
- Search for and select "Virtual network."
- Provide the necessary information such as name, address space, subscription, resource group, and location.
- Define your subnets and specify the address range for each subnet.
- Review and create your VNet.

Configure Subnets:

- After creating your VNet, you can add additional subnets or configure existing ones by specifying address ranges and attaching NSGs for security.

Set Up Route Tables:

- Create and configure route tables if you need to customize how traffic is routed within your VNet or to external locations.

Secure Your VNet with NSGs:

- Define and assign NSGs to subnets or NICs within your VNet to control inbound and outbound traffic.

Connectivity Options:

- For hybrid connectivity, configure VPN gateways or Express-Route to connect your VNet to on-premises networks.
- To connect VNets to each other, use VNet peering, allowing resources in one VNet to communicate with resources in another VNet.

Best Practices for Azure VNet Configuration

- **Use Address Spaces Efficiently**: Choose address spaces that allow for future growth and avoid overlapping with other networks you might connect with.
- **Segmentation**: Use subnets to segment and isolate network traffic, applying the principle of least privilege with NSGs to enhance security.
- **Consistent Naming Convention**: Adopt a consistent naming convention for your VNets and subnets for easier management and identification.
- **Monitor and Manage**: Regularly monitor your VNets for performance and security. Utilize Azure Monitor and Network Watcher to gain insights and diagnostics.

Configuring Azure Virtual Networks is a critical task in setting up a secure, scalable Azure environment. VNets serve as the foundation for your cloud network, enabling secure and efficient communication between Azure resources and beyond. By carefully planning your network architecture, implementing security controls, and adhering to best practices, you can create a robust networking infrastructure that supports your applications and services securely and efficiently in Azure.

Security Practices:

When setting up your Azure environment, incorporating robust security practices from the outset is crucial. Azure offers a comprehensive suite of security tools and features designed to protect your resources, data, and applications. Implementing these security practices ensures that your Azure environment is resilient against threats, compliant with regulations, and optimized for performance and cost-efficiency.

Key Azure Security Practices

Implementing security in Azure involves a multi-layered approach that spans identity and access management, data protection, network security, and threat detection and response. Here's how you can apply these practices in your Azure setup:

Identity and Access Management (IAM) with Azure Active Directory (Azure AD):

- Use Azure AD for managing user identities and access to your Azure resources. Implement Multi-Factor Authentication (MFA) to add an extra layer of security for user sign-ins and transactions.
- Leverage Role-Based Access Control (RBAC) to grant users the least privileges they need to perform their jobs. This minimizes the potential impact of a compromised account.

Secure Your Data:

- Encrypt data at rest using Azure Storage Service Encryption or Azure Disk Encryption for Virtual Machines to protect your data from unauthorized access.
- Use Azure SQL Database's built-in transparent data encryption (TDE) to encrypt database files, backups, and transaction log files without altering application code.
- Implement Azure Key Vault to manage cryptographic keys and secrets used by cloud applications and services securely.

Enhance Network Security:

- Deploy Azure Network Security Groups (NSGs) to filter network traffic to and from Azure resources in an Azure Virtual Network (VNet).
- Use Azure Firewall, a managed, cloud-based network security service, to protect your Azure Virtual Network resources with application and network filtering rules.
- For hybrid networks, utilize Azure VPN Gateway or Azure ExpressRoute to securely connect your on-premises network to the Azure cloud.

Implement Threat Protection and Monitoring:

- Activate Azure Security Center to gain unified security management and advanced threat protection across your hybrid cloud workloads. It provides security recommendations and rapid threat detection.

- Enable Azure Monitor to collect, analyze, and act on telemetry data from your Azure and on-premises environments, helping you understand your security state and quickly respond to events.

Regularly Review and Update Security Policies:

- Regularly review and update your security policies and configurations to adapt to evolving threats and compliance requirements.
- Use Azure Policy to enforce organizational standards and assess compliance at scale across your resources.

Best Practices for Azure Security Configuration

Start with Secure Foundation:

Apply the principle of least privilege and secure defaults when setting up your Azure environment. Regularly review access permissions and network configurations to eliminate unnecessary exposure.

Stay Informed and Responsive: Utilize Azure's security and compliance dashboards to stay informed about the security posture of your resources. Be proactive in responding to alerts and recommendations.

Leverage Azure's Security Benchmarks: Follow Azure security benchmarks and best practices guides to align your security posture with industry standards and best practices.

Educate Your Team: Ensure that your team is aware of the potential security risks and the best practices for mitigating those risks in the Azure environment.

Configuring security practices is an integral part of setting up your Azure environment. By leveraging Azure's comprehensive security tools and following best practices, you can create a secure, resilient cloud environment that protects your resources and data against emerging threats. Remember, security in Azure is a shared responsibility; while Azure provides the tools and services to secure the infrastructure, it's up to you to configure and manage these settings effectively to protect your applications and data.

Step 4: Deploy Your First Resources:

Select and Deploy Services:

After setting up your Azure account, subscriptions, resource groups, and configuring your network and security infrastructure, the next pivotal step in establishing your Azure environment involves deploying your first set of resources. Selecting and deploying services in Azure is a crucial process that sets the foundation for your cloud-based applications and solutions. This stage involves careful planning and execution to ensure that the deployed resources align with your business objectives, operational requirements, and budget constraints.

Understanding Azure Services and Resources

Azure offers a broad spectrum of services and resources that cater to various computing, storage, networking, and application development needs. Before deploying your first resources, it's essential to understand the available services and how they fit into your overall architecture. Services like Azure Virtual Machines for compute, Azure Blob Storage for unstructured data storage, Azure SQL Database for relational databases, and Azure Functions for serverless computing are among the fundamental resources that many organizations start with.

Steps to Select and Deploy Azure Services

Identify Your Requirements:

- **Business Needs**: Define the specific business needs that your Azure resources need to address. Whether it's hosting a website, running a database, or processing big data, understanding your objectives is crucial.
- **Technical Requirements**: Assess the technical requirements, including compute power, storage needs, network configurations, and compliance requirements.
- **Cost Considerations**: Estimate the cost of running your services in Azure. Utilize the Azure Pricing Calculator to forecast

expenses and adjust your selections to fit your budget.

Explore Azure Services:

- Use the Azure Marketplace and Azure Portal to explore the services that meet your identified needs. Azure Marketplace is a great place to find third-party and Microsoft services that extend Azure's capabilities.

Plan for Deployment:

- **Architecture Design**: Design your architecture, considering aspects like scalability, availability, and security. Azure Advisor can provide recommendations to optimize your environment.
- **Resource Group Organization**: Decide how you'll organize resources within your resource groups. A logical organization by function, application, or environment can simplify management and cost tracking.

Deploy Your Services:

- Navigate to the Azure Portal and select "Create a resource" to start the deployment process.
- Search for the service you wish to deploy (e.g., Azure Virtual Machines, Azure SQL Database) and fill in the necessary configuration options, such as names, sizes, and network settings.
- Review and adjust the settings, then click "Create" to deploy the service. Azure will provision the resources according to your specifications.

Configure and Validate:

- After deployment, configure your services as needed, applying any additional settings or security controls.
- Validate the deployment by testing the functionality, performance, and connectivity of your services to ensure they operate as expected.

Best Practices for Deploying Azure Services

- **Start Small and Scale**: Begin with the minimal viable configuration and scale your resources as demand increases. This approach helps manage costs and complexity.
- **Leverage Automation**: Utilize Azure Resource Manager templates or Azure CLI scripts for deploying resources. Automation can ensure consistency and reduce the potential for human error.
- **Monitor and Optimize**: After deployment, continuously monitor your resources using tools like Azure Monitor and Azure Cost Management. Be proactive in optimizing your resources for performance and cost efficiency.

Deploying your first Azure resources is a critical step in leveraging the cloud for your computing needs. By thoroughly understanding your requirements, carefully selecting the appropriate services, and following best practices for deployment, you can establish a robust, scalable, and cost-effective Azure environment. This foundation will support your applications and services, enabling your organization to innovate and grow in the cloud.

Configure Monitoring and Management Tools:

After deploying your initial resources in Microsoft Azure, configuring monitoring and management tools is a crucial next step. These tools are essential for maintaining the health, performance, and cost-effectiveness of your Azure resources. Azure offers a suite of built-in monitoring, management, and governance tools that provide deep insights into your applications and services, ensuring they perform optimally and securely while staying within budget.

Azure Monitor

Azure Monitor is at the core of Microsoft Azure's monitoring service. It collects, analyzes, and acts on telemetry data from your Azure and on-premises environments. Azure Monitor helps you understand how your applications are performing and proactively identifies issues affecting them and the resources they depend on.

Features:

- **Application Insights**: Offers application performance monitoring and user analytics. It helps you understand how your applications are performing and how users interact with them, making it easier to spot and diagnose issues.
- **Log Analytics**: Collects and analyzes data generated by resources in your cloud and on-premises environments. It's crucial for understanding and acting upon the telemetry data your applications and services generate.
- **Alerts**: Set up proactive alerts based on metrics and logs. Alerts notify you about critical conditions and potentially take automated actions to mitigate issues.

Azure Service Health

Azure Service Health provides personalized alerts and guidance when Azure service issues affect you. It informs you about service issues, planned maintenance, and health advisories, allowing for proactive response and preparation.

Benefits:

- **Immediate Notifications**: Receive notifications about any issues that might affect your resources so you can mitigate them as quickly as possible.
- **Detailed Impact Analysis**: Understand the impact of incidents and maintenance on your resources to better manage and respond to them.

Azure Advisor

zure Advisor is a personalized cloud consultant that helps you follow best practices to optimize your Azure deployments. It analyzes your resource configuration and usage telemetry to provide recommendations across four categories: cost optimization, security, performance, and operational excellence.

Key Recommendations Include:

- **Cost Optimization**: Suggestions on how to reduce your costs by identifying idle and underutilized resources.
- **Security**: Recommendations for improving the security of your resources.
- **Performance**: Tips for enhancing the performance of your applications by optimizing Azure resources.

Azure Policy

Azure Policy helps to enforce organizational standards and to assess compliance at scale. Through its policy definitions, you can ensure that resources in your environment are compliant with corporate standards and service level agreements (SLAs).

Use Cases:

- **Enforcing Standards**: Automatically enforce standards for resources in your Azure environment, ensuring consistency and compliance with external regulations and internal policies.
- **Compliance Assessment**: Continuously monitor compliance and manage risk across your Azure resources.

Configuring monitoring and management tools is a critical step in setting up a well-architected Azure environment. By leveraging Azure Monitor, Azure Service Health, Azure Advisor, and Azure Policy, you can ensure that your resources are performing efficiently, securely, and in compliance with your organizational policies. These tools not only help in proactively identifying and mitigating issues but also play a significant role in optimizing the cost and performance of your Azure resources. As you become more familiar with Azure's capabilities, these monitoring and management tools will be invaluable in maintaining the health and efficiency of your cloud environment.

Step 5: Familiarize Yourself with Cost Management and Billing:

Azure Cost Management:

An essential aspect of managing an Azure environment efficiently is understanding and controlling your cloud costs. Azure Cost Management and Billing is a suite of tools provided by Microsoft Azure designed to give you visibility into your cloud spend and to help manage your costs effectively. It's vital for organizations of all sizes to familiarize themselves with Azure Cost Management tools to ensure they can optimize their cloud investments while avoiding unnecessary expenditures.

Overview of Azure Cost Management

Azure Cost Management and Billing provides comprehensive tools to monitor, allocate, and optimize your costs. It offers detailed insights into your spending patterns, allowing you to identify trends, detect inefficiencies, and understand the drivers behind your cloud costs. This suite is integrated directly into the Azure portal, providing a seamless experience for managing your Azure spend alongside your resources.

Key Features of Azure Cost Management

Cost Analysis: This tool offers detailed reports and charts that break down your Azure spending. You can view costs by resource, service, location, and tags, enabling you to pinpoint where and how your budget is being used. Cost Analysis helps in identifying trends over time, facilitating more informed budgeting and spending forecasts.

Budgets: Azure allows you to set up budgets to control cloud spending across your subscriptions, resource groups, or services. You can configure alerts to notify you when your spending approaches or exceeds your budgeted amount. This proactive approach helps in avoiding cost overruns and in making necessary adjustments to stay within budget.

Recommendations: Azure Cost Management includes a recommendations feature that suggests ways to reduce costs. It might recommend resizing underutilized virtual machines, deleting idle resources, or purchasing reserved instances to save on long-term costs.

Cost Allocation: This feature helps in distributing costs across departments, projects, or regions by using tags. Effective cost allocation is crucial for understanding the cost implications of different projects or departments, enabling more accurate chargeback or showback models.

Cloudyn: A tool acquired by Microsoft that provides advanced cost management and optimization features. Cloudyn offers deeper insights and more granular control over your cloud spend, supporting multi-cloud environments beyond just Azure.

Best Practices for Azure Cost Management

Regularly Review Cost Management Data: Make it a habit to regularly review and analyze your spending data through Azure Cost Analysis. Keeping a close eye on your spending can help you catch and address inefficiencies early.

Utilize Tags Effectively: Implement a consistent tagging strategy for your resources. Tags allow you to categorize costs in a way that aligns with your business structure, making it easier to track and manage expenditures.

Optimize Resource Usage: Leverage Azure Advisor recommendations to optimize your resources for cost efficiency. Regularly assess and adjust your resource sizes, and consider using Azure Reserved Instances for predictable workloads.

Implement Governance Policies: Use Azure Policy to enforce governance and cost control measures, such as restricting the types of resources that can be deployed or setting up policies for auto-shutdown of VMs during off-hours.

Familiarizing yourself with Azure Cost Management and Billing is crucial for maintaining control over your cloud costs. By leveraging the tools and best practices outlined above, you can ensure transparency in your cloud spending, make informed decisions to optimize costs, and allocate resources efficiently. Azure Cost Management provides the insights and controls necessary to maximize the value of your cloud investments, making it an essential component of your Azure environment setup.

Billing Alerts:

One of the critical aspects of managing your Azure environment efficiently is keeping track of your spending to avoid unexpected costs. Microsoft Azure provides a powerful toolset for monitoring and controlling your cloud expenditures, with billing alerts playing a pivotal role in this process. These alerts help you stay informed about your Azure consumption and spending patterns, allowing you to make informed decisions and take timely action to manage your costs effectively.

Understanding Billing Alerts in Azure

Billing alerts in Azure are automated notifications that are triggered when your Azure spending reaches a predefined threshold. These alerts are essential for cost management, as they provide real-time visibility into your Azure expenditures and help prevent bill shock by alerting you before costs exceed your budget.

Setting Up Billing Alerts

Access Cost Management + Billing: In the Azure portal, navigate to the "Cost Management + Billing" section. This is your central hub for all things related to Azure billing and cost management.

Configure Cost Alerts: Within the Cost Management + Billing section, you'll find an option for "Cost alerts." Here, you can set up new alerts based on your spending thresholds. Azure allows you to create alerts for both actual and forecasted costs, giving you the flexibility to monitor your spending proactively.

Specify Alert Conditions: When creating a billing alert, you'll need to specify several conditions, including:

- The subscription or resource group you want to monitor.
- The spending threshold that triggers the alert.
- The period over which spending is assessed (e.g., monthly, quarterly).

Determine Alert Recipients: You can specify one or more recipients for the billing alerts. These can be individuals or groups within your organization who need to be informed about cost-related developments.

Review and Save: Before finalizing, review your alert settings to ensure they match your monitoring and notification needs. Once confirmed, save the alert. Azure will now automatically notify the specified recipients when spending reaches the defined threshold.

Best Practices for Using Billing Alerts

Regular Review: Periodically review your billing alert settings to ensure they align with your current budget and spending patterns. Adjust thresholds as necessary to reflect changes in your Azure usage or financial objectives.

Multiple Thresholds: Consider setting up multiple alerts at different spending thresholds to provide early warnings and more critical alerts as spending approaches budget limits.

Integrate with Budgets: Use billing alerts in conjunction with Azure budgets to manage and track your cloud spending more effectively. While budgets help you set spending limits, alerts provide real-time notifications to keep you informed of your financial status.

Actionable Insights: When you receive a billing alert, take the time to analyze the underlying causes of the spending increase. Azure Cost Management tools can help you identify specific resources or services driving up costs, enabling you to take targeted actions to reduce expenditures.

Billing alerts in Azure are an essential tool for managing cloud costs effectively. By providing timely notifications about your spending, they enable you to maintain control over your Azure expenditures, ensuring that you stay within budget and avoid financial surprises. Coupled with Azure's comprehensive cost management tools, billing alerts empower you to optimize your cloud investments, ensuring that you get the most value out of your Azure environment.

Navigating the Azure Dashboard:

The Azure Dashboard is the primary user interface through which you interact with resources, services, and administrative functions in Microsoft Azure. As the hub for managing and monitoring your cloud environment, becoming proficient in navigating the Azure Dashboard is essential for effectively utilizing Azure's vast offerings. This comprehensive guide aims to equip you with the knowledge to confidently navigate and customize the Azure Dashboard, enhancing your productivity and control over your Azure resources.

Overview of the Azure Dashboard

The Azure Dashboard provides a visual interface that aggregates and displays information about your Azure environment. It offers a customizable and interactive experience, allowing you to tailor the dashboard according to your specific needs and preferences. Key components include tiles for quick insights into services, navigation panes for accessing resource groups and services, and toolbars for managing account settings and notifications.

Key Components of the Azure Dashboard

Navigation Pane: Located on the left side of the dashboard, the navigation pane (or sidebar) offers quick access to all Azure services, resource groups, and additional tools like Azure Advisor and Cost

Management. It serves as the primary means of navigating between different areas of your Azure account.

Resource Groups: Effective management of resource groups is crucial for organizing your resources and managing access and policies.

Dashboard Tiles: The main area of the dashboard can be customized with tiles that provide snapshots of key metrics, resource statuses, and quick links to commonly used services. Tiles can be added, removed, or rearranged to create a personalized overview of your environment.

Top Toolbar: The top toolbar includes global search, resource creation shortcuts, cloud shell access, directory and subscription filters, and account settings. It also houses the notifications area, where you can view alerts, billing information, and system notifications.

Customizing the Azure Dashboard

Customization is a powerful feature of the Azure Dashboard, enabling you to create a workspace tailored to your operational needs. Here's how to customize your dashboard:

- **Add or Remove Tiles**: Customize your dashboard view by adding tiles for quick access to frequently used resources, services, or metrics. You can also remove unnecessary tiles to declutter your view.

- **Create Multiple Dashboards**: For different projects or operational focuses, you can create multiple dashboards and switch between them as needed. Each dashboard can be customized to show relevant resources and information for specific tasks or projects.

- **Share Dashboards**: Azure allows you to share custom dashboards with other users in your organization, facilitating collaboration and ensuring that team members have access to the same information and operational views.

Navigating to Key Services and Resources

- **Service Categories**: Use the navigation pane to access different categories of services, such as Compute, Networking, Storage, and Databases. Each category provides a centralized space to manage related Azure services.
- **Search Functionality**: The global search bar at the top of the dashboard enables you to quickly find resources, services, and documentation, saving time and enhancing efficiency in managing your Azure environment.
- **Azure Marketplace**: Accessible from the navigation pane, the Azure Marketplace allows you to find and deploy third-party and Microsoft applications and services, expanding your environment's capabilities.

Navigating the Azure Dashboard is a fundamental skill for managing your cloud environment in Microsoft Azure. By understanding and customizing the dashboard, you can streamline your workflow, quickly access important information, and maintain a high level of control over your resources. The Azure Dashboard's flexibility and customization options make it a powerful tool for cloud management, enabling you to focus on optimizing and expanding your Azure solutions.

Azure Subscriptions:

When setting up your Azure environment, understanding the hierarchy and function of Azure Subscriptions, Resource Groups, and Resources is fundamental. This hierarchical structure is crucial for organizing, managing, and securing your cloud assets efficiently. Here's a detailed exploration of these core components and how they interrelate within the Azure ecosystem.

Azure Subscriptions

An Azure subscription is a logical container used to provision resources in Microsoft Azure. It holds the details of all your resources like virtual machines, databases, and more. A subscription serves two primary purposes: it acts as a boundary for billing and as an access control container.

Billing: Each subscription has its own set of billing rules and limits. All the resources within a subscription are billed together under a single payment method.

Access Control: Subscriptions are associated with Azure Active Directory (Azure AD), allowing you to apply access management policies at the subscription level.

Resource Groups

Within a subscription, resources are organized into resource groups. A resource group is a collection of resources that share the same lifecycle, permissions, and policies. They are a fundamental element of Azure resource management, allowing you to manage and monitor resources as a single entity.

Lifecycle Management: Deploying, updating, or deleting resources as a group simplifies the management of resources that share a common lifecycle.

Access Management: You can apply Role-Based Access Control (RBAC) policies to the entire resource group, thereby uniformly controlling access to the resources within it.

Organizational Clarity: Resource groups provide a way to organize resources by application, department, project, or any other criteria that fit your operational needs.

Resources

Resources are the individual instances of services that you use in Azure, such as virtual machines, SQL databases, or storage accounts. Every resource must belong to a resource group, and you can move resources between groups as needed.

Types and Instances: Azure offers a vast array of resource types, each with specific features, configurations, and pricing. An instance of a resource type is a resource you have provisioned in your subscription.

Configuration and Management: Each resource type has its own set of configuration options and management tasks. Azure provides management tools like the Azure portal, Azure PowerShell, and the Azure CLI for interacting with resources.

Best Practices for Organizing Subscriptions, Resource Groups, and Resources

Use Multiple Subscriptions: For larger organizations or complex projects, consider using multiple subscriptions to separate environments, billing, and access control more effectively.

Logical Resource Grouping: Organize resources into resource groups based on their lifecycle, purpose, or access control requirements. This simplifies management tasks and clarifies organizational structures.

Naming Conventions: Implement consistent naming conventions for subscriptions, resource groups, and resources. This aids in identification, management, and automation.

Tagging: Use tags to add metadata to your resources, subscriptions, and resource groups. Tags can help with categorizing and reporting on cloud spend, ownership, or any custom criteria relevant to your organization.

The structured hierarchy of Azure Subscriptions, Resource Groups, and Resources plays a critical role in managing your Azure environment efficiently. By understanding and utilizing these constructs effectively, you can achieve granular control over billing, access management, and the organization of your cloud assets. Adhering to best practices in structuring and managing these elements ensures a well-organized, secure, and cost-effective Azure environment.

Conclusion

Setting up your Azure environment is a critical first step in your cloud journey, requiring thoughtful planning around subscription management, resource organization, networking, security, and cost control. By following these foundational steps, you can establish a robust, scalable, and secure environment that leverages the full potential of Azure services. As you grow more comfortable with Azure, you can explore more advanced features and services to further enhance your cloud capabilities, always keeping security and cost management at the forefront of your strategy.

Chapter 3: Azure Core Services Overview

Microsoft Azure provides a comprehensive suite of cloud services, enabling businesses and developers to build, deploy, and manage applications through Microsoft's global network of data centers. This extensive array of services covers everything from computing power and storage solutions to artificial intelligence (AI) and Internet of Things (IoT) functionalities. Understanding the core services Azure offers is crucial for leveraging the platform's full potential to drive innovation and efficiency in your cloud-based solutions. Below is an overview of the key service categories within Azure and their primary offerings.

Compute Services:

Compute services form the backbone of Azure, offering scalable computing resources on-demand. These services support a wide range of applications, from simple websites to complex machine learning applications.

Azure Virtual Machines (VMs):

Deploy and manage VMs inside a virtualized environment. Azure VMs offer flexibility for running a wide array of workloads, from development and testing environments to high-performance computing.

Azure Virtual Machines (VMs) stand as one of the cornerstone services in Microsoft Azure's suite of cloud computing offerings. This service provides scalable, on-demand virtualized computing resources, allowing users to deploy and manage applications in the cloud with the same level of control and flexibility as if they were running on physical machines in their own data center. Understanding how to leverage Azure VMs is essential for IT professionals and developers looking to maximize the efficiency and scalability of their cloud-based applications.

What Are Azure Virtual Machines?

Azure Virtual Machines offer the ability to create and use virtual machines in the cloud. These VMs can run Windows, Linux, or other operating systems and can be configured with a wide range of processing power, memory, and storage options to meet various application requirements. Azure VMs are fully integrated with other Azure services, providing a comprehensive environment for deploying, managing, and scaling applications.

Key Features of Azure Virtual Machines

Flexibility and Control: Azure VMs give you full control over the operating system, the VM configuration, and the software that runs on the VM, offering the flexibility to tailor your cloud environment to your specific needs.

Scalability: You can easily scale your VMs up or down based on your computing requirements, and Azure's global infrastructure ensures that your applications can be deployed close to your users to reduce latency.

Integrated Security: Azure VMs come with built-in security and compliance features, including network security groups, encryption, and Azure's Identity and Access Management (IAM) capabilities.

High Availability and Disaster Recovery: Azure ensures high availability for VMs through features like Azure Availability Sets and Azure Site Recovery, minimizing downtime and ensuring that your critical applications remain online.

Examples of Using Azure Virtual Machines

Web Application Hosting: Deploying a web application stack on Azure VMs is a common use case. For example, you can set up a LAMP stack (Linux, Apache, MySQL, PHP) on a series of VMs for hosting a dynamic website or a web application.

Development and Testing Environments: Azure VMs can be used to quickly provision development and testing environments that mimic production environments. This allows developers to develop and test their applications in a cloud environment that can be easily scaled or replicated.

Database Servers: Running database servers on Azure VMs is another typical scenario. Whether it's SQL Server, MySQL, PostgreSQL, or another database system, you can leverage Azure VMs for database hosting, benefiting from Azure's scalability and availability features.

High-Performance Computing (HPC): For compute-intensive tasks such as simulations, modeling, or data analysis, Azure VMs can be configured to provide the necessary computational power. By using Azure's HPC-optimized VMs, you can tackle complex scientific, engineering, or financial computations.

Legacy Application Migration: Azure VMs enable businesses to migrate legacy applications to the cloud without needing to re-architect them for a cloud-native environment. This allows for the preservation of investments in existing software while still benefiting from the scalability and flexibility of cloud computing.

Azure Virtual Machines provide a versatile and powerful platform for deploying a wide range of applications in the cloud. From simple web hosting to complex, compute-intensive workloads, Azure VMs offer the scalability, security, and flexibility needed to support modern cloud computing requirements. By understanding and effectively leveraging Azure VMs, organizations can optimize their cloud infrastructure, ensuring efficient operation and alignment with business goals.

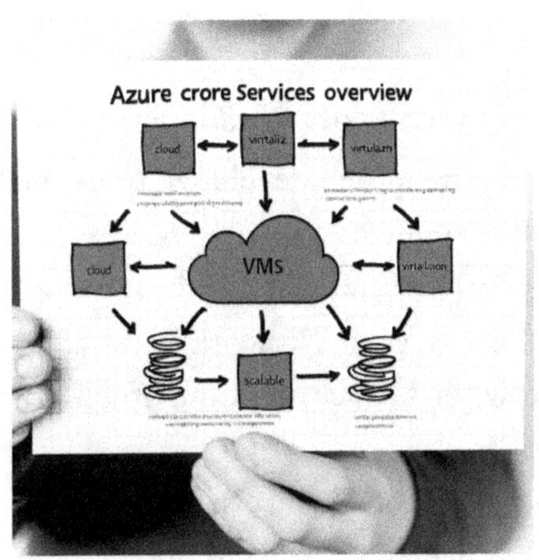

Azure Kubernetes Service (AKS):

Simplify the deployment, management, and scaling of containerized applications using Kubernetes, an open-source container orchestration system.

In the landscape of cloud computing, containerization has emerged as a pivotal technology for deploying and managing applications efficiently. The Azure Kubernetes Service (AKS) is Microsoft Azure's managed container orchestration service, designed to simplify the deployment, scaling, and operations of application containers across clusters of hosts. AKS is built on the open-source Kubernetes system, providing a powerful platform for developers and system administrators to automate the deployment, scaling, and management of containerized applications.

What is Azure Kubernetes Service (AKS)?

AKS manages your hosted Kubernetes environment, making it easier to deploy and manage containerized applications without container orchestration expertise. It eliminates the complexity of handling Kubernetes by offloading much of that responsibility to Azure, allowing you to focus on your applications rather than the infrastructure.

Key Features of Azure Kubernetes Service

Automated Kubernetes Version Upgrades and Patching: AKS simplifies the maintenance of your containerized applications by automatically upgrading the Kubernetes version and applying security patches.

Integrated Developer Tools: AKS integrates with Azure DevOps, Visual Studio Code, and other developer tools, making it easier to build, test, and deploy applications.

Advanced Networking: AKS provides advanced networking features, including Azure Virtual Network integration, enabling secure communication between AKS clusters and other Azure services or on-premises resources.

Elastic Scaling: With AKS, you can automatically scale your application in response to demand, ensuring that your application remains highly available and performs optimally at all times.

Integrated Security and Compliance: AKS integrates with Azure Active Directory and provides built-in security features, including role-based access control (RBAC), ensuring that access to your Kubernetes environment is securely managed.

Examples of Using Azure Kubernetes Service (AKS)

Microservices Architectures: AKS is ideal for running applications based on a microservices architecture. By containerizing each microservice and deploying them on AKS, you can achieve greater scalability, resilience, and deployment agility. For instance, an e-commerce platform can be broken down into microservices such as user authentication, product catalog, order management, and payment processing, each running independently in AKS.

Continuous Integration and Continuous Deployment (CI/CD): AKS can be integrated into a CI/CD pipeline, automating the deployment of containerized applications. With Azure DevOps or GitHub Actions, you can set up workflows that automatically build, test, and deploy applications to AKS whenever code changes are made, streamlining the development process.

Machine Learning Workloads: AKS can host machine learning models as containerized applications, benefiting from the scalability and flexibility of Kubernetes. Data scientists can deploy machine learning models in AKS, making them accessible as web services for applications or users, enabling scenarios like real-time predictions or batch processing.

Application Modernization: Businesses looking to modernize legacy applications can containerize these applications and run them on AKS. This allows for leveraging cloud-native technologies and practices while maintaining existing investments in software and infrastructure.

The Azure Kubernetes Service (AKS) offers a comprehensive solution for managing containerized applications at scale, harnessing the power of Kubernetes without the complexity of managing it. By providing tools for automated scaling, updates, and integrated security, AKS enables organizations to focus on developing and deploying applications more efficiently. Whether you're building new cloud-native applications, modernizing legacy applications, or creating complex microservices architectures, AKS provides the robust, scalable, and secure platform needed to meet modern application deployment and management challenges.

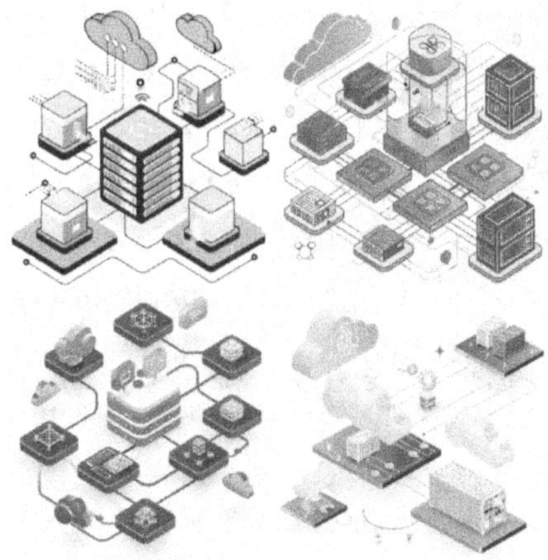

Azure Functions:

A serverless compute service that enables you to run event-triggered code without explicitly provisioning or managing infrastructure, facilitating the development of scalable applications and microservices.

Azure Functions is a pivotal service within Microsoft Azure's compute offerings, embodying the essence of serverless computing. This service allows developers to run small pieces of code ("functions") in response to events, simplifying complex orchestration challenges and allowing for a focus on business logic rather than infrastructure management. Azure Functions supports a variety of programming languages, including C#, JavaScript, Python, and PowerShell, making it a versatile tool for a wide range of applications.

What Are Azure Functions?

Azure Functions is a serverless execution environment that enables you to run event-driven code without explicitly provisioning or managing infrastructure. With Azure Functions, you only pay for the compute time you consume, making it a cost-effective option for many scenarios, from simple tasks to complex integrations.

Key Features of Azure Functions

Event-driven Execution: Azure Functions can automatically run code in response to a wide array of events occurring in Azure services, third-party services, or on-premises systems.

Integration Capabilities: Offers seamless integration with other Azure services, providing out-of-the-box triggers and bindings that simplify connecting your functions to data and services.

Scaling: Automatically scales based on demand, handling thousands of concurrent functions executions without requiring manual intervention. This ensures that applications remain responsive at all times.

Development Flexibility: Supports development in multiple languages and provides tools that enable local testing and debugging of functions on your development machine.

Security and Compliance: Integrates with Azure Active Directory for authentication and compliance, ensuring that functions are secure and meet regulatory requirements.

Examples of Using Azure Functions

Real-time Data Processing: Azure Functions can process real-time data streams from IoT devices, logs, or social media feeds. For instance, functions can analyze tweets for sentiment in real time, providing immediate insights into public perception.

Automated Tasks: Schedule tasks to run at specific intervals using timer triggers, ideal for nightly backups, cleaning up databases, or sending batch email notifications.

Webhooks and APIs: Build APIs and respond to webhooks from third-party services. Azure Functions can serve as a backend for web applications, handling HTTP requests for specific routes or actions.

Database Change Processing: Respond to changes in data within Azure Cosmos DB, SQL Database, or other data stores. Functions can trigger on data insertion or modification, allowing for tasks like data validation, transformation, or synchronization across systems.

Image or File Processing: Trigger functions upon the upload of images or files to Azure Blob Storage, performing actions such as resizing images or processing file content for indexing and analysis.

Azure Functions offers a powerful platform for building scalable, event-driven applications with minimal infrastructure management. Its serverless nature, combined with broad language support and deep integration with Azure services, makes it an ideal choice for a wide variety of computing tasks. From simple automation scripts to complex processing workflows, Azure Functions enables developers to focus on writing code that adds value, rather than managing servers and infrastructure. By leveraging Azure Functions, organizations can build more responsive, efficient, and cost-effective solutions.

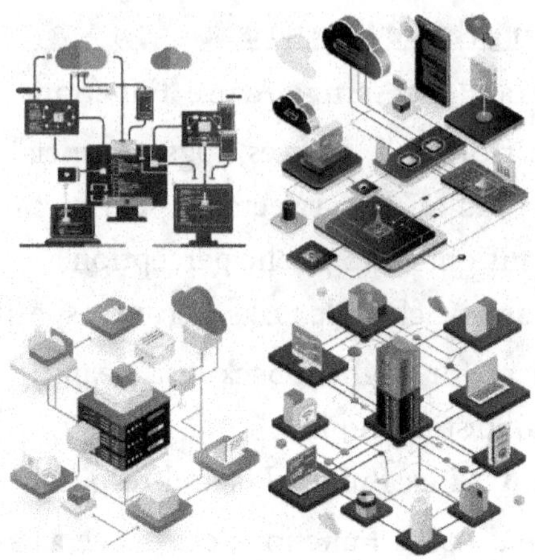

Storage Services:

Azure's storage services provide secure, scalable, and highly available storage solutions for data of all types and sizes.

Azure Blob Storage:

An object storage solution for the cloud that supports a wide range of unstructured data such as text, binary data, documents, and media files.

In the array of Azure Core Services, Azure Blob Storage stands out as a critical component for managing large amounts of unstructured data in the cloud. This service is designed to handle everything from documents and videos to application data and real-time analytics. Understanding Azure Blob Storage is essential for developers, IT professionals, and businesses looking to leverage cloud storage's scalability, reliability, and security.

What is Azure Blob Storage?

Azure Blob Storage is Microsoft Azure's object storage solution for the cloud. It is optimized for storing massive amounts of unstructured data, such as text or binary data. Blob storage is ideal for serving images or documents directly to a browser, storing files for distributed access, streaming video and audio, and performing secure backup and disaster recovery.

Key Features of Azure Blob Storage

Durability and High Availability: Azure Blob Storage is designed for high durability, storing data redundantly in multiple locations within a data center and across geographic regions to ensure data remains available and protected against failures.

Scalability: It offers massive scalability to meet the needs of growing data. You can store petabytes of data in Blob Storage, making it suitable for any scale of application.

Security: Azure provides advanced security features, including role-based access control (RBAC), encryption in transit and at rest, and fine-grained access policies to secure your data.

Cost-Effective: With multiple access tiers (Hot, Cool, and Archive), you can optimize storage costs based on how frequently data is accessed.

Examples of Using Azure Blob Storage

Website Content: Store static content for a website, such as images, CSS files, and JavaScript files, in Blob Storage. This content can be delivered directly to clients, reducing the load on web servers.

Data Lake: Utilize Blob Storage as a data lake to store vast amounts of raw data in its native format. This data can later be processed and analyzed by big data analytics services like Azure Databricks or HDInsight.

Video and Audio Streaming: Store and stream video or audio content directly from Blob Storage. The service's scalability ensures smooth delivery to a global audience, regardless of demand spikes.

Backup and Disaster Recovery: Use Blob Storage for secure backup of files and virtual machine disks. Its geo-redundant storage options make it an ideal choice for disaster recovery plans.

Archiving: Archive infrequently accessed data to the Azure Blob Storage Archive tier, significantly reducing storage costs while ensuring that data is still available when needed.

Azure Blob Storage offers a robust and scalable solution for managing unstructured data in the cloud. Whether you're storing documents, media files, backup copies, or large datasets for analysis, Blob

Storage provides a secure, durable, and cost-effective storage solution. By leveraging Azure Blob Storage, businesses and developers can easily manage their data at scale, ensuring that it is always accessible, protected, and optimized for cost and performance.

Azure File Storage:

Offers fully managed file shares in the cloud that are accessible via the industry-standard Server Message Block (SMB) protocol, ideal for migrating legacy applications to the cloud.

Azure File Storage presents a unique offering within Microsoft Azure's diverse range of storage solutions, specifically designed to cater to the need for managed file shares in the cloud. It bridges the gap between cloud storage and traditional file systems, providing a familiar paradigm for file access and sharing across both cloud-based and on-premises environments. This service is instrumental for scenarios requiring file shares accessible via the SMB (Server Message Block) or NFS (Network File System) protocols, offering seamless integration and flexibility.

What is Azure File Storage?

Azure File Storage is a service that enables you to create, mount, and share file shares in the cloud using the standard SMB protocol or the NFS protocol. It is engineered to provide fully managed file shares that cloud or on-premises deployments can access and use. This service supports scenarios such as sharing application data, storing diagnostic logs, data migration, and more, offering high availability, security, and scalability.

Key Features of Azure File Storage

SMB and NFS Protocol Support: Azure File Storage supports both SMB and NFS protocols, allowing for versatile access options, including from Windows, Linux, and macOS clients.

Integration with Azure Active Directory Domain Services: Offers seamless integration with Azure Active Directory Domain Services for easy authentication and access control, enhancing security and simplification of management.

Snapshot Support: Provides the ability to create snapshots of file shares, enabling point-in-time recovery and backup of files.

Scalability and Performance: File shares in Azure File Storage can scale up to meet demand, ensuring high performance for read-heavy or write-heavy scenarios.

Hybrid Cloud Scenarios: Supports hybrid cloud deployments, enabling on-premises applications to access file shares in the cloud as if they were located within the local network.

Examples of Using Azure File Storage

Lift and Shift Applications: Migrate traditional applications to the cloud without modifications. Azure File Storage can host shared data that these applications rely on, ensuring minimal disruption during the migration process.

Development and Testing Environments: Share code bases, test data, and diagnostic outputs across development and testing environments hosted in Azure. Developers and testers can access these files from any location, facilitating collaboration.

Web Server Shared Storage: Use Azure File Storage to store web content such as media files, documents, and templates, making them accessible to web servers deployed across multiple regions for high availability and load balancing.

Diagnostics and Log Storage: Collect and store logs and diagnostic data from virtual machines and applications. This centralized storage solution simplifies log management and analysis, especially in large-scale deployments.

Hybrid File Sharing: Set up a hybrid file sharing scenario where on-premises and cloud-based applications access the same file shares seamlessly. This is particularly useful for organizations transitioning to the cloud while maintaining some on-premises infrastructure.

Azure File Storage offers a versatile and highly accessible solution for managing file shares in the cloud, providing a familiar experience for those used to working with traditional file servers. By leveraging this service, businesses can achieve greater flexibility, scalability, and efficiency in their storage strategies, accommodating a wide range of scenarios from application data sharing to hybrid cloud storage solutions. With Azure File Storage, organizations can simplify their storage infrastructure while benefiting from the advanced features and global reach of Azure.

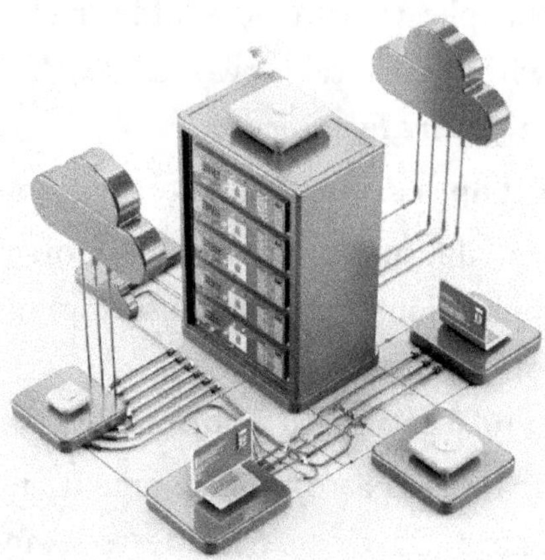

Azure Queue Storage:

A messaging store for reliable messaging between application components, whether they are within the cloud, on the desktop, on-premises, or on mobile devices.

Azure Queue Storage is a key component of Microsoft Azure's storage solutions, designed to provide a reliable messaging queue for large-scale applications. It enables asynchronous communication between application components, whether they're running in the cloud, on desktops, on-premises, or on mobile devices. This service is particularly useful for managing a large volume of messages and tasks, ensuring that high-volume workloads are processed efficiently and reliably.

What is Azure Queue Storage?

Azure Queue Storage is a service that offers a simple REST-based interface for queueing and reliably delivering messages between different parts of an application. It supports programmatically accessing message queues and adding, removing, and peering messages. This service is engineered to enhance application scalability and reliability by decoupling components and ensuring smooth operation even under variable loads.

Key Features of Azure Queue Storage

Decoupling of Application Components: By using message queues, Azure Queue Storage helps decouple application components, making the system more resilient and scalable.

Reliable Message Delivery: Ensures messages are reliably delivered to and processed by application components, supporting a wide range of communication patterns.

Scalability: Automatically scales to meet demand, capable of storing millions of messages per queue. This scalability is critical for applications with variable workloads.

Simple REST API: Offers a straightforward REST-based API for queue operations, making it accessible from any application that can send and receive HTTP/HTTPS requests.

Examples of Using Azure Queue Storage

Web Application Order Processing: In an e-commerce web application, orders placed by customers are added to a queue. A separate background service reads from the queue and processes orders, such as payment processing and inventory updates. This decouples the order placement mechanism from the order processing logic, improving responsiveness and scalability.

Video Processing: For a video sharing platform, videos uploaded by users are queued for processing, including encoding and thumbnail generation. A background process reads from the queue and performs these tasks asynchronously, ensuring that the user interface remains responsive.

IoT Device Message Collection: In IoT scenarios, messages from thousands of devices can be collected in Azure Queue Storage. A back-end service processes these messages, which might include sensor data or device status updates, ensuring timely and reliable data processing.

Log Data Aggregation: Collect log data from multiple sources into a queue. Background processing services can then aggregate, analyze, or store the log data as needed, providing a centralized approach to log management.

Task Scheduling: Use Azure Queue Storage to implement simple task scheduling. Tasks can be queued with specific instructions, and worker roles can process these tasks asynchronously based on priority or other criteria.

Azure Queue Storage provides a robust, scalable, and simple solution for message queuing needs, facilitating asynchronous communication and processing within applications. Its ability to decouple application components not only enhances scalability and reliability but also improves overall application design. By leveraging Azure Queue Storage, developers can build more responsive, efficient, and resilient applications capable of handling variable workloads and complex communication patterns. Whether for web applications, IoT ecosystems, or any scenario requiring reliable message delivery and processing, Azure Queue Storage offers a versatile messaging backbone.

Networking Services:

Networking services in Azure provide a range of options to connect cloud and on-premises infrastructure and services securely.

Azure Virtual Network (VNet):

Create your private network in the cloud, enabling Azure resources to securely communicate with each other, the internet, and on-premises networks.

Azure Virtual Network (VNet) is a fundamental building block of Microsoft Azure's Networking Services, providing the backbone for many types of cloud-based and hybrid networking solutions. It offers the ability to create isolated and highly secure networks in the cloud, enabling Azure resources, such as virtual machines (VMs) and applications, to securely communicate with each other, the internet, and on-premises networks. Understanding how to leverage Azure VNet is crucial for architects and developers aiming to design robust, scalable, and secure cloud architectures.

What is Azure Virtual Network (VNet)?

Azure VNet is a customizable network service that provides private, isolated networking environments in the Azure cloud. It allows you to create your own private space in Azure, which is crucial for many cloud networking scenarios. With VNet, you can control IP address ranges, subnets, route tables, and network gateways within your virtual network, offering a wide range of networking functionalities such as segmentation, peering, and connectivity to on-premises networks.

Key Features of Azure Virtual Network

Isolation and Segmentation: Azure VNet provides a secure, isolated environment for your Azure resources. You can further divide your VNet into subnets, allowing for detailed network segmentation and organization.

Interconnectivity: VNets facilitate secure connections between Azure resources, between VNets (VNet peering), and between Azure and on-premises networks (VPN Gateway and ExpressRoute).

Customizable IP Address Ranges: You have the freedom to define your own private IP address space, using public and private (RFC 1918) addresses as needed.

Integration with Azure Services: VNet integrates seamlessly with many Azure services, ensuring that resources such as VMs, databases, and web apps can securely communicate within the VNet.

Controlled Routing: You can control how traffic is routed within and outside of your VNet using route tables and network appliances.

Examples of Using Azure Virtual Network

Multi-tier Application Architecture: For a traditional three-tier application (web, application, and database layers), you can use VNets and subnets to isolate and control traffic flow between each tier, enhancing security and reducing the risk of exposure.

Hybrid Cloud Connectivity: Connect your on-premises data center to Azure using VPN Gateway or ExpressRoute within a VNet to extend your data center and run hybrid applications that leverage both on-premises and cloud resources.

Disaster Recovery: Implement disaster recovery solutions by connecting VNets across different Azure regions. This ensures that if one region goes down, traffic can be rerouted to another region, keeping your applications running.

Development and Testing Environments: Create isolated VNets for development, testing, and production environments. This separation helps prevent accidental cross-environment transactions and provides a safe space for development and testing without impacting production workloads.

Microservices Architectures: For applications built using a microservices architecture, VNets and subnets can provide network isolation for each service, improving security and allowing for microservice-specific scaling and policies.

Azure Virtual Network (VNet) is a powerful and versatile tool in the Azure Networking Services portfolio, providing the foundational networking infrastructure necessary for deploying and managing cloud and hybrid applications. By offering control over private networking environments, connectivity options, and integration with Azure services, VNets enable businesses to create sophisticated, secure, and scalable network architectures in the cloud. Whether for segregating development environments, connecting on-premises data centers, or architecting complex applications, Azure VNet serves as a critical component in realizing your cloud networking strategy.

Azure ExpressRoute:

Establish private connections between Azure data centers and infrastructure on your premises or in a colocation environment.

Azure ExpressRoute stands out as a pivotal service within Microsoft Azure's Networking Services, offering a private, dedicated network connection between on-premises networks and the Azure cloud. This service bypasses the public internet, providing more reliability, faster speeds, lower latencies, and higher security than typical internet connections. Understanding the benefits and applications of Azure ExpressRoute is essential for organizations looking to optimize their cloud connectivity and performance.

What is Azure ExpressRoute?

Azure ExpressRoute allows you to extend your on-premises networks into the Microsoft cloud over a private connection facilitated by a connectivity provider. With ExpressRoute, data that would normally traverse the public internet is sent through a private link to Azure data centers, ensuring enhanced security and performance for enterprise-grade applications and services.

Key Features of Azure ExpressRoute

Private Connectivity: ExpressRoute connections do not go over the public internet. This private nature of the connection ensures more predictable performance and enhanced security.

Higher Bandwidth Options: ExpressRoute provides a range of connectivity speeds from 50 Mbps up to 100 Gbps, catering to the demands of high-throughput applications.

Global Reach Expansion: Azure's global network can be leveraged to connect your on-premises network to Azure services across the world, not limited to the region you're directly connected to.

Redundancy and Reliability: ExpressRoute connections offer built-in redundancy and a 99.95% uptime SLA, ensuring high availability for your critical applications.

Integration with Microsoft Cloud Services: Beyond Azure, ExpressRoute also provides private connectivity to Microsoft 365 and Dynamics 365, optimizing performance and security for these services.

Examples of Using Azure ExpressRoute

Hybrid Cloud Deployments: For enterprises operating both on-premises data centers and Azure cloud services, ExpressRoute provides a seamless and reliable connection between these environments. It enables scenarios like hybrid cloud applications, disaster recovery, and data migration without compromising on performance or security.

High-Performance Computing (HPC): Organizations running compute-intensive workloads such as simulations, analytics, or graphics rendering can use ExpressRoute to transfer large datasets between on-premises HPC clusters and Azure compute resources with minimal latency.

Secure Access to Cloud-hosted Applications: Financial institutions, healthcare organizations, and other sectors with strict regulatory requirements for data privacy and security can leverage ExpressRoute for secure access to applications and data hosted in Azure, ensuring compliance and data protection.

Global Network Expansion: Companies with a global presence can use ExpressRoute to connect their geographically dispersed offices and data centers to Azure, facilitating secure and efficient inter-office collaboration and data sharing.

Optimized Connectivity to Microsoft 365: Businesses can enhance the performance and reliability of their Microsoft 365 deployments by routing traffic over ExpressRoute, improving user experience for applications like Outlook, Teams, and SharePoint online.

Azure ExpressRoute provides a robust solution for organizations looking to enhance their connectivity to Azure and other Microsoft cloud services. By offering a dedicated, private connection, ExpressRoute ensures superior performance, security, and reliability for enterprise-grade applications and services. Whether for hybrid cloud architectures, data-intensive workloads, or secure access to cloud-hosted applications, ExpressRoute offers a compelling choice for businesses aiming to optimize their cloud connectivity and performance.

Azure DNS:

Host your DNS domains in Azure for seamless integration with your other Azure services.

Azure DNS is a pivotal component of Microsoft Azure's Networking Services, offering a hosting service for DNS domains that provides name resolution using Microsoft Azure infrastructure. By integrating seamlessly with other Azure services, Azure DNS enables Azure customers to use the same credentials, billing, and support contract for their DNS needs. Understanding Azure DNS is essential for architects and developers aiming to ensure their applications and services are reliably accessible and performant.

What is Azure DNS?

Azure DNS allows you to host your DNS domain in Azure, enabling you to manage your DNS records using the same credentials, billing, and support contract as your other Azure services. It supports hosting your domain and provides name resolution using Microsoft's global network of DNS servers. Azure DNS is built on the robust, scalable, and global Azure infrastructure, ensuring high availability and quick response times for your domain.

Key Features of Azure DNS

Global Reach and Reliability: Leverages the global distribution of Azure data centers to provide high availability and performance for your DNS domains.

Integration with Azure Services: Offers seamless integration with other Azure services, like Azure Virtual Machines and Azure Traffic Manager, for a cohesive cloud service experience.

Security and Privacy: Azure DNS benefits from the security and privacy features of the Azure platform. It supports integration with Azure Role-Based Access Control (RBAC) for managing access to DNS zones and records.

Zone and Record Management: Allows for easy management of DNS zones and records using the Azure portal, Azure PowerShell, and Azure CLI tools. This includes support for a wide range of DNS record types.

Examples of Using Azure DNS

Web Application Hosting: Host the DNS domain for your web application in Azure DNS. This allows you to manage your web application and its domain in a single place, leveraging Azure's global network to ensure your application is always accessible and performs well.

Custom Domain Names for Azure Services: Use Azure DNS to configure custom domain names for Azure services like Azure Blob Storage or Azure Web Apps. This can help provide a more professional and recognizable domain name for your services.

Domain Name System for Virtual Networks: Deploy Azure DNS within your Azure Virtual Network (VNet) to provide name resolution for VMs and applications hosted in your VNet. This can be particularly useful for internal applications that require DNS but do not need to be accessible from the internet.

Load Balancing with Traffic Manager: Integrate Azure DNS with Azure Traffic Manager to provide high availability and load balancing for your applications. By using DNS-based traffic routing, you can ensure that users are directed to the closest or most performant application instance.

Azure DNS is a robust and reliable solution for hosting and managing your DNS domains within the Azure ecosystem. By offering global distribution, integration with other Azure services, and the security features of the Azure platform, Azure DNS provides a comprehensive DNS solution for Azure customers. Whether you're hosting a global web application, configuring custom domain names for Azure services, or setting up DNS for internal networks, Azure DNS offers the features and performance needed to support your networking requirements.

Databases:

Azure offers fully managed database services for a variety of database management systems (DBMS), supporting both relational and non-relational databases.

Azure SQL Database:

A fully managed relational database service that offers SQL Server compatibility, automated backups, and global scalability.

In the spectrum of Azure Core Services, Azure SQL Database emerges as a highly scalable, relational database service built for the cloud. It's designed to automate a significant amount of maintenance tasks, security provisioning, and scaling while ensuring global availability and fault tolerance. Azure SQL Database is based on the latest stable version of the Microsoft SQL Server database engine, providing a fully managed SQL database service that allows developers and businesses to focus on application development without worrying about infrastructure management.

What is Azure SQL Database?

Azure SQL Database is a Platform as a Service (PaaS) offering that provides a relational database service in the cloud. It offers a blend of

SQL Server's capabilities with additional benefits such as managed instance models, elastic pools for resource sharing among databases, and built-in intelligence that optimizes performance and secures data.

Key Features of Azure SQL Database

Managed Database Service: Automates updates, patching, backups, and monitoring, reducing the administration effort needed from database administrators.

Scalability: Offers dynamic scalability options, allowing databases to scale up or down based on demand without downtime.

Built-in Intelligence: Utilizes built-in features like automatic tuning to optimize performance by automatically adjusting query plans and indexes.

High Availability: Built on a globally distributed infrastructure, ensuring high availability with built-in automatic failover.

Security and Compliance: Provides advanced security features, including data encryption, threat detection, and network isolation, while meeting a broad set of compliance standards.

Examples of Using Azure SQL Database

Web and Mobile Applications: Azure SQL Database is ideal for powering the back-end databases of web and mobile applications, providing global scalability, security, and performance. For example, an e-commerce platform can utilize Azure SQL Database to store customer data, product catalogs, and order histories, ensuring fast, secure access to data.

Microservices Architecture: In applications built using a microservices architecture, individual microservices can utilize separate Azure SQL databases. This setup allows each microservice to independently scale and ensures that the databases can be managed and updated without impacting other components of the application.

Data Warehousing and Analytics: Azure SQL Database can serve as a scalable cloud data warehouse for storing and analyzing large volumes of data. Businesses can use SQL queries and integration with

Azure Analysis Services to derive insights from their data, supporting business intelligence and decision-making processes.

Dev/Test Environments: Developers can quickly spin up instances of Azure SQL Database for development and testing purposes, ensuring that the database environment mirrors production settings. This use case is particularly beneficial for continuous integration and delivery pipelines.

Legacy Database Migration: Azure SQL Database supports the migration of existing SQL Server databases to the cloud, enabling businesses to modernize their applications and benefit from the cloud's scalability, reliability, and cost-efficiency.

Azure SQL Database stands as a cornerstone of Azure's database offerings, providing a robust, scalable, and secure relational database service for a wide range of applications. Whether for new development projects or the migration of existing databases to the cloud, Azure SQL Database offers the performance, availability, and features needed to support modern, data-driven applications. By leveraging Azure SQL Database, businesses and developers can significantly reduce the complexity of database management, focusing instead on creating innovative solutions and driving value.

Azure Cosmos DB:

A globally distributed, multi-model database service designed for high availability and low latency at global scale, supporting document, key-value, graph, and column-family data models.

Azure Cosmos DB stands prominently within the Azure Core Services as a globally distributed, multi-model database service designed for high availability, low latency, and scalable applications. It offers turnkey global distribution across any number of Azure regions, providing transparent multi-master replication, and is designed from the ground up with global distribution and horizontal scale at its core. Understanding how to leverage Azure Cosmos DB is crucial for developers and architects aiming to build highly responsive and globally distributed applications.

What is Azure Cosmos DB?

Azure Cosmos DB is Microsoft's proprietary globally-distributed, multi-model database service. It enables you to build and scale applications with multiple data models, including document, key-value, graph, and column-family models. Its global distribution capabilities and multi-model support make it uniquely positioned to solve problems that involve large amounts of distributed data and users around the world.

Key Features of Azure Cosmos DB

Global Distribution: Easily replicate your data globally and place it close to your users to ensure fast access regardless of location.

Multi-Model Support: Use the API that best fits your application needs, including SQL (DocumentDB), MongoDB, Cassandra, Gremlin (Graph), and Table (Key-value).

Automatic Scaling: Azure Cosmos DB automatically scales throughput and storage as needed, providing incredible flexibility and performance.

Comprehensive SLAs: Offers comprehensive Service Level Agreements (SLAs) for throughput, latency, availability, and consistency.

Multi-Master Replication: Provides support for multi-master replication, enabling multiple write regions, automatic conflict resolution, and active-active replication patterns.

Examples of Using Azure Cosmos DB

Real-Time IoT Device Telemetry: Store and process IoT device telemetry in real-time, leveraging Cosmos DB's capability to ingest massive amounts of data at low latency. This setup is ideal for scenarios where sensor data from globally distributed devices must be aggregated and analyzed quickly.

Global E-Commerce Platform: Build a global e-commerce platform where product catalogs, user profiles, and order histories are stored in Cosmos DB. The global distribution ensures that users experience low latency when accessing the platform, regardless of their geographical location.

Personalized Recommendations: Use the Gremlin API for graph data in Cosmos DB to model user preferences and relationships in a social network or e-commerce site. This allows for building complex queries to generate personalized recommendations based on user interactions.

Gaming Leaderboards: Implement globally distributed gaming leaderboards that scale to millions of players. Cosmos DB can handle rapid writes and reads, ensuring that player scores are updated and retrieved in real-time with minimal latency.

Multi-Tenant SaaS Applications: Develop multi-tenant applications where each tenant's data is isolated and independently scalable. Cosmos DB's multi-model approach and automatic scaling capabilities allow for efficiently managing diverse datasets across tenants.

Azure Cosmos DB is a powerful solution for any application that requires global distribution, high availability, and the ability to scale seamlessly with demand. Its multi-model support and comprehensive SLAs make it a versatile choice for a wide range of applications, from IoT and e-commerce to social networks and gaming. By leveraging Azure Cosmos DB, architects and developers can significantly simplify the complexity associated with managing distributed databases, focusing instead on building responsive, scalable, and globally distributed applications.

AI and Machine Learning:

Azure provides a rich set of AI and machine learning services that enable the development of intelligent applications capable of seeing, hearing, speaking, understanding, and interpreting needs using natural methods of communication.

Azure Machine Learning:

Build, train, and deploy machine learning models quickly using Azure's scalable cloud resources.

In the expansive realm of Azure Core Services, Azure Machine Learning (Azure ML) represents a cutting-edge platform designed to empower developers, data scientists, and AI researchers to build, train, and deploy machine learning models at scale. Azure ML stands out for its comprehensive approach to machine learning, providing a wide array of tools and services that streamline the end-to-end machine learning lifecycle, from data preparation and model training to deployment and monitoring.

What is Azure Machine Learning?

Azure Machine Learning is a cloud-based service that facilitates the creation, experimentation, and deployment of machine learning models. It leverages the power of the Azure cloud to provide scalable compute resources, integrated data services, and a robust set of machine learning and AI tools. Azure ML supports a wide range of machine learning frameworks and languages, including TensorFlow, PyTorch, Scikit-learn, and R, making it a flexible and powerful platform for developing advanced machine learning solutions.

Key Features of Azure Machine Learning

Automated Machine Learning (AutoML): Azure ML's AutoML automatically selects the best machine learning algorithms and hyper-parameters for your data, significantly reducing the time and expertise required to build high-quality models.

Scalable Training and Inference: Leverage Azure's scalable compute resources to train complex models and deploy them for real-time or batch inference across a global network of data centers.

MLOps (DevOps for Machine Learning): Integrates with tools and practices for MLOps, enabling you to automate and monitor the machine learning lifecycle, including model versioning, deployment, and monitoring.

Data and AI Services Integration: Seamlessly integrates with other Azure services, such as Azure Data Lake Storage, Azure Databricks, and Azure Cognitive Services, providing a comprehensive ecosystem for building AI-driven applications.

Visual Interface and Notebooks: Offers a visual interface for constructing machine learning pipelines, as well as Jupyter notebooks for more granular control and experimentation with code.

Examples of Using Azure Machine Learning

Predictive Maintenance: Develop models to predict when industrial equipment requires maintenance before failures occur, minimizing downtime and maintenance costs. Azure ML can process historical sensor data from equipment to identify patterns that precede failures.

Customer Churn Prediction: Use Azure ML to analyze customer data and predict which customers are likely to churn. This enables businesses to proactively engage at-risk customers with retention strategies, improving customer satisfaction and loyalty.

Financial Fraud Detection: Train models on transaction data to identify potentially fraudulent activities. By deploying these models as real-time scoring services, financial institutions can detect and prevent fraud in transactions as they occur.

Personalized Marketing: Analyze customer behavior and preferences to build personalized marketing campaigns. Machine learning models can segment customers and predict the most effective marketing strategies for different segments, increasing conversion rates and customer engagement.

Healthcare Diagnostics: Leverage Azure ML to develop diagnostic tools that analyze medical images, lab results, and patient data to assist healthcare professionals in diagnosing diseases more quickly and accurately.

Azure Machine Learning offers a robust platform for developing sophisticated machine learning models and AI solutions, catering to a wide spectrum of applications across industries. By providing tools for the entire machine learning lifecycle, integrated with Azure's powerful cloud infrastructure and services, Azure ML enables organizations to harness the power of AI and machine learning to drive innovation, efficiency, and competitive advantage. Whether for predictive analytics, personalized experiences, fraud detection, or healthcare diagnostics,

Azure Machine Learning simplifies and accelerates the journey from data to insights and action.

Azure Cognitive Services:

A collection of APIs and services that allow applications to see, hear, respond, translate, and make decisions in more human-like ways.

Azure Cognitive Services is a suite of artificial intelligence (AI) services and APIs that enable developers to easily add AI capabilities to their applications without needing deep knowledge of machine learning models or data science. These services provide pre-built, high-quality AI models designed by experts and trained on vast datasets, making it straightforward to integrate vision, speech, language, and decision-making abilities into applications across a variety of platforms.

What are Azure Cognitive Services?

Azure Cognitive Services are cloud-based services that provide capabilities to solve complex problems with AI, using simple API calls. These services are categorized into several domains, including Vision, Speech, Language, and Decision, each offering a set of functionalities that enable applications to see, hear, interpret, and interact with the user environment in more human-like ways.

Key Features of Azure Cognitive Services

Ease of Integration: Designed to be easily integrated into applications with REST APIs and client library SDKs available in popular programming languages.

Scalability: Built on Azure's scalable infrastructure, ensuring that the services can handle high volumes of requests and scale with your application's needs.

Customizability: While offering pre-built models, many Cognitive Services allow for customization, enabling you to train models on your own data, thereby improving accuracy for specific scenarios.

Examples of Using Azure Cognitive Services

Content Moderation: Use the Content Moderator service to automatically scan user-generated content (text, images, videos) in your application for potentially offensive or risky content, ensuring a safe and positive user environment.

Speech-Enabled Applications: Integrate speech recognition and synthesis capabilities into your applications using the Speech Service. This can transform customer service bots into more interactive voice assistants or enable hands-free operation in applications.

Visual Product Search: Implement the Computer Vision service in e-commerce platforms to allow users to search for products using images instead of text queries, enhancing the shopping experience.

Real-Time Translation for Global Communication: Utilize the Translator Text API to provide real-time text translation in chat applications, breaking down language barriers in global communications.

Personalized Recommendations: Leverage the Personalizer service to create more engaging user experiences by providing personalized content and recommendations based on user behavior and preferences.

Language Understanding for Conversational AI: Build sophisticated conversational interfaces with the Language Understanding (LUIS) service, enabling applications to understand user intents from natural language input.

Azure Cognitive Services democratizes AI by providing a set of powerful, ready-to-use AI capabilities that can be easily integrated into applications, bringing sophisticated AI functionalities within reach of every developer. By leveraging these services, businesses and developers can enhance their applications with features that engage users more naturally, make sense of data, and make decisions based on insights drawn from real-world inputs. Whether it's through enhancing user interfaces with speech and language understanding, automating content moderation, or creating personalized user experiences, Azure Cognitive Services opens up a world of possibilities for enriching applications with AI.

Conclusion

Microsoft Azure's core services offer a powerful and flexible platform for building a wide range of applications and solutions. By leveraging Azure's computing, storage, networking, database, and AI services, businesses can accelerate their digital transformation, optimize their operations, and innovate at scale. Understanding these core services is essential for effectively utilizing Azure to meet your specific business needs and objectives.

8

Chapter 4: Managing Azure with the Azure Portal and PowerShell

Part II: Diving Deeper into Azure

In the vast ecosystem of Microsoft Azure, efficient management of resources is key to leveraging the platform's full potential. The Azure Portal and PowerShell are two primary tools provided by Microsoft for managing Azure resources. Each offers a unique set of capabilities catering to different preferences and requirements, from graphical user interface-based management to command-line automation and scripting.

<u>Azure Portal Overview</u>

The Azure Portal is a web-based, user-friendly interface that provides a comprehensive and integrated environment for accessing and managing all of your Azure resources. It allows users to create, configure, and monitor the services within their Azure subscriptions visually. The portal is designed for administrators and developers who prefer a graphical interface for cloud management tasks.

Dashboard Customization: Users can customize dashboards to monitor resources and services that are most important to them.

Resource Management: Easily create, configure, and delete Azure resources such as VMs, storage accounts, and databases through intuitive wizards and panels.

Access Control and Monitoring: Manage access to resources using Role-Based Access Control (RBAC) and monitor the health and performance of services with integrated monitoring tools.

Using Azure Portal for Resource Management:

The Azure Portal stands as a central hub for managing all aspects of your Microsoft Azure environment. It offers an intuitive, web-based user interface that allows users to create, manage, and monitor Azure resources with ease. The portal is designed to accommodate both beginners and experienced cloud professionals, providing a rich set of tools for comprehensive resource management.

<u>Overview of Resource Management in the Azure Portal</u>

Resource management through the Azure Portal involves the creation, configuration, monitoring, and deletion of Azure resources such as virtual machines, storage accounts, databases, and more. The portal's user-friendly interface simplifies these tasks, making cloud management accessible to users with varying levels of technical expertise.

<u>Key Features for Resource Management</u>

Dashboard Customization:

Users can personalize their Azure Portal dashboard to display the most relevant resources and metrics, providing quick access to frequently used services and monitoring tools.

Dashboard customization in the Azure Portal is a powerful feature that significantly enhances the resource management experience. It allows users to tailor the Azure Portal interface to their specific needs, providing quick access to the most frequently used resources, tools, and information. By personalizing their dashboard, users can streamline their workflows, improve productivity, and keep a close eye on the health and performance of their Azure resources.

Overview of Dashboard Customization

The Azure Portal dashboard is the first thing users see upon logging in. It serves as a control panel where various widgets and shortcuts can be added, moved, and removed to create a personalized view of the Azure environment. This customization capability allows for a highly tailored experience, ensuring that users have immediate access to the resources and data most relevant to their roles and tasks.

Key Features of Dashboard Customization

Personalized Layouts: Users can drag and drop tiles and widgets to arrange their dashboard according to their preferences, creating layouts that highlight the resources, metrics, and tools they use most often.

Multiple Dashboards: The Azure Portal allows users to create and switch between multiple dashboards. This is particularly useful for managing different projects, environments (e.g., development, testing, production), or roles (e.g., administrator, developer, analyst) within the same Azure account.

Shared Dashboards: Users can share their customized dashboards with other team members, promoting collaboration and ensuring that everyone has access to the same set of tools and information.

Integration of Azure Services: The dashboard can incorporate a wide range of Azure services and features, from resource groups and virtual machines to cost management and Azure Advisor recommendations. Users can add, configure, and interact with tiles for these services directly from their dashboard.

Examples of Using Dashboard Customization for Resource Management

Monitoring Resource Health: Add tiles for Azure Monitor and Service Health to the dashboard for real-time visibility into the performance and health of Azure resources. This setup helps in quickly identifying and responding to issues.

Cost Management: Incorporate the Cost Management tile to keep track of spending and ensure that Azure usage stays within budget. Users can easily access detailed cost reports and alerts from their dashboard.

Quick Access to Frequently Used Resources: Pin frequently accessed resources, such as specific virtual machines or storage accounts, directly to the dashboard. This enables one-click access to these resources, saving time and reducing navigation effort.

Project-Specific Dashboards: Create separate dashboards for different projects, each configured with tiles relevant to that project's resources, metrics, and tools. This organization helps users focus on the specific information needed for each project.

Dashboard customization in the Azure Portal is a versatile feature that enhances the management of Azure resources by allowing users to create a tailored and efficient workspace. By personalizing their dashboards, users can ensure that critical information and tools are readily accessible, streamlining the monitoring, management, and optimization of Azure resources. Whether for individual productivity or team collaboration, customized dashboards play a crucial role in effective cloud resource management within the Azure ecosystem.

Resource Groups:

The Azure Portal allows users to organize resources into resource groups, a logical container that holds related resources for an Azure solution. This organization facilitates easier management, deployment, and monitoring of resources that share a common lifecycle.

Resource groups in Azure play a critical role in organizing and managing cloud resources efficiently. Through the Azure Portal, resource groups provide a systematic approach to grouping related resources for an Azure solution, making it simpler to manage their lifecycle, access control, billing, and more.

What Are Resource Groups?

A resource group in Azure is a container that holds related resources for an Azure solution. It serves as a logical collection where Azure resources like virtual machines, databases, and storage accounts can be deployed and managed collectively. Each resource can only belong to one resource group, and resource groups can be used to apply policies, access control, and configure settings across multiple resources simultaneously.

Key Benefits of Using Resource Groups

Simplified Management: By organizing resources that share a common lifecycle into a resource group, you can deploy, update, and delete them as a single unit, simplifying management tasks.

Consistent Access Control: Resource groups work seamlessly with Azure Role-Based Access Control (RBAC) to provide a unified way to manage access permissions across multiple resources within the group.

Effective Cost Management: Resource groups enable you to monitor and manage costs more effectively by providing a single lens to view and analyze the costs associated with a group of resources.

Logical Organization: They allow for organizing resources according to their purpose, environment, application, or any other criteria that align with your organizational needs, making it easier to keep your Azure environment structured and manageable.

Using Resource Groups in the Azure Portal

Creating Resource Groups: The Azure Portal offers a straightforward process for creating resource groups. You can specify the resource group name, subscription, and the region where it will be hosted. This sets the stage for deploying resources within the newly created resource group.

Deploying Resources: When deploying new resources via the Azure Portal, you have the option to select an existing resource group or create a new one. This ensures that resources are organized according to your project or application architecture from the outset.

Managing Resources within a Group: The Azure Portal provides detailed views and tools for managing the resources within a resource group. You can easily add or remove resources, apply tags, and adjust settings across resources collectively.

Access Control and Policy Assignment: Within the Azure Portal, resource groups can be targeted for specific access control configurations and policy assignments. This allows administrators to enforce security and compliance standards across resources efficiently.

Monitoring and Cost Management: The portal facilitates monitoring of resource utilization and performance at the resource group level. It also allows for analyzing and exporting cost data, helping to ensure that resources are being used efficiently and within budget.

Resource groups are a foundational element of resource management in Azure, providing a logical framework for grouping and managing resources. Through the Azure Portal, users can leverage resource groups to simplify management tasks, enforce security and compliance policies, and monitor costs effectively. By utilizing resource groups wisely, organizations can ensure their Azure environments are well-organized, secure, and cost-efficient, supporting the successful deployment and operation of cloud-based solutions.

Tagging Resources:

Users can apply tags to resources, enabling categorization and management at scale. Tags can be used for cost tracking, grouping resources across different projects, departments, or environments.

In the complex and dynamic environment of cloud computing, maintaining clarity and organization across a multitude of resources is paramount. Azure's resource tagging feature, accessible through the Azure Portal, stands as a critical tool in achieving this organizational clarity. Tagging allows users to assign metadata to Azure resources, enabling more effective tracking, management, and reporting on resource usage and expenditures.

What Are Azure Resource Tags?

Azure resource tags are key-value pairs assigned to Azure resources. These tags can be used to annotate resources with additional information such as ownership, environment, project, or cost center. By employing tags, you can categorize resources in ways that align with your business and operational structures, making it easier to manage and monitor resources across your Azure subscriptions.

Key Benefits of Tagging Resources

Improved Resource Organization: Tags help organize resources across different dimensions such as project, department, application, or environment, simplifying the management of resources in a large-scale cloud environment.

Enhanced Cost Management and Billing: By tagging resources with cost-related information, you can gain better insights into where and how resources are being consumed, facilitating more accurate cost allocation and budgeting.

Simplified Resource Management: Tags enable you to filter and group resources within the Azure Portal, streamlining operations such as monitoring, automation, and policy enforcement.

Operational and Compliance Reporting: Tags can be used to generate detailed reports for operational monitoring and compliance purposes, providing visibility into resource utilization and adherence to governance policies.

Using the Azure Portal for Tagging Resources

Assigning Tags to Resources: The Azure Portal provides a user-friendly interface for assigning tags to resources at the time of creation or to existing resources. You can navigate to any resource's "Overview" page and select "Tags" to add, edit, or remove tags.

Tag Management at Scale: For managing tags across multiple resources, the Azure Portal offers tools such as the "All resources" page, where you can select multiple resources and apply tags in bulk, ensuring consistency and saving time.

Filtering and Grouping by Tags: The portal allows users to filter and group resources based on tags. This capability is invaluable for managing resources across different projects, environments, or cost centers, providing a segmented view of resources based on chosen criteria.

Automating Tagging: While manual tagging is supported, Azure also offers capabilities for automating the tagging process through policies. For example, you can create Azure policies that enforce tagging rules, ensuring that all resources within a subscription or resource group are automatically tagged according to predefined standards.

Examples of Tagging Strategies

Cost Center Allocation: Tag resources with **CostCenter:Finance** or **CostCenter:Marketing** to track cloud spending by department, facilitating accurate chargebacks and financial planning.

Project Lifecycle Management: Use tags like **Project:Project-Name** and **Environment:Dev/Test/Prod** to organize resources by project and environment, supporting structured deployment workflows and environment-specific policies.

Ownership and Responsibility: Assign tags such as **Owner:TeamName** or **ManagedBy:IndividualName** to clarify ownership and operational responsibility for resources, improving accountability and response times for management tasks.

Tagging resources in Azure provides a powerful mechanism for organizing, managing, and reporting on cloud resources. Through the Azure Portal, users can easily apply, manage, and utilize tags to bring order to their cloud environments, enhancing operational efficiency, cost management, and compliance. By adopting a consistent and thoughtful tagging strategy, organizations can significantly improve their resource management practices in Azure, ensuring that their cloud resources are aligned with their business and operational objectives.

Access Control and Security:

The portal integrates seamlessly with Azure Role-Based Access Control (RBAC), allowing administrators to define fine-grained access permissions for resources and services. This ensures that users have the appropriate level of access to manage resources securely.

Effective access control and robust security mechanisms are paramount in managing cloud resources, ensuring that sensitive data and critical infrastructures are shielded from unauthorized access while enabling legitimate users to perform their roles efficiently. The Azure Portal provides a comprehensive set of tools for managing access control and enhancing security across Azure resources, making it easier for administrators to enforce security policies and compliance standards.

Overview of Access Control and Security in the Azure Portal

The Azure Portal offers an integrated environment for configuring access control and security settings for Azure resources. It leverages Azure Active Directory (Azure AD) for identity and access management, providing role-based access control (RBAC), conditional access policies, and integration with other security services like Azure Policy and Azure Security Center to create a fortified security posture.

Key Features for Managing Access Control and Security

Role-Based Access Control (RBAC): Azure RBAC enables fine-grained access management for Azure resources, allowing administrators to grant users, groups, and applications access to specific resources, services, and operations within a defined scope.

Conditional Access: Conditional access policies in Azure AD allow administrators to apply automated access decisions based on conditions such as user location, device state, and risk level, further securing resource access.

Azure Policy: Azure Policy helps enforce organizational standards and assess compliance at scale. It allows administrators to create policies that automatically enforce rules for resource properties during deployment and throughout their lifecycle.

Azure Security Center: Provides unified security management and advanced threat protection across hybrid cloud workloads. The Azure Portal integrates with Azure Security Center to offer recommendations, monitor security configurations, and alert administrators to potential vulnerabilities.

Using the Azure Portal for Access Control and Security: Examples

Assigning Roles to Users and Groups: Administrators can assign predefined or custom RBAC roles to users and groups directly from the

Azure Portal, granting them specific permissions to manage resources within a subscription, resource group, or an individual resource.

Configuring Conditional Access Policies: Through the Azure Portal, administrators can configure conditional access policies that require multi-factor authentication (MFA) for users accessing Azure resources from outside the corporate network, enhancing security for remote access.

Enforcing Compliance with Azure Policy: Administrators can use the Azure Portal to create and assign policies that ensure all deployed resources adhere to organizational standards, such as enforcing specific network configurations or ensuring that only allowed types of resources are created.

Monitoring Security Posture with Azure Security Center: The Azure Portal allows administrators to monitor the security posture of their Azure environment using Azure Security Center. They can view security alerts, recommendations, and configure security policies to enhance the protection of their cloud resources.

The Azure Portal provides a powerful and user-friendly interface for managing access control and security across Azure resources. By leveraging RBAC, conditional access, Azure Policy, and Azure Security Center, organizations can create a robust security framework that protects their cloud environment from threats while enabling productivity. Through diligent management of access permissions and proactive security practices, administrators can ensure that their Azure resources remain secure, compliant, and accessible to authorized users, supporting the organization's overall security and compliance objectives.

Using the Azure Portal for Resource Management: Examples

Creating a Virtual Machine: From the Azure Portal, users can easily create a virtual machine by specifying the VM's configuration details such as the operating system, size, and network settings through a guided process. The portal also provides options for advanced configurations, including disk options, networking, and management tools.

Setting up Azure SQL Databases: The portal simplifies the setup of Azure SQL Databases, guiding users through selecting the appropriate compute and storage options, configuring security settings, and defining scalability preferences. Users can monitor database performance, set up alerts, and manage backups directly from the portal.

Monitoring Resource Utilization: The Azure Portal offers integrated monitoring and analytics tools, such as Azure Monitor and Azure Advisor, enabling users to track resource utilization, identify performance bottlenecks, and receive recommendations for optimizing resource configurations and reducing costs.

Managing Access with Azure Active Directory: Through the portal, administrators can manage user identities and access to resources using Azure Active Directory. This includes creating user accounts, assigning roles, and configuring multi-factor authentication for enhanced security.

The Azure Portal provides a comprehensive and user-friendly environment for managing Azure resources. With its customizable dashboard, intuitive navigation, and integrated tools for resource management, monitoring, and security, the portal empowers users to effectively manage their cloud resources. Whether deploying new services, monitoring application performance, or securing access to resources, the Azure Portal offers a centralized platform for streamlined cloud management.

Automating Tasks with Azure PowerShell:

In the versatile and extensive world of Azure, the ability to automate tasks and streamline deployment processes is indispensable for efficient cloud management. Azure PowerShell and the Azure Command-Line Interface (CLI) are powerful tools provided by Microsoft that cater to this need, enabling administrators and developers to manage Azure resources through scripts and command lines.

Azure PowerShell Overview

Azure PowerShell is a module offering a set of cmdlets for managing Azure resources directly from the PowerShell command line. Designed for the automation of repetitive tasks, it enables scripting complex deployment and management tasks, making it a preferred tool for administrators who are familiar with PowerShell scripting.

Azure PowerShell represents a pivotal tool within Microsoft Azure's suite of services for the automation and management of Azure resources. It is a module that provides cmdlets for virtually every Azure service, allowing administrators, developers, and IT professionals to script operations in PowerShell, a widely used command-line shell and scripting language.

What is Azure PowerShell?

Azure PowerShell is a set of modules that provide cmdlets to manage Azure resources directly from the PowerShell command line interface. Built on the .NET Framework, it enables users to interact with Azure resources in a scriptable manner, making it an indispensable tool for automating deployment, configuration, and management tasks within Azure. Azure PowerShell is designed to offer a comprehensive scripting environment that aligns with the operational needs and workflows of IT professionals accustomed to PowerShell.

Key Features of Azure PowerShell

Comprehensive Coverage: Azure PowerShell offers cmdlets for managing all aspects of Azure, including virtual machines, web apps, databases, and networking resources, among others. This extensive coverage ensures that administrators can script operations for any Azure service.

Scriptable Automation: Facilitates the creation of scripts that automate repetitive or complex tasks, improving efficiency and accuracy in Azure resource management. Scripts can be reused and shared, standardizing operations across teams.

Integration with Azure Services: Seamlessly integrates with Azure services, providing a unified approach to managing resources.

It allows for the automation of tasks across different Azure services within a single script.

Support for Hybrid Environments: Enables the management of not just cloud resources but also supports scenarios where on-premises and cloud environments need to be managed together, facilitating hybrid cloud automation.

Practical Uses of Azure PowerShell for Automating Tasks

Resource Deployment: Automate the deployment of Azure resources such as virtual networks, VMs, and storage accounts. Scripts can define the entire infrastructure required for an application, enabling consistent deployments across development, testing, and production environments.

Example: Using Azure PowerShell to script the deployment of a multi-tier application infrastructure, including network configurations, VMs, and database services.

Configuration Management: Script the configuration of resources to meet specific requirements. This includes network settings, security policies, and application configurations.

Example: Automating the setup of network security groups (NSGs) and rules across a set of virtual machines to ensure compliance with security policies.

Operational Tasks: Automate routine operational tasks such as backups, updates, and monitoring. Scripts can handle these tasks across multiple resources, ensuring that operational standards are maintained.

Example: Writing a PowerShell script to automate the backup of Azure SQL databases on a scheduled basis.

Scaling Operations: Leverage Azure PowerShell to automate scaling operations for Azure services based on demand, performance metrics, or schedules.

Example: Automating the scaling of Azure Web Apps during peak usage times to ensure application performance and user experience.

Azure PowerShell is a powerful tool for the automation of Azure resource management, offering a scriptable interface to the full range of Azure services. Its integration capabilities, combined with the scripting prowess of PowerShell, provide IT professionals with the means to automate complex deployments, manage configurations, perform operational tasks, and implement scaling strategies efficiently. By leveraging Azure PowerShell, organizations can achieve not only operational efficiency but also consistency and reliability in their Azure resource management practices.

Azure CLI Overview

The Azure CLI is a cross-platform command-line tool that provides a similar set of capabilities for managing Azure resources but is designed to be used from a terminal or script on any operating system. It offers a comprehensive, easy-to-use set of commands, making it accessible for users who prefer command-line interfaces or are working within Linux or macOS environments.

In the array of tools available for managing Microsoft Azure, the Azure Command-Line Interface (CLI) stands out as an essential instrument for developers, system administrators, and DevOps engineers who prefer a command-line approach. Azure CLI complements Azure PowerShell by offering a cross-platform command-line tool designed to manage Azure resources. It caters to a wide audience by providing a straightforward, scriptable interface that works across macOS, Linux, and Windows.

What is Azure CLI?

Azure CLI is a set of commands used to manage Azure resources. It provides a command-line interface that allows users to execute simple one-line commands for complex tasks with just a few keystrokes. The CLI is designed to be idempotent, enabling the same command to be executed repeatedly with the same results, a feature that is particularly useful for scripting and automation.

Key Features of Azure CLI

Cross-Platform Support: Azure CLI is designed to run on Windows, macOS, and Linux, offering a consistent experience across all platforms. This ensures that scripts are portable and can be run on any system.

Comprehensive Resource Management: It covers a wide range of Azure services, allowing for the management of virtually all aspects of Azure, including compute, networking, storage, and more.

Batch Processing and Scripting: The CLI supports batch processing and scripting, enabling users to automate repetitive tasks and orchestrate complex deployments through scripts.

Integration with Azure Services: Works seamlessly with other Azure services and management tools, providing a unified approach to cloud resource management.

Practical Uses of Azure CLI for Automating Tasks

Simplified Resource Deployment: Azure CLI can be used to deploy resources such as VMs, web apps, and databases quickly. Scripts can be developed to automate the provisioning of entire environments, enhancing efficiency and consistency.

Example: Deploying a scalable web application environment that includes an Azure App Service, Azure SQL Database, and associated networking components using a single Azure CLI script.

Configuration and Updates: Automate the configuration and updating of Azure resources to meet specific operational or security requirements.

Example: Using Azure CLI to update the configuration of an Azure Cosmos DB account to enable multi-region writes, ensuring global scalability and availability.

Monitoring and Diagnostics: Leverage Azure CLI to automate the collection and analysis of monitoring data, aiding in the proactive management of resource performance and health.

Example: Scripting periodic retrieval of diagnostic logs from Azure Blob Storage and analyzing them for specific error patterns or performance metrics.

Scaling Operations: Utilize Azure CLI to automate scaling operations based on performance metrics or predefined schedules, ensuring resources are optimized for both performance and cost.

Example: Automatically scaling Azure Kubernetes Service (AKS) node pools in response to increased application load, ensuring that the application remains responsive under heavy traffic conditions.

The Azure CLI offers a powerful, flexible, and cross-platform tool for managing Azure resources directly from the command line. With its comprehensive coverage of Azure services and its ease of use for scripting and batch processing, Azure CLI is an indispensable tool for automating cloud management tasks. Whether deploying new resources, managing configurations, monitoring performance, or scaling services, Azure CLI provides the command-line capabilities necessary to automate these tasks efficiently, helping organizations to streamline their Azure operations and achieve greater operational agility.

Automating Tasks with Azure PowerShell and CLI

Resource Deployment and Configuration:

Both Azure PowerShell and CLI can be used to automate the deployment and configuration of Azure resources. Scripts can be written to create, configure, and manage resources such as virtual machines, storage accounts, and web apps, allowing for consistent setups across different environments.

In the world of cloud computing, the ability to automate the deployment and configuration of resources significantly enhances efficiency, reduces the potential for human error, and ensures consistency across environments. Azure PowerShell and the Azure Command-Line Interface (CLI) are instrumental tools provided by Microsoft Azure for automating these crucial tasks. Both tools offer comprehensive capabilities for scripting and executing commands that manage Azure resources, but they cater to different preferences in terms of syntax and operating environments.

Azure PowerShell: Utilizes cmdlets, PowerShell's command-line tools, for deploying resources. For instance, creating a new virtual machine can be achieved through a script that specifies the VM's configuration, such as size, image, and network settings.

Example:

```
New-AzVm `
-ResourceGroupName "MyResourceGroup" `
-Name "MyVM" `
-Location "East US" `
-VirtualNetworkName "MyVNet" `
-SubnetName "MySubnet" `
-SecurityGroupName "MySecurityGroup" `
-PublicIpAddressName "MyPublicIpAddress" `
-OpenPorts 80,443
```

Azure CLI: Commands in the CLI are designed to be intuitive and easy to script for similar deployment tasks. The CLI's advantage lies in its simplicity and cross-platform support.

Example:

```
az vm create \
--resource-group MyResourceGroup \
--name MyVM \
--location eastus \
--vnet-name MyVNet \
--subnet MySubnet \
--nsg MySecurityGroup \
--public-ip-address MyPublicIpAddress \
--open-ports 80 443
```

Automating Resource Configuration

Once resources are deployed, they often require further configuration to meet specific operational, security, or compliance requirements. Automation plays a key role in ensuring these configurations are applied consistently and efficiently.

Azure PowerShell: PowerShell scripts can be used to modify resource configurations, such as updating a web app's settings or resizing a virtual machine according to performance metrics.

Example:

```
Set-AzWebApp `
-ResourceGroupName "MyResourceGroup" `
-Name "MyWebApp" `
-AppSettings @{"WEBSITE_TIME_ZONE"="Eastern Standard Time"}
```

Azure CLI: Similarly, the Azure CLI can execute commands to adjust configurations, offering a streamlined syntax that is easy to incorporate into scripts for batch processing or automation pipelines.

Example:

```
az webapp config appsettings set \
--resource-group MyResourceGroup \
--name MyWebApp \
--settings WEBSITE_TIME_ZONE="Eastern Standard Time"
```

Automating resource deployment and configuration through Azure PowerShell and CLI not only speeds up the provisioning process but also enhances reliability and consistency across deployments. Both tools offer robust scripting capabilities that cater to different user preferences and environments, enabling developers and administrators to select the tool that best fits their workflow. Whether deploying a single resource or orchestrating the provisioning of entire environments, Azure PowerShell and CLI provide the necessary commands and flexibility to automate these tasks, driving efficiency and accuracy in managing Azure resources.

Automating Resource Deployment

Resource deployment involves provisioning and setting up various Azure resources like virtual machines, storage accounts, web apps, and databases. Automating this process ensures rapid and consistent deployments, essential for agile development practices and operational efficiency.

In the rapidly evolving landscape of cloud computing, the automation of resource deployment stands as a cornerstone of efficient cloud management. Azure PowerShell and Azure Command-Line Interface

(CLI) empower users to streamline the provisioning and setup of Azure resources, encapsulating complex deployment tasks into reusable, scriptable commands. This automation not only accelerates deployment processes but also ensures consistency and repeatability across different environments, a critical aspect for development, testing, and production workflows.

The Role of Azure PowerShell and CLI in Resource Deployment

Azure PowerShell and CLI offer a comprehensive set of commands tailored for managing Azure resources. These tools enable the scripting of deployment tasks, from simple resource provisioning to orchestrating complex, multi-resource deployments. The choice between PowerShell and CLI often boils down to user preference, environment, or specific task requirements, with PowerShell being a favorite in Windows-centric environments and CLI offering cross-platform flexibility.

Advantages of Automating Resource Deployment

Consistency and Accuracy: Automated scripts reduce manual errors and ensure deployments are consistent across different environments or subscriptions.

Speed and Efficiency: Scripting the deployment process saves time, especially when dealing with complex infrastructures or multiple environments.

Repeatability and Scalability: Automation scripts can be executed multiple times, simplifying the process of scaling up resources or replicating environments.

Documentation and Version Control: Scripts can be version-controlled and serve as documentation for infrastructure setups, facilitating collaboration and compliance.

Implementing Automated Deployments

Azure PowerShell: Utilizing cmdlets, Azure PowerShell scripts can define every aspect of the Azure resource configuration, allowing for detailed customization and control. Scripts can include commands for creating virtual networks, storage accounts, VMs, and configuring additional settings like firewall rules or diagnostics.

Example:

```
# Create a resource group
New-AzResourceGroup -Name "MyResourceGroup" -Location "East US"
# Create a virtual network
$vnet = New-AzVirtualNetwork -ResourceGroupName "MyResourceGroup" -Location "East US" -Name "MyVNet" -AddressPrefix "10.0.0.0/16"
# Deploy a VM
New-AzVm `
-ResourceGroupName "MyResourceGroup" `
-Name "MyVM" `
-Location "East US" `
-VirtualNetworkName $vnet.Name `
-Image "Win2019Datacenter"
```

Azure CLI: Similar to PowerShell, Azure CLI scripts can automate the deployment of resources. The CLI's syntax is optimized for readability and succinctness, making it an excellent choice for quick scripting in any operating system.

Example:

```
# Create a resource group
az group create --name MyResourceGroup --location "East US"
# Create a virtual network
az network vnet create --resource-group MyResourceGroup --name MyVNet --address-prefix "10.0.0.0/16"
# Deploy a VM
az vm create \
--resource-group MyResourceGroup \
--name MyVM \
--location "East US" \
--image Win2019Datacenter \
```

--vnet-name MyVNet

Automating resource deployment with Azure PowerShell and CLI is a powerful strategy to enhance the management of Azure resources. It provides a structured, efficient, and error-reducing approach to provisioning resources, crucial for maintaining agility and compliance in the cloud. Whether leveraging the detailed control of PowerShell or the cross-platform capabilities of CLI, automation scripts serve as a foundation for scalable, repeatable, and manageable cloud infrastructures, driving operational efficiencies and enabling faster time-to-market for services and applications.

Batch Processing:

Automate tasks that need to be executed on a set of resources, such as starting or stopping virtual machines outside of business hours to save costs.

Batch processing in the context of Azure resource management is a powerful technique to execute operations on a large set of resources simultaneously. This approach is essential for efficient cloud management, especially when dealing with a high volume of resources or when repetitive tasks need to be performed. Azure PowerShell and the Azure Command-Line Interface (CLI) are instrumental tools for implementing batch processing, enabling administrators and developers to automate complex workflows and operational tasks across numerous Azure resources with precision and efficiency.

Understanding Batch Processing with Azure PowerShell and CLI

Batch processing involves the execution of a single command or script that applies to multiple resources. This can include deploying, updating, monitoring, or deleting resources in bulk, rather than managing each resource individually. Azure PowerShell and CLI support batch processing through scripting capabilities that allow for looping constructs, conditional logic, and integration with other Azure services or external data sources.

Advantages of Batch Processing in Azure

Efficiency and Time Savings: Automating repetitive tasks across multiple resources reduces manual effort and significantly speeds up operational workflows.

Consistency and Reliability: Applying operations uniformly across resources ensures consistency in configurations and settings, reducing the risk of human error and configuration drift.

Scalability: As the Azure environment grows, the ability to manage resources in batch becomes crucial for scaling operations and maintaining control over the cloud infrastructure.

Implementing Batch Processing

Azure PowerShell: Utilizes cmdlets in conjunction with Power-Shell scripting constructs like **ForEach-Object** or **ForEach** loops to process multiple resources. This approach is ideal for scenarios requiring conditional logic or integration with other PowerShell-based tools or scripts.

Example:

```
# Retrieve a list of all VMs in a resource group and stop them
Get-AzVm -ResourceGroupName "MyResourceGroup" | ForEach-Object {
    Stop-AzVm -ResourceGroupName "MyResourceGroup" -Name $_.Name -Force
}
```

Azure CLI: Employs Azure CLI commands within shell scripting loops (**for** loops in bash, for example) to perform operations on a set of resources. This method is particularly effective in cross-platform environments or when integrating with other CLI tools.

Example:

```
# Retrieve a list of all VM names in a resource group and stop them
vms=$(az vm list -g MyResourceGroup --query '[].name' -o tsv)
for vm in $vms; do
az vm stop --resource-group MyResourceGroup --name $vm
done
```

Use Cases for Batch Processing

Resource Clean-up: Automatically delete temporary or unused resources across multiple subscriptions or resource groups to manage costs and maintain a clean Azure environment.

Bulk Updates: Apply configuration changes or updates to a large set of resources, such as modifying network security rules, resizing VMs, or updating application settings in App Services.

Monitoring and Reporting: Collect and aggregate metrics or logs from multiple resources for analysis, reporting, or alerting purposes, ensuring comprehensive visibility across the Azure environment.

Batch processing with Azure PowerShell and CLI is a cornerstone of effective Azure resource management, offering a scalable, consistent, and efficient approach to managing cloud resources. By leveraging these tools for automating batch operations, organizations can enhance their cloud operational workflows, maintain tighter control over their Azure environments, and free up valuable time for more strategic activities. Whether dealing with routine maintenance tasks, complex deployments, or compliance audits, batch processing empowers teams to manage their Azure resources more effectively and with greater precision.

Monitoring and Diagnostics:

Scripts can be created to automate the collection of metrics and logs for analysis, facilitating proactive monitoring and troubleshooting of Azure resources.

Effective monitoring and diagnostics are fundamental to maintaining the health, performance, and security of applications and services running in Azure. The ability to automate these aspects not only ensures proactive management of resources but also enables rapid response to potential issues before they impact users or services. Azure PowerShell and the Azure Command-Line Interface (CLI) provide powerful tools for automating monitoring and diagnostic tasks, allowing for comprehensive oversight of Azure resources.

Azure PowerShell and CLI for Monitoring and Diagnostics

Azure PowerShell and CLI extend beyond resource management to encompass monitoring and diagnostics, offering commands and cmdlets to retrieve metrics, logs, and alerts. These tools can automate the collection of diagnostic data, configure monitoring settings on Azure resources, and create or manage alert rules, making it easier to keep a pulse on the state of your Azure environment.

Advantages of Automating Monitoring and Diagnostics

Proactive Management: Automated monitoring allows for the early detection of issues, enabling proactive management of resources and minimizing downtime.

Operational Efficiency: Automating the collection and analysis of diagnostic data reduces manual effort, freeing up time for more strategic activities.

Consistency and Coverage: Applying monitoring configurations uniformly across resources ensures comprehensive coverage and consistent monitoring practices.

Implementing Automated Monitoring and Diagnostics

Azure PowerShell: Utilizes cmdlets to configure monitoring settings, retrieve performance metrics, manage diagnostic settings, and create alert rules. PowerShell scripts can be developed to automate these tasks across multiple resources or subscriptions.

Example:

```
# Configure diagnostic settings on a storage account to send logs and metrics to a Log Analytics workspace
$storageId = (Get-AzStorageAccount -ResourceGroupName "MyResourceGroup" -Name "MyStorageAccount").Id
$logWorkspaceId = (Get-AzOperationalInsightsWorkspace -ResourceGroupName "MyResourceGroup" -Name "MyWorkspace").ResourceId

Set-AzDiagnosticSetting -ResourceId $storageId -WorkspaceId $logWorkspaceId -Enabled $true
```

Azure CLI: Offers commands to manage monitoring and diagnostic settings, including the retrieval of metrics and logs and the management of alert rules. CLI scripts provide a cross-platform solution for automating monitoring tasks.

Example:

Configure diagnostic settings to send logs and metrics to a Log Analytics workspace

az monitor diagnostic-settings create \

--resource "/subscriptions/{SubID}/resourceGroups/MyResourceGroup/providers/Microsoft.Storage/storageAccounts/MyStorageAccount" \

--workspace "/subscriptions/{SubID}/resourceGroups/MyResourceGroup/providers/Microsoft.OperationalInsights/workspaces/MyWorkspace" \

--name "MyDiagnosticsSetting" \

--logs '[{"category": "Write", "enabled": true}, {"category": "Delete", "enabled": true}]' \

--metrics '[{"category": "Transaction", "enabled": true, "retentionPolicy": {"enabled": true, "days": 0}}]'

Use Cases for Automated Monitoring and Diagnostics

Performance Monitoring: Automate the collection of performance metrics across various resources to identify trends, bottlenecks, and opportunities for optimization.

Log Management: Configure resources to automatically send logs to Azure Monitor Logs or a Log Analytics workspace for centralized log management, analysis, and retention.

Alert Management: Automatically create or update alert rules based on specific metrics or log patterns to notify administrators of potential issues, ensuring rapid response to operational or security incidents.

Automating monitoring and diagnostics tasks with Azure PowerShell and CLI enables organizations to maintain a high level of visibility and control over their Azure resources. By leveraging these tools, administrators can ensure that monitoring practices are consistently applied, operational efficiencies are realized, and the Azure environment remains secure, performant, and reliable. Through proactive management and automated oversight, businesses can better manage the complexities of their cloud infrastructure and respond more effectively to the dynamic needs of their applications and services.

Security Management:

Automate the management of security policies and access controls, ensuring that your Azure environment complies with organizational security standards.

In the realm of cloud computing, maintaining a robust security posture is paramount. As Azure environments grow in complexity and scale, the automation of security management tasks becomes essential for ensuring that resources remain protected against potential threats while complying with organizational security policies. Azure PowerShell and the Azure Command-Line Interface (CLI) provide powerful tools for automating a wide range of security management tasks, from configuring network security policies to managing access controls and responding to security alerts.

Leveraging Azure PowerShell and CLI for Security Automation

Azure PowerShell and CLI enable administrators to script and automate various security-related operations, ensuring consistent application of security configurations across all Azure resources and subscriptions. These tools offer commands and cmdlets to interact directly with Azure's security services, such as Azure Security Center, Azure Active Directory, and network security groups, allowing for a programmable approach to security management.

Key Benefits of Security Automation

Consistency: Ensures uniform security configurations across your Azure environment, reducing the risk of misconfigurations and vulnerabilities.

Efficiency: Automates repetitive and time-consuming security tasks, allowing security teams to focus on strategic security initiatives.

Scalability: Facilitates the management of security policies and practices as your Azure environment scales, maintaining a strong security posture without additional overhead.

Responsiveness: Enables rapid response to detected threats or security incidents by automating alert responses and mitigation actions.

Implementing Security Automation

Azure PowerShell: Utilizes a comprehensive set of cmdlets designed for managing Azure security services and resources. Administrators can script the creation and configuration of network security groups, role-based access controls, and integration with Azure Security Center for automated threat detection and response.

Example:

```
# Create a new network security group and rule
$nsg = New-AzNetworkSecurityGroup -ResourceGroupName "MyResourceGroup" -Location "East US" -Name "MyNSG"
$rule = New-AzNetworkSecurityRuleConfig -Name "AllowSSH" -Access "Allow" -Protocol "Tcp" -Direction "Inbound" -Priority 100 -SourceAddressPrefix "*" -SourcePortRange "*" -DestinationAddressPrefix "*" -DestinationPortRange 22
$nsg | Add-AzNetworkSecurityRuleConfig -NetworkSecurityRule $rule | Set-AzNetworkSecurityGroup
```

Azure CLI: The CLI offers a straightforward syntax for managing security configurations and integrating with Azure security services. It's particularly useful for scripting across different platforms and environments.

Example:

```
# Create a new network security group and rule
az network nsg create --resource-group MyResourceGroup --name MyNSG --location eastus
az network nsg rule create --resource-group MyResourceGroup --nsg-name MyNSG --name AllowSSH --priority 100 --direction Inbound --access Allow --protocol Tcp --source-address-prefix "*"
```

--source-port-range "*" --destination-address-prefix "*" --destination-port-range 22

Use Cases for Security Automation

Access Management: Automate the assignment of role-based access controls to ensure that only authorized users have access to specific resources, based on their roles and responsibilities.

Security Configuration and Compliance: Script the deployment of security configurations and policies across resources to meet compliance requirements, ensuring that all resources adhere to organizational security standards.

Threat Detection and Response: Integrate with Azure Security Center to automate the detection of and response to security threats. Scripts can be used to analyze alerts, apply security updates, and quarantine affected resources automatically.

Encryption and Data Protection: Automate the configuration of encryption settings for storage accounts and databases to protect sensitive data at rest and in transit.

Automation of security management tasks using Azure PowerShell and CLI is crucial for maintaining a secure and compliant Azure environment. By leveraging these tools, organizations can ensure consistent application of security policies, enhance the efficiency of security operations, and respond more rapidly to emerging threats. The programmable nature of Azure PowerShell and CLI transforms security management from a manual, time-consuming process into a streamlined, automated workflow, enabling a proactive and robust security posture in the cloud.

Backup and Disaster Recovery:

Automate the backup of data and applications, as well as the orchestration of disaster recovery drills, to ensure business continuity.

In the cloud era, safeguarding data against loss and ensuring business continuity are paramount concerns. Azure's robust capabilities for backup and disaster recovery can be fully leveraged through automation, ensuring that critical data is protected and that services can be quickly restored in the event of an outage. Azure PowerShell and the Azure Command-Line Interface (CLI) offer powerful mechanisms for automating backup and disaster recovery processes, providing a proactive approach to data protection and minimizing downtime.

Leveraging Azure PowerShell and CLI for Backup and Disaster Recovery Automation

Azure PowerShell and CLI enable administrators to script and automate the deployment of backup policies, the recovery of data, and the orchestration of disaster recovery plans. These tools interface directly with Azure Backup, Azure Site Recovery, and other Azure services designed for data protection and recovery, allowing for the comprehensive automation of backup and disaster recovery tasks.

Key Benefits of Automation in Backup and Disaster Recovery

Consistent Policy Application: Automating the deployment of backup policies ensures that all critical data across Azure resources is protected according to organizational standards.

Efficient Recovery Processes: Automation speeds up the recovery process, reducing downtime and operational impact in the event of data loss or a disaster.

Scalable Protection Strategies: As Azure environments grow, automation enables the scalable application of backup and disaster recovery strategies to new resources without manual intervention.

Reduced Human Error: Scripting backup and recovery tasks minimizes the risk of human error, ensuring that data protection measures are correctly and consistently applied.

Implementing Backup and Disaster Recovery Automation

Azure PowerShell: Utilizes cmdlets to manage backups, restore operations, and configure Site Recovery. PowerShell scripts can automate the scheduling of backups, the recovery of individual items or entire resources, and the setup of disaster recovery replication.

Example: Automating Azure VM backups with Azure PowerShell.

Create a Recovery Services vault

$recoveryVault = New-AzRecoveryServicesVault -ResourceGroup-Name "MyResourceGroup" -Name "MyRecoveryVault" -Location "East US"

Enable backup for an Azure VM

$vm = Get-AzVM -Name "MyVM" -ResourceGroupName "MyResourceGroup"

Enable-AzRecoveryServicesBackupProtection -ResourceGroup-Name "MyResourceGroup" -Name "MyRecoveryVault" -Target $vm -PolicyName "DefaultPolicy"

Azure CLI: Offers commands to configure backups and manage disaster recovery scenarios. CLI scripts are useful for integrating backup and disaster recovery operations into deployment pipelines or for cross-platform scripting.

Example: Setting up Azure VM backup with Azure CLI.

Create a Recovery Services vault

az backup vault create --resource-group MyResourceGroup --name MyRecoveryVault --location eastus

Enable backup for an Azure VM

az backup protection enable-for-vm --resource-group MyResource-Group --vault-name MyRecoveryVault --vm MyVM --policy-name DefaultPolicy

Use Cases for Backup and Disaster Recovery Automation

Automated Backups: Schedule and manage backups for Azure VMs, SQL databases, and Azure file shares, ensuring that data is regularly backed up without manual intervention.

Automated Disaster Recovery Testing: Script the orchestration of disaster recovery drills to test the readiness and effectiveness of recovery plans in a non-disruptive manner.

Rapid Recovery: Automate the recovery process to minimize downtime in the event of data loss, system failures, or disasters, quickly restoring services to their operational state.

Cross-Region Replication: Manage the replication of critical workloads to secondary regions for disaster recovery purposes, ensuring that applications can be quickly failed over and recovered in another region if necessary.

Automating backup and disaster recovery tasks using Azure Power-Shell and CLI is an essential strategy for safeguarding data and ensuring business continuity in the cloud. By leveraging these tools, organizations can apply consistent data protection strategies, efficiently recover from data loss or disasters, and scale their backup and disaster recovery operations in line with their Azure environment's growth. Automation not only enhances the reliability and effectiveness of backup and disaster recovery processes but also contributes to operational resilience, protecting against the potential impact of unforeseen events.

The automation capabilities provided by Azure PowerShell and the Azure CLI are critical for managing Azure resources efficiently and effectively. By leveraging these tools to automate repetitive and complex tasks, organizations can achieve greater operational efficiency, reduce the potential for human error, and ensure consistent deployment and management practices across their Azure environments. Whether for deploying new resources, managing security, or ensuring business continuity, Azure PowerShell and CLI offer the flexibility and power to streamline your cloud management tasks.

Conclusion

The Azure Portal and PowerShell cater to different management styles and requirements within the Azure ecosystem. The Azure Portal offers an intuitive, graphical interface for managing resources, suitable for users who prefer visual interaction. In contrast, Azure PowerShell provides powerful scripting capabilities for automation, complex management tasks, and users comfortable with command-line interfaces. Together, they offer flexible options for managing Azure resources effectively, whether through interactive GUI sessions or automated scripts. By leveraging these tools, organizations can streamline their Azure resource management, enhance productivity, and ensure their cloud environments are optimally configured and maintained.

9

Chapter 5: Azure Security and Compliance

In today's digital landscape, security and compliance stand as critical pillars for any cloud platform, with Microsoft Azure leading the way through its comprehensive suite of security features and compliance certifications. Azure's security and compliance framework is designed to protect data, applications, and infrastructure from potential threats while ensuring that organizations can meet the stringent regulatory requirements governing their industries. This comprehensive overview explores the multifaceted approach of Azure to security and compliance, highlighting key features, tools, and certifications that make Azure a trusted platform for businesses worldwide.

Azure's Approach to Security

Azure's security philosophy is built on a foundation of shared responsibility, where security is a joint task between Microsoft and the customer. Microsoft secures the cloud infrastructure and services, while customers are responsible for securing their data and access to Azure resources.

Key Features of Azure Security:

Identity and Access Management (IAM): Azure Active Directory (Azure AD) provides robust IAM capabilities, enabling organizations to control access to resources through multi-factor authentication, conditional access policies, and role-based access control (RBAC).

Network Security: Azure offers a range of network security tools, including Azure Firewall, Network Security Groups (NSGs), and Azure DDoS Protection, to safeguard network resources and protect against a variety of network attacks.

Data Security: Azure provides encryption in transit and at rest, alongside Azure Key Vault for managing encryption keys and secrets. Additionally, Azure offers tools for data classification, privacy, and protection against data leaks.

Threat Protection and Detection: Azure Security Center and Azure Sentinel offer advanced threat detection, providing real-time security analytics, threat intelligence, and automated threat response capabilities.

Information Protection: Azure Information Protection (AIP) helps organizations classify, label, and protect documents and emails, ensuring that sensitive information is safeguarded wherever it resides.

Azure's Approach to Compliance

Azure's global infrastructure is designed to meet the compliance needs of the most security-sensitive organizations. By achieving a broad set of international and industry-specific compliance standards, Azure enables customers to comply with regulatory requirements and to leverage the compliance documentation provided by Azure to support their own compliance activities.

Key Aspects of Azure Compliance:

Comprehensive Compliance Portfolio: Azure maintains an extensive portfolio of compliance certifications, including ISO/IEC 27001, HIPAA, FedRAMP, SOC 1, SOC 2, and GDPR, among others.

Regulatory Compliance: Azure provides specific features and services to help organizations meet regulatory requirements, such as those in the financial services, healthcare, and government sectors.

Compliance Tools and Resources: Azure offers tools like Azure Policy, Azure Blueprints, and the Compliance Manager to help organizations assess and manage their compliance posture, automate compliance tasks, and simplify audits.

Transparency and Trust: Microsoft provides detailed documentation on its compliance offerings, security practices, and data protection measures, fostering transparency and building trust with customers.

Understanding Azure Security Center:

In the landscape of cloud computing, securing cloud resources against evolving threats is paramount. Azure Security Center plays a crucial role in Microsoft Azure's security and compliance framework, offering a unified security management system that strengthens the security posture of data centers, and provides advanced threat protection across hybrid cloud workloads. This comprehensive exploration delves into Azure Security Center, its capabilities, and how it underpins the broader ecurityy and compliance objectives of organizations leveraging Azure.

What is Azure Security Center?

Azure Security Center is a cloud-based tool that provides comprehensive visibility and control over the security of Azure resources. It extends beyond Azure to on-premises environments and other cloud platforms, making it a versatile solution for securing hybrid cloud deployments. At its core, Azure Security Center aims to provide continuous security assessment, actionable security recommendations, and rapid threat detection and response.

Key Features of Azure Security Center

Continuous Assessment and Security Recommendations:

Azure Security Center continuously assesses the security state of your Azure resources, identifying potential vulnerabilities and providing actionable recommendations to improve your security posture.

In the rapidly evolving cloud environment, maintaining a strong security posture requires constant vigilance and proactive management. Azure Security Center addresses this need through its Continuous Assessment and Security Recommendations feature, a cornerstone of its security and compliance capabilities. This functionality enables organizations to continuously evaluate their Azure and hybrid environments against security best practices and regulatory standards, providing actionable insights to mitigate potential vulnerabilities and enhance overall security.

Continuous Assessment in Azure Security Center

Continuous assessment is a process where Azure Security Center scans Azure resources, identifying potential security misconfigurations and vulnerabilities. This scanning extends across a wide range of services, including virtual machines (VMs), networking, data services, and identity services. The assessment leverages Microsoft's extensive security knowledge base, incorporating best practices and the latest threat intelligence to evaluate the security state of resources.

Key Aspects of Continuous Assessment

Comprehensive Coverage: Continuous assessment covers a broad spectrum of Azure services and settings, ensuring a thorough evaluation of the cloud environment's security posture.

Integration with Azure Services: The assessment process is deeply integrated with Azure services, allowing for seamless evaluation of service-specific configurations and security settings.

Real-time Insights: Organizations receive real-time insights into their security posture, enabling immediate identification of issues and vulnerabilities that could potentially expose resources to threats.

Security Recommendations in Azure Security Center

Based on the findings from the continuous assessment, Azure Security Center generates a set of tailored security recommendations. These recommendations are prioritized based on the potential impact and severity of the identified issues, guiding administrators on where to focus their remediation efforts.

Key Features of Security Recommendations

Actionable Guidance: Each recommendation includes detailed guidance on how to address the identified issue, often with direct links to the relevant Azure configuration pages.

Prioritization: Recommendations are prioritized, helping organizations focus on fixing the most critical vulnerabilities first to maximize the impact of their security efforts.

Automated Remediation: In some cases, Azure Security Center offers automated remediation scripts or the ability to fix issues directly from within the portal, simplifying the process of securing resources.

Enhancing Security Posture with Continuous Assessment and Recommendations

Proactive Vulnerability Management: Continuous assessment and the resulting recommendations enable organizations to proactively manage vulnerabilities, reducing the risk of exploitation and improving the security of cloud workloads.

Compliance Alignment: By aligning security practices with industry standards and regulatory requirements, organizations can ensure compliance and avoid potential penalties or breaches.

Security Awareness: Continuous assessment fosters a culture of security awareness, encouraging developers and administrators to adopt security best practices in their daily operations.

Azure Security Center's Continuous Assessment and Security Recommendations feature is a powerful tool for maintaining and enhancing the security posture of Azure and hybrid environments. By providing real-time insights into potential vulnerabilities and offering actionable guidance for remediation, Azure Security Center helps organizations proactively address security risks. This continuous vigilance not only strengthens cloud security but also aligns with compliance objectives, making it an indispensable component of an effective cloud security strategy.

Advanced Threat Protection (ATP):

Leveraging global threat intelligence from Microsoft, Azure Security Center offers advanced threat detection capabilities, identifying and alerting on potential security threats to your resources.

Within the expansive suite of Azure's security services, Advanced Threat Protection (ATP) offered by Azure Security Center stands out as a crucial line of defense against sophisticated cyber threats. ATP is designed to detect, investigate, and respond to advanced threats, malicious actions, and security breaches across Azure and hybrid environments.

What is Advanced Threat Protection in Azure Security Center?

Advanced Threat Protection in Azure Security Center is a feature that provides an additional layer of security intelligence that leverages Microsoft's vast threat intelligence data, analytics, and machine learning capabilities to identify and respond to emerging and sophisticated attacks. ATP extends beyond traditional security measures by focusing on detecting and mitigating threats that may bypass other security controls.

Key Features of ATP in Azure Security Center

Behavioral Analytics: ATP utilizes behavioral analytics and anomaly detection to identify unusual activities that could indicate a breach or an advanced threat. By analyzing patterns and behaviors, it can pinpoint activities that deviate from the norm.

Threat Intelligence: Leveraging Microsoft's global threat intelligence, ATP can identify known malicious actors, software, and activities. This intelligence is continuously updated, ensuring protection against the latest threats.

Integration with Other Azure Services: ATP works in concert with other Azure services, such as Azure Active Directory and Azure Sentinel, to provide a comprehensive security analysis and response mechanism.

Customizable Security Alerts: Organizations can customize alert rules to focus on specific threats relevant to their environment. Alerts provide detailed information on the nature of the threat, the affected resources, and recommended actions for mitigation.

Automated Security Investigations: When a threat is detected, ATP automatically generates a security incident and begins an investigation process, mapping out the attack timeline and involved resources to aid in understanding and remediation.

Enhancing Security with ATP

Advanced Threat Protection plays a pivotal role in enhancing the security framework of Azure deployments by:

Early Detection of Advanced Threats: ATP's ability to detect suspicious activities and known malicious threats early in the attack chain allows organizations to respond before significant damage can occur.

Reduced False Positives: Through behavioral analytics and machine learning, ATP can more accurately distinguish between legitimate activities and potential threats, reducing the noise from false positives and focusing attention on genuine security concerns.

Streamlined Incident Response: The automated investigation and detailed alerts provided by ATP enable security teams to quickly understand the scope and impact of an attack, facilitating a faster and more effective response.

Comprehensive Security Posture: By integrating with other Azure security services, ATP provides a layered security approach that enhances the overall security posture of Azure environments, protecting against a wide range of threats.

Advanced Threat Protection within Azure Security Center is an essential component of Azure's security and compliance framework, offering sophisticated capabilities to detect and respond to advanced threats. ATP's integration of behavioral analytics, threat intelligence, and automated investigations empowers organizations to proactively safeguard their cloud environments against emerging cyber threats. As cyber threats continue to evolve in complexity and stealth, leveraging ATP's advanced security capabilities will be indispensable for maintaining the integrity and resilience of Azure deployments, ensuring that organizations can navigate the digital landscape with confidence.

Regulatory Compliance Dashboard:

The compliance dashboard within Azure Security Center evaluates your resources against a set of compliance standards and benchmarks, providing insights into your compliance posture and recommendations for improvement.

In the realm of cloud computing, navigating the complexities of regulatory compliance is a critical challenge for many organizations. The Regulatory Compliance Dashboard within Azure Security Center represents a pivotal tool in addressing this challenge, providing organizations with comprehensive insights into their compliance posture across a variety of standards and regulations.

What is the Regulatory Compliance Dashboard?

The Regulatory Compliance Dashboard in Azure Security Center is a feature designed to give organizations a centralized view of their compliance status with various regulatory standards and benchmarks. It automatically assesses Azure resources against a set of controls derived from common compliance frameworks, offering detailed reports on compliance gaps and actionable recommendations to improve the overall compliance posture.

Key Features of the Regulatory Compliance Dashboard

Comprehensive Compliance Coverage: The dashboard covers a wide range of compliance standards, including but not limited to ISO 27001, NIST SP 800-53, PCI DSS, and GDPR, providing organizations with insights into their compliance status across multiple frameworks.

Automated Compliance Assessments: Utilizing Azure's security and audit data, the dashboard automatically evaluates the compliance of Azure resources, reducing the manual effort required for compliance assessments.

Actionable Recommendations: For each identified compliance gap, the dashboard provides actionable recommendations on how to address the issue, including direct links to the relevant Azure security controls and configurations.

Continuous Compliance Monitoring: The dashboard offers continuous monitoring of compliance status, ensuring that organizations can maintain compliance over time and quickly address any new compliance issues that arise.

Enhancing Compliance with the Regulatory Compliance Dashboard

The Regulatory Compliance Dashboard plays a crucial role in helping organizations manage their compliance efforts effectively:

Streamlined Compliance Reporting: By offering a consolidated view of compliance across multiple standards, the dashboard simplifies the process of compliance reporting, making it easier for organizations to demonstrate compliance to auditors and regulatory bodies.

Prioritized Remediation Efforts: The dashboard prioritizes compliance gaps based on their potential impact, enabling organizations to focus their remediation efforts where they are needed most, thereby optimizing the allocation of security resources.

Improved Compliance Posture: The detailed recommendations provided by the dashboard guide organizations in implementing best practices and security controls that not only address compliance requirements but also enhance the overall security posture.

Reduced Compliance Costs: Automation of compliance assessments and continuous monitoring help reduce the costs associated with compliance efforts, including the costs of manual audits and potential non-compliance penalties.

The Regulatory Compliance Dashboard within Azure Security Center is an invaluable tool for organizations navigating the complexities of regulatory compliance in the cloud. By providing automated assessments, actionable insights, and continuous monitoring, the dashboard empowers organizations to improve their compliance posture efficiently and effectively. As regulatory landscapes continue to evolve, leveraging the capabilities of the Regulatory Compliance Dashboard will be essential for organizations aiming to achieve and maintain compliance, safeguarding their operations against compliance risks while building trust with customers and regulatory bodies.

Just-In-Time (JIT) VM Access:

This feature reduces exposure to attacks by locking down inbound traffic to your Azure VMs, allowing access to ports only when needed and for a specified amount of time.

In the dynamic and often vulnerable digital landscape, securing virtual machines (VMs) against unauthorized access is paramount. Azure Security Center's Just-In-Time (JIT) VM Access is a pivotal security feature designed to minimize the attack surface of Azure VMs by controlling access to them. This feature dramatically enhances the security posture of cloud environments by allowing access to VMs only when needed and for a specified duration

What is Just-In-Time (JIT) VM Access?

Just-In-Time VM Access is a feature within Azure Security Center that helps protect your Azure Virtual Machines from potential attacks by managing access to them. JIT VM Access reduces exposure to attacks by enabling you to lock down inbound traffic to your VMs, essentially closing all ports by default and allowing access only when needed for a limited time.

How Does JIT VM Access Work?

JIT VM Access works by controlling access to VMs through network security group (NSG) rules or Azure Firewall rules. When access to a VM is requested, JIT dynamically adjusts the NSG or Firewall rules to allow inbound traffic to the requested ports, but only for the approved amount of time. After the access period expires, JIT automatically reverts the rules, effectively closing the ports again.

Key Features of JIT VM Access

Request-Based Access Control: Access to VMs must be explicitly requested through Azure Security Center, and can be granted for specific ports over a limited time frame.

Dynamic NSG Rule Management: JIT automatically manages NSG rules to temporarily allow access, reducing the risk of misconfiguration or oversight leaving VMs vulnerable.

Audit Logs for Access Requests: Every access request is logged, providing an audit trail that includes the requester's identity, the reason for access, and the duration for which access was granted.

Integration with Azure RBAC: Access to request JIT VM Access can be controlled using Azure Role-Based Access Control (RBAC), ensuring that only authorized users can request access to VMs.

Benefits of Using JIT VM Access

Minimized Attack Surface: By keeping VM ports closed except when needed, JIT VM Access significantly reduces the VMs' exposure to potential attacks, such as brute force or port scanning attacks.

Enhanced Security Posture: JIT VM Access complements other security measures, contributing to a robust security posture that protects critical cloud resources.

Streamlined Access Management: The automated management of NSG rules simplifies the process of providing temporary access to VMs, ensuring efficiency without compromising security.

Compliance and Auditability: The logging of access requests aids in compliance efforts, providing clear evidence of who accessed what resources, when, and why.

Implementing JIT VM Access

Implementing JIT VM Access involves enabling the JIT policy for your VMs through Azure Security Center, specifying the ports to be controlled, the maximum allowed access duration, and any other configurations relevant to your security policies. Once enabled, users must request access through Azure Security Center, specifying their required access duration within the limits defined.

Just-In-Time VM Access is a testament to Azure's commitment to providing advanced security features that meet the complex demands of protecting cloud environments. By granting temporary access to VMs on an as-needed basis, JIT VM Access effectively shrinks the attack surface, enhancing the overall security and compliance of Azure deployments. This feature is instrumental for organizations aiming to fortify their cloud resources against unauthorized access, aligning with broader security strategies that safeguard data and infrastructure in the evolving threat landscape.

Adaptive Application Controls:

Azure Security Center helps in whitelisting safe applications, allowing you to control which applications can run on your VMs, thereby reducing the surface area for attacks.

In the multifaceted domain of cloud security, safeguarding applications against unauthorized or malicious activities is paramount. Azure Security Center's Adaptive Application Controls (AAC) are a vital feature designed to enhance the security of virtual machines (VMs) and other cloud workloads by controlling which applications can run, thereby significantly reducing the surface area for potential attacks.

What are Adaptive Application Controls?

Adaptive Application Controls are an advanced security feature within Azure Security Center that employs machine learning to understand and control application behavior on Azure VMs and non-Azure servers connected to Azure Security Center. By creating, enforcing, and monitoring application whitelists, AAC enables organizations to ensure that only known, safe applications are allowed to execute, effectively blocking unauthorized software and reducing the risk of malware or other malicious code execution.

Key Features of Adaptive Application Controls

Automated Whitelisting: Leveraging machine learning, AAC can automatically generate whitelists of safe applications based on the observed behavior of VMs and servers, simplifying the process of maintaining application controls.

Custom Whitelisting Policies: Organizations can customize whitelisting policies to meet their specific security requirements, adding or removing applications from the whitelist as needed.

Group Management: AAC allows for the grouping of similar VMs for simplified policy management. Application control policies can then be applied to groups of VMs, ensuring consistent application control across similar environments.

Audit and Enforcement Modes: Adaptive Application Controls can operate in audit mode, where execution attempts of unauthorized applications are logged for review, or enforcement mode, where such executions are actively blocked.

Alerts and Reporting: Azure Security Center provides alerts and detailed reports on attempts to run unauthorized applications, offering insights into compliance with whitelisting policies and potential security threats.

Enhancing Security with Adaptive Application Controls

Adaptive Application Controls strengthen the security framework of Azure deployments by:

Minimizing Attack Vectors: By ensuring that only authorized applications can run, AAC significantly reduces the attack surface available to potential attackers, mitigating the risk of malware infections and other security breaches.

Facilitating Compliance: For organizations subject to regulatory requirements that mandate strict control over software execution, AAC helps in achieving and demonstrating compliance with such regulations.

Streamlining Security Operations: The machine learning-based automation and group management features of AAC reduce the operational burden on security teams, allowing for more efficient management of application controls across large-scale deployments.

Proactive Threat Mitigation: By monitoring and blocking unauthorized application executions, AAC provides an additional layer of defense, enabling organizations to proactively mitigate potential security threats before they can impact the environment.

Adaptive Application Controls within Azure Security Center represent a sophisticated approach to application security, harnessing the power of machine learning to automate and enforce application whitelisting policies. By limiting application execution to authorized software, AAC plays a crucial role in minimizing the attack surface, enhancing regulatory compliance, and bolstering the overall security posture of Azure and hybrid cloud environments. As part of Azure's comprehensive security and compliance offerings, Adaptive Application Controls empower organizations to secure their cloud workloads more effectively, ensuring the integrity and resilience of their digital assets in the clou

Integrated Security Solutions:

It integrates with a range of security solutions and services, both from Microsoft and third-party vendors, offering a comprehensive approach to cloud security.

Azure Security Center stands as a pivotal component within Microsoft Azure's security architecture, offering a holistic approach to cloud security by integrating a wide array of security solutions. This integration not only streamlines security management across Azure resources but also enhances the overall security posture through a comprehensive, layered defense strategy. Integrated Security Solutions within Azure Security Center are designed to provide seamless security coverage, from identity and access management to data protection and threat intelligence.

The Essence of Integrated Security Solutions in Azure Security Center

Integrated Security Solutions in Azure Security Center refer to the cohesive blend of Azure's native security features and third-party security products and services, all unified under the Security Center's management umbrella. This integration facilitates a centralized, unified security management experience, enabling organizations to leverage the strengths of various security technologies in a coordinated manner.

Key Components of Integrated Security Solutions

Azure Active Directory (Azure AD): Integration with Azure AD enhances identity and access management, providing robust capabilities for multi-factor authentication, conditional access, and identity protection.

Azure Policy and Azure Blueprints: These tools are integrated to ensure compliance and governance across Azure resources, enabling organizations to enforce and automate security policies and standards.

Azure Firewall and Network Security Groups (NSGs): Seamlessly integrated into the Security Center, these network security solutions offer capabilities to control inbound and outbound traffic, protect against network threats, and isolate resources.

Azure Information Protection (AIP): Integration with AIP allows for classification, labeling, and protection of sensitive information, ensuring data security and compliance with regulatory requirements.

Third-Party Security Solutions: Azure Security Center allows for the integration of a wide range of third-party security products, including firewall appliances, anti-malware solutions, and vulnerability assessment tools, providing a flexible and extensible security framework.

Advantages of Integrated Security Solutions

Comprehensive Security Coverage: By integrating various security technologies, Azure Security Center provides comprehensive coverage across all layers of the cloud environment, from the network to applications to data.

Streamlined Security Management: Centralized management of both Azure-native and third-party security solutions simplifies the security administration process, offering a unified view of the security posture across Azure and hybrid environments.

Enhanced Threat Detection and Response: The aggregation of security intelligence from multiple sources improves the detection of sophisticated threats, enabling faster and more effective response to security incidents.

Customized Security Strategy: The flexibility to integrate third-party solutions allows organizations to tailor their security strategy to fit their specific needs, leveraging the best tools available for their unique environment.

The Integrated Security Solutions within Azure Security Center represent a strategic approach to cloud security, emphasizing the importance of a unified, layered defense mechanism. By integrating Azure-native security features with a broad ecosystem of third-party security solutions, Azure Security Center enables organizations to achieve a robust, comprehensive security posture. This integrated approach not only enhances the effectiveness of security measures but also simplifies the management of security across complex cloud and hybrid environments. As cybersecurity threats continue to evolve, the ability to seamlessly manage and coordinate diverse security technologies will be crucial for protecting Azure resources and ensuring compliance with industry standards and regulations.

Enhancing Security and Compliance with Azure Security Center

Azure Security Center plays a pivotal role in enhancing the security and compliance of Azure deployments:

Streamlining Security Management: By providing a central view of the security state across Azure, on-premises, and other clouds, it simplifies the complexity of managing security in diverse environments.

Proactive Threat Prevention: Through its continuous assessment and recommendations, Azure Security Center helps organizations proactively address potential vulnerabilities before they can be exploited.

Rapid Threat Detection and Response: With its ATP capabilities, Azure Security Center quickly identifies threats and provides tools and guidance for rapid response, minimizing the potential impact of security incidents.

Compliance Assurance: The compliance dashboard enables organizations to track their compliance status in real time, ensuring that they meet regulatory and policy requirements.

Azure Security Center stands as a cornerstone of Azure's security and compliance offerings, providing a robust set of tools designed to enhance the security posture of organizations' cloud environments. By offering comprehensive visibility, continuous assessment, advanced threat protection, and compliance monitoring, Azure Security Center empowers organizations to address the modern security challenges of cloud computing. As threats evolve and regulatory requirements become more stringent, leveraging Azure Security Center will be critical for organizations aiming to protect their cloud resources and ensure compliance with industry standards and regulations.

Implementing Azure Role-Based Access Control (RBAC):

In the realm of cloud security and compliance, managing who has access to your resources and what they can do with those resources is foundational. Azure Role-Based Access Control (RBAC) is a critical security feature within Microsoft Azure that enables fine-grained access management for Azure resources. By assigning specific roles to users, groups, and applications, Azure RBAC ensures that only authorized entities can perform actions within Azure environments, thereby enforcing the principle of least privilege and enhancing overall security.

Understanding Azure RBAC

Azure RBAC is an authorization system built on Azure Resource Manager that provides built-in roles, each encapsulating a specific set of permissions to perform operations like read, write, and delete on Azure resources. These roles can be assigned at various scopes, from management groups to individual resources, offering flexibility in how access is granted and managed across Azure subscriptions.

Azure Role-Based Access Control (RBAC) is an essential feature within Microsoft Azure's security and compliance framework, designed to provide granular access management for Azure resources. It allows organizations to precisely define who can access Azure resources, what they can do with those resources, and the scope at which access permissions are applied. This in-depth understanding of Azure RBAC is crucial for maintaining a secure and compliant Azure environment, ensuring that only authorized users can perform specific actions.

Core Concepts of Azure RBAC

Roles: At the heart of RBAC are roles, which are sets of permissions that can be assigned to users, groups, service principals, and managed identities. These permissions determine the operations that can be performed on Azure resources, such as reading, writing, and deleting.

Scope: RBAC allows roles to be assigned at different levels of scope - from an entire Azure subscription down to an individual resource. This hierarchical approach enables fine-grained control over access to resources within Azure.

Built-in Roles: Azure provides several predefined roles that cater to common user scenarios, such as the Owner, Contributor, and Reader roles. These built-in roles are designed to facilitate common access management tasks without the need for custom role definitions.

Custom Roles: For scenarios where built-in roles do not meet specific access requirements, Azure RBAC allows for the creation of custom roles. Custom roles can be tailored with precise permissions to fit the unique needs of an organization.

Implementing Effective Access Management with Azure RBAC

Assessment of Access Needs: The first step in implementing Azure RBAC is to assess the access requirements of your users and applications. This involves determining the least privileges necessary for them to perform their functions effectively.

Role Assignment: Once access needs are understood, the appropriate roles can be assigned to users, groups, service principals, and managed identities. Assignments should be made with the principle of least privilege in mind, granting only the permissions necessary to perform required tasks.

Use of Custom Roles: In cases where predefined roles do not align perfectly with access requirements, custom roles can be created and assigned. Custom roles should be crafted carefully to ensure they provide access to the right resources without overprivileged permissions.

Regular Review and Audit: To maintain a secure and compliant environment, it's essential to regularly review and audit RBAC role assignments. Azure provides tools and logs for monitoring RBAC configurations and changes, enabling organizations to adjust roles and permissions as needed.

Integration with Governance Policies: RBAC should be integrated with broader Azure governance policies, such as those enforced through Azure Policy, to ensure comprehensive compliance and security posture. Policies can be used to audit and enforce necessary RBAC configurations across the environment.

Azure Role-Based Access Control is a powerful tool for managing access to Azure resources, offering the granularity and flexibility needed to enforce security and compliance requirements. By understanding and effectively implementing Azure RBAC, organizations can ensure that users have the right level of access to perform their duties, while minimizing the risk of unauthorized access or data breaches. As cloud environments become increasingly complex, leveraging RBAC alongside other Azure security and compliance features will be crucial for maintaining the integrity and security of cloud resources.

Key Features of Azure RBAC

Built-in Roles:

Azure RBAC comes with several predefined roles that cater to common access management scenarios, such as Owner, Contributor, Reader, and User Access Administrator, among others.

In the Azure cloud ecosystem, managing access and permissions efficiently is fundamental to maintaining a secure and compliant environment. Azure Role-Based Access Control (RBAC) plays a crucial role in this aspect by providing a mechanism to assign specific permissions to users, groups, service principals, and managed identities. Among the features that make Azure RBAC particularly powerful are its built-in roles, predefined sets of permissions that simplify the assignment of access rights within Azure.

Overview of Built-in Roles in Azure RBAC

Built-in roles in Azure RBAC are predefined roles that encompass common sets of permissions needed for various tasks and responsibilities within Azure. These roles are designed to cover a broad spectrum of common use cases, allowing administrators to quickly and efficiently assign appropriate access levels without needing to create custom roles for every scenario.

Key Built-in Roles

Owner: Grants full access to manage all resources, including the rights to delegate access to others. This role is typically reserved for administrators who need complete control over resources in a subscription or resource group.

Contributor: Allows users to create and manage all types of Azure resources but does not allow them to grant access to others. This role is suitable for individuals who need to work with resources without requiring full administrative rights.

Reader: Provides read-only access to Azure resources, making it ideal for users who need to view but not modify resources.

User Access Administrator: Enables users to manage user access to Azure resources. This role is crucial for managing permissions and ensuring that individuals have the appropriate level of access.

Advantages of Using Built-in Roles

Simplicity and Efficiency: Built-in roles simplify the process of granting access to Azure resources by providing ready-to-use sets of permissions that cater to common operational needs.

Security and Compliance: By offering a granular level of control over permissions, built-in roles help organizations adhere to the principle of least privilege, reducing the risk of unauthorized access and potential security breaches.

Scalability: As organizations grow and evolve, the ability to quickly assign and manage access using built-in roles becomes essential for scaling operations securely and efficiently.

Best Practices for Using Built-in Roles

Assess Access Needs Carefully: Before assigning roles, assess the specific access requirements of users and applications to ensure that they are granted only the permissions necessary for their tasks.

Use the Principle of Least Privilege: Opt for roles that provide the minimum level of access needed for users to perform their duties, minimizing potential exposure to sensitive resources.

Regularly Review and Audit Role Assignments: Periodically review role assignments to ensure they still align with users' current responsibilities. Leverage Azure's audit logs and governance tools to monitor and adjust permissions as needed.

Combine Roles Strategically: In scenarios where a single built-in role does not meet all access requirements, consider combining roles thoughtfully to achieve the desired level of access without over privileging.

Built-in roles in Azure RBAC represent a fundamental element of Azure's security and compliance strategy, enabling administrators to manage access to cloud resources effectively and securely. By leveraging these predefined roles, organizations can streamline access management processes, enhance security posture, and ensure compliance with internal and external regulations. Understanding and utilizing built-in roles appropriately is key to achieving a balanced approach to cloud resource management, security, and compliance in Azure.

Custom Roles:

Beyond the built-in roles, Azure RBAC allows the creation of custom roles to meet specific organizational needs, enabling precise control over the actions that users can perform.

While Azure provides a robust set of built-in roles designed to meet most common access control requirements, there are scenarios where the predefined permissions of these roles do not align perfectly with the specific needs of an organization. This is where Azure Role-Based Access Control (RBAC)'s capability to create custom roles becomes invaluable. Custom roles in Azure RBAC allow for the granular tailoring of permissions, providing organizations the flexibility to define access precisely as needed for their unique operational contexts.

Understanding Custom Roles in Azure RBAC

Custom roles are user-defined roles that allow for a bespoke set of permissions to be created. These roles can be defined based on the fine-grained access control needs of an organization, allowing for specific actions to be included or excluded from a role's capabilities. Custom roles can be assigned at various scopes within Azure, including management groups, subscriptions, resource groups, and individual resources, providing flexibility in how access is granted.

Key Considerations for Custom Roles

Granularity: Custom roles can be as granular as needed, specifying exact actions that the role can perform on Azure resources. This includes creating, reading, updating, and deleting resources or even more specific actions within those categories.

Scalability: Like built-in roles, custom roles are scalable across the organization. Once created, they can be assigned to any number of users or groups, making them highly effective for widespread use cases that are not covered by the built-in roles.

Management: Custom roles are managed through the Azure portal, Azure PowerShell, or the Azure CLI, offering various ways to create, update, and assign these roles within your Azure environment.

Steps to Implement Custom Roles

Identify the Need for a Custom Role: Before creating a custom role, clearly identify the gap in the built-in roles that necessitates a custom solution. This typically involves a specific set of permissions that are either not encapsulated by a single built-in role or involve a combination of permissions across multiple roles.

Define the Custom Role: Using the Azure portal, PowerShell, or CLI, define the new custom role. This involves specifying a name, description, and the set of actions (permissions) that the role should allow. It's also important to define any notActions, which explicitly prevent certain actions from being performed by the role.

Example using Azure PowerShell:

```
$actions = @("Microsoft.Storage/*/read","Microsoft.Storage/storageAccounts/write")

$notActions = @("Microsoft.Storage/storageAccounts/blobServices/delete")

$roleDefinition = @{
Name = "Custom Storage Account Contributor"
IsCustom = $true
Description = "Can manage storage accounts but not delete them."
Actions = $actions
NotActions = $notActions
AssignableScopes = @("/subscriptions/your_subscription_id")
}
New-AzRoleDefinition @roleDefinition
```

Test the Custom Role: Before broadly assigning the new role, test it with a limited set of users or in a controlled environment to ensure it behaves as expected, granting the intended permissions without exposing additional privileges.

Deploy and Monitor: Once verified, deploy the custom role across the required scopes and monitor its usage. Regularly review custom roles to ensure they remain aligned with organizational needs and security policies.

Custom roles in Azure RBAC represent a powerful mechanism for organizations to tailor their access control policies precisely. By defining custom roles, organizations can ensure that their Azure resources are accessed securely and compliantly, adhering to the principle of least privilege. Properly implemented, custom roles enhance the security posture of Azure environments, providing a bespoke solution to meet specific operational and security requirements.

Scoped Assignments:

Roles can be assigned at different scopes – subscription, resource group, or specific resource, providing granular control over access to resources within Azure.

In the realm of Azure Security and Compliance, the precision with which access control can be applied is a cornerstone of maintaining a secure and compliant cloud environment. Scoped assignments in Azure Role-Based Access Control (RBAC) empower administrators to tailor access permissions with a high degree of granularity, ensuring that users, groups, service principals, and managed identities have access only to the resources necessary for their roles. This focused approach to access management is crucial for adhering to the principle of least privilege, a key practice in minimizing potential attack surfaces and ensuring compliance with regulatory standards.

Understanding Scoped Assignments in Azure RBAC

Scoped assignments in Azure RBAC allow for the assignment of roles within specific contexts or "scopes." These scopes can range from broad to very specific, including management groups, subscriptions, resource groups, or individual resources. By defining the scope of a role assignment, administrators can control access permissions with precision, ensuring that the assigned roles are effective only within the defined boundaries.

Levels of Scope

Management Group Scope: This is the broadest level, where roles assigned at a management group scope apply to all subscriptions and resources within that management group.

Subscription Scope: Roles assigned at the subscription scope are effective across all resource groups and resources within the specified subscription.

Resource Group Scope: Assigning roles at the resource group level limits the permissions to all resources within that particular resource group.

Resource Scope: The most granular level, where roles are assigned directly to a single resource, such as a virtual machine, storage account, or database.

Benefits of Scoped Assignments

Granular Access Control: Scoped assignments enable administrators to apply permissions precisely where needed, avoiding overprivileged access and reducing security risks.

Flexible Management: By allowing for role assignments at various levels, Azure RBAC supports flexible access management that can adapt to organizational structures and project requirements.

Efficient Resource Segregation: Scoped assignments facilitate the segregation of resources for different projects, departments, or environments, ensuring that users have access only to the resources relevant to their roles.

Enhanced Compliance: Scoped role assignments help organizations meet compliance requirements by enforcing strict access controls that limit exposure of sensitive resources and data.

Implementing Scoped Assignments

When implementing scoped assignments, it's important to follow a structured approach:

Identify Access Requirements: Clearly define the access needs of users, groups, and applications, considering their roles and responsibilities within the organization.

Determine Appropriate Scopes: Based on the access requirements, determine the most appropriate scope for each role assignment, whether it be at the management group, subscription, resource group, or resource level.

Assign Roles: Utilize the Azure portal, Azure PowerShell, or Azure CLI to assign the chosen roles at the determined scopes. Ensure that the principle of least privilege is applied, granting only the permissions necessary for users to perform their tasks.

Review and Adjust: Regularly review scoped role assignments to ensure they continue to align with users' roles and the organization's security policies. Adjust scopes and permissions as necessary to adapt to changes within the organization or project.

Scoped assignments in Azure RBAC are a powerful mechanism for administering precise access control within the Azure environment. By leveraging scoped assignments, organizations can enhance their security posture, ensure compliance with regulatory standards, and maintain operational efficiency in managing cloud resources. As Azure environments become increasingly complex, the ability to apply roles with such granularity will remain essential for safeguarding resources and data in the cloud.

Multiple Assignments:

A user, group, service principal, or managed identity can have multiple role assignments, allowing for flexible access configurations that match complex organizational structures and requirements.

In the dynamic and diverse ecosystem of Azure, managing access control with granularity and precision is paramount for upholding security and ensuring operational efficiency. Azure Role-Based Access Control (RBAC) stands as a fundamental component in this process, enabling the assignment of specific roles to users, groups, service principals, and managed identities across different scopes. An advanced feature within this realm is the capability for multiple role assignments, which allows entities to hold more than one role simultaneously, each potentially scoped differently. This feature is instrumental in tailoring access rights to the complex needs of large-scale, multifaceted cloud environments.

Understanding Multiple Role Assignments in Azure RBAC

Multiple role assignments refer to the practice of assigning more than one RBAC role to a single security principal (a user, group, service principal, or managed identity) within Azure. This capability is essential for accommodating nuanced access requirements, where a single role does not suffice to cover the spectrum of permissions an entity needs to perform its functions across various resources or resource groups.

Advantages of Multiple Role Assignments

Granular Access Control: Allows for the precise tailoring of access rights, ensuring entities have exactly the permissions they need—no more, no less—across different areas of the Azure environment.

Flexibility and Scalability: As organizations grow and their cloud deployments become more complex, multiple role assignments provide the flexibility needed to scale access control mechanisms efficiently.

Simplified Management: By using combinations of roles, administrators can streamline access management, reducing the need to create numerous custom roles for specific scenarios.

Implementing Multiple Role Assignments

When implementing multiple role assignments, it is crucial to follow best practices to maintain security and compliance:

Assess and Plan Access Requirements: Carefully evaluate the specific access needs of users or services across all areas of your Azure environment. Consider the operations they need to perform and the resources they need to access.

Use the Principle of Least Privilege: Combine roles in a way that adheres to the principle of least privilege, ensuring that each assignment contributes only the necessary permissions, avoiding unnecessary access rights.

Monitor and Review Assignments Regularly: Utilize Azure's monitoring tools to keep track of role assignments. Regularly review these assignments to ensure they remain aligned with current operational roles and responsibilities, adjusting as necessary.

Leverage Azure Policy for Governance: Implement Azure policies to audit and enforce proper role assignments across your subscriptions and resource groups, ensuring compliance with your organization's access control policies.

Practical Use Case Scenario

Consider a scenario where a team member requires access to manage virtual machines in a production environment (requiring the "Virtual Machine Contributor" role), while also needing to read network configurations (requiring the "Network Contributor" role) across several resource groups. By assigning both roles to this team member, you can ensure they have all the necessary permissions to perform their job without granting excessive rights that could pose a security risk.

Multiple role assignments in Azure RBAC represent a powerful feature for managing complex access control requirements in large and diverse Azure environments. By thoughtfully combining roles and carefully scoping these assignments, organizations can ensure their users and services have the precise access needed to perform their functions efficiently and securely. This approach not only enhances operational flexibility but also reinforces the organization's security posture by adhering to the principle of least privilege, a cornerstone of cloud security and compliance.

Implementing Azure RBAC for Enhanced Security

Implementing RBAC effectively is crucial for securing your Azure environment and ensuring compliance with your organization's access control policies.

Assessing Access Requirements: Begin by understanding the minimum necessary permissions each user or group needs to perform their tasks. Apply the principle of least privilege to limit excessive access rights.

Assigning Roles: Utilize the Azure Portal, Azure PowerShell, or Azure CLI to assign the appropriate built-in or custom roles to users, groups, service principals, and managed identities based on their access requirements.

Custom Role Creation: For specific access needs not covered by built-in roles, create custom roles with precisely defined permissions. This involves identifying the necessary Azure Resource Manager actions and notActions that encapsulate the desired permissions.

Monitoring and Auditing: Leverage Azure activity logs and Azure Policy to monitor role assignments and ensure they comply with your organization's access policies. Regularly review and adjust role assignments and custom roles to adapt to changing requirements and maintain optimal security.

Integration with Azure AD: For comprehensive identity and access management, integrate Azure RBAC with Azure Active Directory (Azure AD) to manage user identities and group memberships effectively. This integration simplifies access management across Azure services.

Azure Role-Based Access Control is a cornerstone of Azure's security and compliance strategy, providing the mechanisms necessary to manage access to Azure resources securely. By carefully implementing RBAC, organizations can ensure that users have the right level of access to perform their jobs, without exposing resources to unnecessary risk. Regularly reviewing and managing access controls, in line with the principle of least privilege, is essential for maintaining a secure and compliant Azure environment. As Azure continues to evolve, leveraging RBAC will remain a critical practice for safeguarding cloud resources and enabling secure, efficient cloud operations.

Compliance, Privacy, and Data Protection in Azure:

In the current digital era, where data breaches and compliance failures can have significant legal and reputational consequences, the importance of compliance, privacy, and data protection cannot be overstated. Microsoft Azure provides a robust framework to support these critical areas, ensuring that organizations can leverage cloud computing while adhering to regulatory requirements and safeguarding sensitive information. This comprehensive overview explores how Azure facilitates compliance, privacy, and data protection, showcasing the platform's commitment to securing user data and assisting organizations in meeting their compliance obligations.

Compliance in Azure

Azure's compliance offerings are designed to simplify the complex landscape of regulatory requirements for organizations across various industries and regions. By achieving certifications for a broad range of global, regional, and industry-specific standards, Azure provides a compliance-ready environment that organizations can leverage to meet their regulatory obligations.

In the complex and rapidly evolving landscape of global business and technology, compliance stands as a critical pillar ensuring that organizations adhere to legal, regulatory, and technical standards. Microsoft Azure, as a leading cloud service provider, places a strong emphasis on compliance, providing tools, certifications, and frameworks to help organizations meet their compliance obligations while leveraging the cloud. Understanding how compliance is managed and supported in Azure is essential for businesses operating in regulated industries or handling sensitive data.

The Foundation of Compliance in Azure

Azure's compliance framework is built on a foundation of trust, transparency, and control, enabling organizations to confidently use Azure services while meeting their compliance requirements. This foundation is supported by a comprehensive set of compliance certifications and attestations that Azure has achieved across various regions and industries.

Key Aspects of Compliance in Azure

Global and Industry-specific Certifications: Azure maintains an extensive portfolio of compliance certifications, including global standards such as ISO/IEC 27001, GDPR, HIPAA for healthcare, FedRAMP for US federal agencies, and many more. These certifications are evidence of Azure's commitment to maintaining the highest standards of security and compliance.

Compliance Manager: Azure provides the Compliance Manager tool, a feature within the Microsoft Service Trust Portal that helps organizations assess and manage their compliance posture. Compliance Manager offers detailed insights into compliance performance, actionable guidance, and simplified compliance reporting.

Regulatory Compliance Dashboard: Within Azure Security Center, the regulatory compliance dashboard offers a comprehensive view of an organization's compliance status against a set of built-in standards and benchmarks. It provides actionable recommendations to improve compliance and reduce potential risks.

Data Protection and Privacy: Azure's approach to compliance extends to data protection and privacy, ensuring that customer data is handled in accordance with strict privacy standards. Azure offers features like encryption, access control, and network security to safeguard data, alongside privacy assurances that comply with regulations such as GDPR.

Implementing Compliance in Azure

Assessment and Planning: Begin by understanding the specific compliance requirements that apply to your organization based on industry, region, and the type of data handled. Utilize Azure's compliance resources to plan your compliance strategy.

Leverage Azure's Compliance Certifications: Align your compliance efforts with Azure's certifications, utilizing the platform's inherent compliance capabilities to fulfill regulatory requirements.

Use Compliance Manager: Take advantage of Compliance Manager to assess your compliance stance, get recommendations, and track progress toward compliance goals.

Regular Monitoring and Reporting: Continuously monitor your compliance posture using tools like the regulatory compliance dashboard in Azure Security Center. Regular reporting and audits are crucial for maintaining compliance over time.

Compliance in Azure represents a critical aspect of cloud security and operations, providing organizations with the framework, tools, and certifications needed to meet complex regulatory requirements confidently. By leveraging Azure's comprehensive compliance offerings, organizations can ensure their cloud environments are secure, private, and compliant with applicable standards, thereby protecting their data and maintaining trust with customers and stakeholders. As regulatory landscapes evolve, Azure continues to adapt, offering updated and new certifications and compliance capabilities to meet emerging requirements.

Broad Range of Certifications: Azure maintains an extensive portfolio of compliance certifications, including but not limited to ISO/IEC 27001, HIPAA, GDPR, FedRAMP, SOC 1, SOC 2, and PCI DSS. These certifications cover various aspects of information security, privacy, and compliance, providing a solid foundation for organizations to build upon.

Azure Compliance Documentation: Azure offers detailed compliance documentation through the Azure Trust Center, which includes compliance offerings, audit reports, and other resources to help organizations understand how Azure services can be used in a compliant manner.

Azure Compliance Manager: This tool helps organizations assess and manage their compliance posture regarding Azure services. It provides detailed insights and actionable recommendations to improve compliance with various standards and regulations.

Privacy in Azure

Privacy is a cornerstone of Azure's design, with Microsoft committed to being transparent about data collection, use, and protection. Azure provides several features and tools to help organizations manage privacy and control their data effectively.

In an era where data privacy has become a forefront concern for organizations worldwide, Microsoft Azure's commitment to privacy is a cornerstone of its cloud services. Azure's privacy policies and practices are designed to ensure that customers retain control over their data, understand how it is used, and feel confident that their information is protected according to the highest standards. This comprehensive overview delves into how Azure addresses privacy, providing the tools and assurances needed to manage data responsibly in the cloud.

Core Principles of Privacy in Azure

Azure's approach to privacy is built on a foundation of trust and transparency, guided by four core principles:

Control: Azure gives customers control over the collection, use, and distribution of their data. Tools and settings allow customers to manage privacy effectively, ensuring that data handling aligns with their privacy requirements.

Transparency: Microsoft provides clear information about how customer data is handled in Azure, including data collection practices, data usage, and how data is protected. This transparency is key to building trust with customers.

Security: The security of customer data in Azure is paramount. Azure employs advanced security technologies and practices to protect data against unauthorized access and threats, thereby supporting customers' privacy and compliance efforts.

Compliance: Azure's privacy practices are aligned with global data protection regulations, such as the General Data Protection Regulation (GDPR), providing a compliant platform for customers operating across different regulatory environments.

Implementing Privacy in Azure

Data Management and Sovereignty: Azure provides mechanisms to manage data throughout its lifecycle, from creation to deletion. Customers can choose the regions in which their data is stored and processed, addressing data sovereignty concerns and regulatory requirements.

Consent and Data Access: Azure enables customers to obtain consent where necessary for data collection and use, and provides tools for customers to access and manage their data, supporting rights such as the right to be forgotten under GDPR.

Data Protection and Encryption: Azure offers a range of data protection features, including encryption in transit and at rest, to safeguard customer data. Azure Key Vault allows customers to manage cryptographic keys and secrets, further enhancing data privacy.

Privacy by Design: Azure incorporates privacy by design and by default into its services, ensuring that privacy considerations are integrated into the development and operation of cloud services. This proactive approach to privacy is essential for meeting regulatory expectations and protecting customer data.

Azure and GDPR

As a global leader in cloud computing, Azure has taken significant steps to ensure its services are compliant with GDPR, setting a benchmark for data protection and privacy in the cloud. Azure provides detailed documentation and guidance to help customers understand GDPR requirements and how Azure services can support compliance, including data processing agreements (DPAs), data subject rights, and data breach notifications.

Privacy in Azure is a multifaceted commitment, encompassing rigorous data management practices, advanced security measures, transparency, and compliance with global data protection regulations. By prioritizing customer control over data and providing comprehensive privacy protections, Azure enables organizations to leverage cloud services while upholding their privacy obligations. As privacy regulations continue to evolve, Azure's ongoing investments in privacy-enhancing technologies and practices demonstrate its dedication to securing customer trust and ensuring that data privacy remains at the forefront of its cloud services.

Data Sovereignty: Azure's global infrastructure allows organizations to choose the regions where their data is stored, helping to meet data residency requirements and ensure data sovereignty.

Privacy Controls: Azure offers a range of privacy controls that allow organizations to manage who has access to their data and how it is used. These controls are integral to maintaining data privacy and preventing unauthorized access.

Data Protection Agreement (DPA): Microsoft provides a robust DPA that outlines its commitments to protecting customer data, ensuring that privacy considerations are transparent and in line with regulatory expectations.

Data Protection in Azure

Protecting data, both at rest and in transit, is a key focus of Azure's security model. Azure implements several mechanisms and services to ensure the highest levels of data protection.

In an era where data is both an invaluable asset and a potential liability, the protection of data within cloud environments like Microsoft Azure is paramount. Azure provides a comprehensive suite of features and services designed to ensure the integrity, confidentiality, and availability of data, aligning with the highest standards of security and compliance. This exploration into data protection in Azure outlines the mechanisms and strategies that Azure employs to safeguard data against threats and unauthorized access, ensuring that organizations can leverage the cloud with confidence.

Core Pillars of Data Protection in Azure

Encryption: Azure implements encryption both at rest and in transit to secure data. At rest, Azure uses industry-standard protocols such as AES-256 to encrypt data stored in Azure services, including Azure Blob Storage, Azure Files, and Azure SQL Database. For data in transit, Azure secures communications with TLS and other encryption protocols, ensuring that data moving between Azure data centers and users is protected against interception and eavesdropping.

Access Control: Azure employs robust access control mechanisms, including Azure Role-Based Access Control (RBAC) and Azure Active Directory, to manage who has access to data and resources. These tools allow for fine-grained permissions and policies, ensuring that only authorized users and applications can access or modify data.

Threat Protection and Monitoring: Azure Security Center provides advanced threat protection and monitoring capabilities, leveraging global threat intelligence and machine learning to detect and respond to potential data breaches and security threats. Azure Sentinel, a cloud-native SIEM service, further enhances data protection by providing real-time security analytics and threat detection across enterprise environments.

Backup and Disaster Recovery: Azure offers comprehensive solutions for data backup and disaster recovery, including Azure Backup and Azure Site Recovery. These services enable organizations to protect their data from accidental deletion, corruption, and disasters, ensuring business continuity and data availability.

Data Sovereignty and Residency: Recognizing the importance of data sovereignty, Azure provides options for data residency, allowing customers to select specific geographic regions for data storage based on compliance and regulatory requirements. Azure's global infrastructure supports data residency and sovereignty needs across a wide range of jurisdictions.

Implementing Data Protection Strategies in Azure

Leverage Encryption Features: Utilize Azure's encryption capabilities to protect your data at rest and in transit. Ensure encryption is enabled for all storage and database services, and use Azure Key Vault to manage encryption keys securely.

Define and Enforce Access Policies: Implement strict access policies using Azure RBAC and Azure Active Directory. Regularly review and update access permissions to reflect changes in roles and responsibilities.

Monitor for Threats: Enable Azure Security Center and Azure Sentinel for continuous monitoring and threat detection. Configure alerts to notify administrators of suspicious activities that could indicate a potential data breach.

Regularly Backup Data: Schedule regular backups of critical data using Azure Backup, and test your disaster recovery procedures using Azure Site Recovery to ensure you can quickly restore data and services in the event of a loss.

Understand Data Residency Requirements: Be aware of your organization's data residency and sovereignty requirements. Choose Azure regions and services that comply with these requirements to ensure data is stored and processed in accordance with legal and regulatory mandates.

Data protection in Azure encompasses a multifaceted approach, integrating encryption, access control, threat detection, backup, and data residency to safeguard data against a wide array of risks. By leveraging Azure's comprehensive data protection features, organizations can secure their data throughout its lifecycle, from creation and storage to transmission and deletion. As the digital landscape continues to evolve, Azure remains committed to enhancing its data protection capabilities, ensuring that organizations can trust Azure as a secure and compliant platform for their cloud computing needs.

Encryption: Azure employs encryption to protect data at rest and in transit. Azure Storage Service Encryption and Azure Disk Encryption are examples of how Azure secures data stored within its services, while TLS/SSL encryption protects data as it moves across networks.

Azure Key Vault: This service allows organizations to manage cryptographic keys and other sensitive information securely. By using Azure Key Vault, organizations can enhance the security of their data encryption practices and streamline key management processes.

Azure Information Protection: Part of Microsoft's suite of information protection technologies, Azure Information Protection (AIP) helps classify, label, and protect documents and emails based on their content and sensitivity, further enhancing data protection measures.

Compliance, privacy, and data protection form the pillars of trust in cloud computing. Azure's comprehensive approach to these areas demonstrates Microsoft's commitment to providing a secure, compliant, and privacy-respecting platform. By leveraging Azure's extensive compliance certifications, privacy controls, and data protection features, organizations can confidently navigate the complexities of regulatory requirements, safeguard sensitive information, and maintain customer trust in an increasingly digital world.

Conclusion

Azure's comprehensive approach to security and compliance empowers organizations to protect their data, applications, and infrastructure from threats while ensuring they can meet complex regulatory requirements. By leveraging Azure's robust security features and taking advantage of its extensive compliance certifications, businesses can confidently migrate to the cloud, secure in the knowledge that their critical assets are protected in a compliant and trusted cloud environment. Azure's continuous investment in security and compliance innovation further ensures that its customers are equipped to face the evolving landscape of cyber threats and regulatory demands.

10

Chapter 6: Developing Applications in Azure

Developing applications in Azure leverages the cloud's power to provide scalable, resilient, and globally accessible software solutions. Azure, Microsoft's cloud computing service, offers an expansive array of services and tools designed to support developers in building, deploying, and managing applications with ease and efficiency. This comprehensive exploration will delve into the key aspects of developing applications in Azure, highlighting the platform's capabilities, services, and best practices for developers.

Core Services for Application Development in Azure

Azure App Services: A fully managed platform for building, deploying, and scaling web applications and APIs. It supports multiple programming languages and frameworks, providing a high-productivity development model without worrying about the underlying infrastructure.

Azure Functions: Enables the development of event-driven, serverless applications that can scale automatically. It's ideal for microservices architectures, allowing developers to focus on the code while Azure handles the execution based on triggers and bindings.

Azure Kubernetes Service (AKS): Offers a managed Kubernetes environment for deploying and managing containerized applications, simplifying the deployment, scaling, and operations of Kubernetes.

Azure DevOps: Provides a suite of development tools for continuous integration and continuous delivery (CI/CD), agile project management, and version control, enabling teams to build and deliver software faster and more reliably.

Azure SQL Database: A managed relational database service that supports SQL Server and offers built-in intelligence, scalability, and security for modern app development.

Azure Cosmos DB: A globally distributed, multi-model database service for building highly responsive and scalable applications with guaranteed single-digit-millisecond response times.

Best Practices for Developing Applications in Azure

Leverage Azure's PaaS Offerings: Take advantage of Azure's Platform as a Service (PaaS) offerings, such as Azure App Services and Azure Functions, to reduce the overhead of managing infrastructure and focus on developing application logic.

Implement Microservices Architectures: Utilize services like Azure Functions and AKS to build applications based on microservices architectures. This approach enhances scalability, agility, and the ability to update components independently.

Utilize DevOps Practices: Integrate Azure DevOps into your development workflow to automate builds, testing, and deployments, ensuring continuous delivery and reducing the time to market.

Incorporate Security Best Practices: Use Azure Security Center and implement Azure's security features early in the development process to ensure your applications are secure by design.

Design for Scalability and Resilience: Architect your applications to be scalable and resilient, utilizing Azure's global infrastructure, load balancers, and services like Azure Traffic Manager to ensure high availability and performance.

Optimize for Cost: Monitor and optimize your Azure resources and services using Azure Cost Management to ensure you are efficiently utilizing resources and managing costs effectively.

Building and Deploying Web Applications:

Azure offers a robust environment for building, deploying, and managing web applications, providing developers with scalable, secure, and high-performance solutions. This comprehensive guide explores how to leverage Azure services for web application development, accompanied by examples to illustrate the process.

Azure App Service for Web Applications

Scenario: You're developing a web application using .NET Core that needs to scale based on demand and requires integration with SQL databases.

Example:

Create an Azure App Service Plan: Begin by setting up an App Service plan, specifying the scale tier based on your expected traffic.

az appservice plan create --name myAppServicePlan --resource-group myResourceGroup --sku S1 --is-linux

Deploy Your Web Application: Use Azure DevOps or GitHub Actions to set up CI/CD pipelines that build your .NET Core application and deploy it to Azure App Service.

Example YAML for Azure Pipelines

trigger:

- main

pool:

vmImage: 'ubuntu-latest'

steps:

- script: dotnet build --configuration Release
- script: dotnet publish --configuration Release --output publish
- task: AzureWebApp@1

inputs:

azureSubscription: '<Your-Azure-Subscription>'

appType: 'webAppLinux'

appName: 'myWebApp'

runtimeStack: 'DOTNETCORE|3.1'

package: 'publish'

Configure Auto-scaling: Set up auto-scaling rules in the Azure Portal to automatically increase or decrease the number of instances based on metrics like CPU usage or request rate.

Azure Static Web Apps for SPA

Scenario: You're developing a Single Page Application (SPA) with React that calls serverless APIs for data.

Example:

Create a Static Web App: Deploy your SPA to Azure Static Web Apps directly from your GitHub repository.

- In the Azure Portal, create a new Static Web App.
- Connect your GitHub repository and select the branch to deploy.
- Configure the build details, specifying the app location and API location if using Azure Functions for serverless APIs.

Setup CI/CD with GitHub Actions: Azure automatically configures a GitHub Actions workflow in your repository for building and deploying your application upon code pushes.

Generated GitHub Actions YAML

name: Azure Static Web Apps CI/CD

on:

push:

branches:

- main

pull_request:

types: [opened, synchronize, reopened, closed]

branches:

- main

jobs:

build_and_deploy_job:

if: github.event_name == 'push' || (github.event_name == 'pull_request' && github.event.action != 'closed')

runs-on: ubuntu-latest

name: Build and Deploy Job

Integrating Azure SQL Database

Scenario: Your web application requires a relational database to store user data securely.

Example:

Create an Azure SQL Database: Provision a new SQL database in Azure.

az sql db create --name myDatabase --resource-group myResourceGroup --server myServer --edition GeneralPurpose --family Gen5 --capacity 2 --zone-redundant false

Connect Your Web Application: Use the connection string provided by Azure to integrate the database with your web application.

For .NET Core applications, configure the connection string in the **appsettings.json** file.

{

"ConnectionStrings": {

"MyDbConnection": "Server=tcp:myServer.database.windows.net,1433;Initial Catalog=myDatabase;Persist Security Info=False;User ID={your_username};Password={your_password};MultipleActiveResultSets=False;Encrypt=True;TrustServerCertificate=False;Connection Timeout=30;"

}

}

Developing and deploying web applications in Azure enables developers to leverage the cloud's power for creating scalable, high-performance, and secure applications. Whether you're building a dynamic web app with Azure App Service, a SPA with Azure Static Web Apps, or integrating databases like Azure SQL Database, Azure provides a comprehensive set of tools and services to streamline the development process. By following these examples and best practices, developers can efficiently deploy web applications that meet modern demands for scalability, reliability, and performance.

Working with Azure SQL Database and Cosmos DB:

Azure provides a wide array of data storage and management services, among which Azure SQL Database and Azure Cosmos DB stand out due to their flexibility, scalability, and robust features tailored for modern application development. Understanding how to effectively utilize these databases within your applications can significantly enhance performance, scalability, and the overall user experience.

Azure SQL Database

Azure SQL Database is a fully managed relational database service that offers SQL Server database capabilities in the cloud. It's an ideal choice for applications that require complex queries, transactional support, and relational data structures.

Key Features:

Scalability and Performance: Automatically scale resources with minimal downtime, and leverage built-in intelligence to optimize performance.

High Availability: Built-in automatic backups and geo-replication ensure data is always available and durable.

Security: Advanced security features, including data encryption, threat detection, and fine-grained access control.

Example: Integrating Azure SQL Database into a .NET Core Web Application

Create an Azure SQL Database:

Use the Azure portal or Azure CLI to create a SQL Database instance.

az sql db create --name MyDatabase --resource-group MyResource-Group --server mySqlServer --edition GeneralPurpose

Obtain the Connection String:

Navigate to the Azure portal, find your database, and copy the ADO.NET (SQL authentication) connection string from the "Connection strings" section.

Configure the Connection String in Your Application:

Place the connection string in your application's **appsettings.json** file, ensuring you replace the placeholders with your actual username and password.

```
{
"ConnectionStrings": {
"MyDbContext":              "Server=tcp:mySqlServer.database.windows.net,1433;Initial      Catalog=MyDatabase;Persist      Security Info=False;User      ID={your_user};Password={your_password};Encrypt=True;TrustServerCertificate=False;Connection Timeout=30;"
}
}
```

Use Entity Framework Core:

Add the Entity Framework Core package and the SQL Server database provider to your project to work with the database using LINQ queries.

```
dotnet add package Microsoft.EntityFrameworkCore.SqlServer
```

Define Your DbContext and Models:

Create your data models and DbContext, then use migrations to create your database schema.

```
public class MyDbContext : DbContext
{
public MyDbContext(DbContextOptions<MyDbContext> options) : base(options) {}
public DbSet<MyModel> MyModels { get; set; }
}
```

Azure Cosmos DB

Azure Cosmos DB is a globally distributed, multi-model database service designed for high availability, low latency, and scalable applications. It supports document, key-value, graph, and column-family data models.

Key Features:

Global Distribution: Easily replicate data across multiple regions to bring data closer to users.

Multi-Model Support: Use document, key-value, graph, and column-family data models in a single service.

Elastic Scalability: Scale throughput and storage automatically based on demand.

Example: Integrating Azure Cosmos DB into a Node.js Application

Create an Azure Cosmos DB Account:

Use the Azure portal or Azure CLI to create a Cosmos DB account.

az cosmosdb create --name MyCosmosDbAccount --resource-group MyResourceGroup --kind GlobalDocumentDB --locations regionName='East US' failoverPriority=0 isZoneRedundant=False

Obtain the Connection Details:

In the Azure portal, navigate to your Cosmos DB account and copy the URI and primary key from the "Keys" section.

Install the Cosmos DB SDK:

Add the Azure Cosmos DB SDK to your Node.js project.

npm install @azure/cosmos

Initialize the Cosmos Client and Define the Database and Container:

const { CosmosClient } = require("@azure/cosmos");

const client = new CosmosClient({ endpoint: "your-cosmos-db-uri", key: "your-primary-key" });

const database = client.database("YourDatabase");

const container = database.container("YourContainer");

Perform Operations:

Use the SDK to interact with your database, such as creating and querying documents.

async function addItem(item) {

```
const { resource: createdItem } = await container.items.create(item);
console.log(`\Created new item: ${createdItem.id}\n`);
}
```

Integrating Azure Functions for Serverless Computing:

Azure Functions is a key service in Azure that enables serverless computing, allowing developers to run event-driven code without explicitly provisioning or managing infrastructure. This paradigm shift not only optimizes costs by charging only for the compute resources consumed during the execution of the function but also significantly simplifies scaling, deployment, and development processes. Azure Functions supports a wide array of application scenarios, from simple webhooks to complex integrations with Azure services and third-party tools. This comprehensive exploration discusses how to integrate Azure Functions into your application development workflow, illustrated with practical examples.

Key Features of Azure Functions

Event-driven Execution:

Azure Functions triggers automatically in response to events from a wide range of Azure services, HTTP requests, webhooks, and external services.

Azure Functions, a cornerstone of serverless computing in Azure, excels in event-driven execution, allowing developers to create applications that respond automatically to a wide array of events. This capability enables the construction of highly responsive, efficient, and scalable applications without the overhead of managing server infrastructure. By focusing on the code that matters most and letting Azure handle the scaling and hosting, developers can significantly streamline application development and deployment processes.

Understanding Event-driven Execution in Azure Functions

Event-driven execution refers to the paradigm where functions are invoked in response to specific events. These events can originate from various sources within Azure, such as storage blobs, queues, HTTP requests, and more, as well as from external services via webhooks. This model is particularly powerful for building applications that need to react in real-time to changes in data, user input, or system state.

Key Benefits of Event-driven Execution

Scalability: Azure Functions automatically scales your application in response to the number of events, ensuring that your function can handle the load without manual intervention.

Flexibility: With support for multiple event sources, Azure Functions allows developers to build a wide range of applications, from web APIs to data processing pipelines.

Efficiency: By executing code only when needed, Azure Functions optimizes resource usage, reducing costs by charging only for the compute resources used during function execution.

Common Event Sources for Azure Functions

HTTP Requests: Functions can be triggered by HTTP requests, making it simple to build APIs and webhooks.

Azure Storage Blobs: Functions can respond to the creation or modification of files in Azure Blob Storage, ideal for scenarios like image processing or data import.

Azure Queues: Respond to messages added to Azure Queue Storage, useful for decoupled applications and background task processing.

Timers: Execute functions on a schedule, perfect for recurring tasks like daily reports or database cleanups.

Cosmos DB: React to changes in Cosmos DB documents, enabling real-time data processing and analytics.

Example: Processing Orders with an Event-driven Function

Consider an e-commerce platform where orders are stored in Azure Queue Storage. An Azure Function can automatically process these orders as they arrive, updating inventory and sending confirmation emails.

Function Trigger: Azure Queue Storage trigger.

Language: C#.

```csharp
public static class OrderProcessingFunction
{
[FunctionName("ProcessOrder")]
public static async Task Run([QueueTrigger("orders", Connection = "AzureWebJobsStorage")]string orderQueueItem, ILogger log)
{
log.LogInformation($"C# Queue trigger function processed: {orderQueueItem}");
// Parse the order details
Order order = JsonConvert.DeserializeObject<Order>(orderQueueItem);
// Update inventory and send confirmation email
await UpdateInventory(order);
await SendConfirmationEmail(order);
log.LogInformation("Order processed successfully.");
}
}
```

In this example, the function **ProcessOrder** is triggered whenever a new order is added to the "orders" queue. The function deserializes the order data, updates the inventory, and sends a confirmation email, all without requiring a server to be explicitly provisioned or managed.

Event-driven execution in Azure Functions offers a powerful, efficient, and scalable approach to developing applications in the cloud. By leveraging Azure Functions, developers can focus on writing the code that delivers value, secure in the knowledge that Azure will scale their application in response to real-world events. This paradigm is instrumental in building modern, responsive applications that can react in real time to a wide array of events.

Multi-language Support:

Write functions in your choice of languages, including C#, Java, JavaScript, PowerShell, Python, and TypeScript.

Azure Functions stands out as a versatile serverless computing solution largely due to its multi-language support, enabling developers to write functions in the language they are most comfortable with or that best suits their application's requirements. This inclusivity fosters a broader adoption by accommodating diverse development ecosystems and promoting best practices across different programming languages. Here, we explore the multi-language capabilities of Azure Functions, underscored by a coding example to illustrate this flexibility in action.

Supported Languages in Azure Functions

Azure Functions supports a variety of programming languages, including but not limited to:

C#: A popular language for .NET developers, offering robustness and a comprehensive ecosystem.

JavaScript/Node.js: Widely used for web and backend development, making it a go-to for full-stack developers.

Python: Favored in scientific computing, machine learning, and automation for its simplicity and powerful libraries.

Java: A choice for enterprise-level applications, known for its portability and extensive use in large systems.

PowerShell: Ideal for automation scripts, especially in Windows-centric environments.

TypeScript: Offers strong typing on top of JavaScript, enhancing code quality and maintainability.

F#: A functional-first language, providing concise syntax for complex computational logic.

This broad support ensures that teams can leverage existing skills and codebases, integrate with diverse tools and frameworks, and choose the most suitable language for each particular function or application.

Example: A Multi-language Azure Functions Scenario

Consider a scenario where an organization is developing a microservices architecture for their e-commerce platform. They decide to use Azure Functions to handle various services such as order processing, inventory management, and user notifications. Given the team's diverse skill set and the specific requirements of each service, Azure Functions' multi-language support becomes advantageous.

Order Processing in C#

```csharp
using Microsoft.Azure.WebJobs;
using Microsoft.Extensions.Logging;
public static class ProcessOrder
{
[FunctionName("ProcessOrder")]
public static async Task Run([QueueTrigger("orders", Connection = "AzureWebJobsStorage")] string myQueueItem, ILogger log)
{
log.LogInformation($"C# Queue trigger function processed: {myQueueItem}");
// Order processing logic here
}
}
```

Inventory Management in Python

```python
import azure.functions as func
import logging
def main(msg: func.QueueMessage) -> None:
logging.info('Python queue trigger function processed a queue item: %s',
msg.get_body().decode('utf-8'))
# Inventory management logic here
```

User Notifications in JavaScript (Node.js)

```javascript
module.exports = async function (context, myQueueItem) {
context.log('JavaScript queue trigger function processed work item', myQueueItem);
// User notification logic here
};
```

Integrating Multi-language Functions

Integrating functions written in different languages into a single application architecture showcases Azure Functions' flexibility. Each function can be deployed and scaled independently, reacting to events such as HTTP requests, database changes, or messages in a queue.

Best Practices for Multi-language Development in Azure Functions

Consistent Coding Standards: Even with multiple languages in use, maintain consistent coding, naming, and design standards across your functions for readability and maintainability.

Shared Resources: Utilize Azure services (e.g., Azure Blob Storage, Azure SQL Database) or external storage solutions to share data and state between functions in different languages.

Monitoring and Logging: Leverage Azure Application Insights across all functions, regardless of language, to ensure consistent monitoring, logging, and diagnostics.

The multi-language support offered by Azure Functions empowers developers to build serverless applications using the languages they prefer or that best fit the task at hand. This flexibility, coupled with Azure's comprehensive set of integrations and services, enables a seamless development experience for building scalable, efficient, and maintainable applications. By leveraging the strengths of each supported language, teams can deliver robust solutions that meet diverse business requirements in the Azure cloud environment.

Scalability: Automatically scales based on demand, managing the infrastructure needed to run your functions with optimal performance.

Integration: Seamlessly integrates with other Azure services, offering a robust backend for applications and processes.

Example Scenarios for Azure Functions

Scenario 1: HTTP-triggered Function for Processing Web Requests

Imagine creating a RESTful API endpoint for a web application without provisioning a server.

Creating the Function: Use the Azure portal, CLI, or Visual Studio Code with the Azure Functions extension to create a new function app and an HTTP-triggered function within it.

Example Code (JavaScript):

```javascript
module.exports = async function (context, req) {
context.log('HTTP trigger function processed a request.');
const name = (req.query.name || (req.body && req.body.name));
const responseMessage = name
? "Hello, " + name + ". This HTTP triggered function executed successfully."
: "This HTTP triggered function executed successfully. Pass a name in the query string or in the request body for a personalized response.";
context.res = {
// status: 200, /* Defaults to 200 */
body: responseMessage
};
};
```

Deploying and Testing: Deploy the function using Azure CLI or through the Azure portal. Test the function by making an HTTP request to the function's URL.

Scenario 2: Timer-triggered Function for Scheduled Tasks

Automate a scheduled task, such as daily data cleanup or sending reports via email, without setting up a cron job on a server.

Creating the Function: Within your function app, add a new timer-triggered function, specifying the schedule using a CRON expression.

Example Code (C#):

```csharp
public static class DataCleanupFunction
{
[FunctionName("DataCleanupFunction")]
public static async Task Run([TimerTrigger("0 0 23 * * *")]TimerInfo myTimer, ILogger log)
{
log.LogInformation($"C# Timer trigger function executed at: {DateTime.Now}");
// Data cleanup logic here
```

}

}

Deploying and Testing: After deploying the function, Azure Functions automatically executes it based on the defined schedule.

Scenario 3: Integrating with Azure Blob Storage

Process or transform files as they are uploaded to Azure Blob Storage, such as resizing images or parsing text files.

Creating the Function: Set up a new function triggered by Azure Blob Storage, specifying the Blob container to monitor.

Example Code (Python):

```python
import logging
import azure.functions as func
def main(myblob: func.InputStream):
logging.info(f"Python blob trigger function processed blob \n"
f"Name: {myblob.name}\n"
f"Blob Size: {myblob.length} bytes")
# Processing logic here
```

Deploying and Testing: Upon uploading a file to the specified Blob container, the function triggers, processing the file according to your logic.

Azure Functions is a powerful tool for adding serverless computing capabilities to your Azure applications, offering flexibility, scalability, and integration with a broad range of services. By leveraging Azure Functions, developers can focus on building application logic rather than managing infrastructure, optimizing both development time and operational costs. Whether handling web requests, automating scheduled tasks, or integrating with Azure services, Azure Functions provides a versatile platform for serverless application development.

Conclusion

Developing applications in Azure provides developers with a robust, flexible, and scalable platform that supports the full spectrum of cloud development scenarios, from simple web apps to complex microservices architectures and serverless applications. By leveraging Azure's comprehensive suite of services and tools, developers can accelerate the development lifecycle, automate deployments, and deliver highly available, secure, and performant applications. As cloud technologies continue to evolve, Azure remains at the forefront, offering innovative solutions that empower developers to build the next generation of applications.

11

Chapter 7: Azure DevOps and CI/CD

Part III: Advanced Azure Topics

In the contemporary landscape of software development, maintaining a rapid, reliable, and efficient pipeline for code integration and deployment is crucial. Azure DevOps, a suite of development tools provided by Microsoft, stands at the forefront of enabling Continuous Integration (CI) and Continuous Deployment (CD) practices. These practices, collectively known as CI/CD, form the backbone of modern development methodologies, particularly in agile environments where the demand for quick market releases and iterative improvements is high. This comprehensive overview explores Azure DevOps' role in facilitating CI/CD, illustrating how it transforms the development lifecycle.

Understanding CI/CD

Continuous Integration (CI) involves automatically building and testing code changes as soon as they are committed to a repository, ensuring early detection of errors or integration issues.

Continuous Integration (CI) is a foundational practice within modern software development, particularly within the CI/CD (Continuous

Integration/Continuous Deployment) pipeline. CI aims to increase software delivery quality and speed by automatically integrating code changes from multiple contributors into a shared repository early and often. This practice is instrumental in identifying and addressing errors, improving code quality, and reducing the time to release new software updates.

The Role of Continuous Integration In Software Development

CI plays a pivotal role in modern software development methodologies, especially in agile environments where the emphasis is on rapid, iterative releases. The core idea behind CI is to encourage developers to frequently merge their code changes into a central repository, where automated builds and tests are run. This approach has several key benefits:

Early Detection of Errors: By integrating and testing code changes regularly, issues and integration bugs are identified early, significantly reducing the cost and effort required to fix them.

Improved Code Quality: Continuous feedback from automated tests ensures code quality is maintained, encouraging best practices and standards among the development team.

Increased Transparency: Regular integration provides visibility into the application's development progress and its current state, enabling better collaboration and decision-making.

Enhanced Collaboration: CI fosters a collaborative environment where code changes are shared and integrated frequently, reducing the likelihood of conflicting changes and encouraging team members to work together more effectively.

Implementing CI with Azure DevOps

Azure DevOps provides a comprehensive set of tools to implement and manage Continuous Integration effectively through Azure Pipelines. Azure Pipelines is a CI/CD service that supports automatic builds and testing for any language or platform. Here's how Azure DevOps supports CI:

Automated Builds: Azure Pipelines can automatically trigger builds whenever code is pushed to the repository, ensuring that the codebase is always in a buildable state.

Automated Testing: Along with building the application, Azure Pipelines can run automated tests to validate code changes, including unit tests, integration tests, and UI tests, providing immediate feedback on the impact of changes.

Integration with Version Control: Azure DevOps seamlessly integrates with various version control systems, including Azure Repos, GitHub, and others, facilitating easy setup of CI processes for projects hosted on these platforms.

Example Workflow for CI in Azure DevOps

Create a Build Pipeline: Start by setting up a build pipeline in Azure Pipelines. This pipeline defines how your application is built and tested. You can configure the pipeline using the YAML syntax or through the visual designer.

Trigger Builds Automatically: Configure the pipeline to trigger automatically upon a commit or pull request to the main branch. This ensures that every code change is integrated and tested promptly.

```
trigger:
- main
pool:
vmImage: 'ubuntu-latest'
steps:
- script: echo Building the project...
displayName: 'Build step'
- script: echo Running tests...
displayName: 'Test step'
```

Run Automated Tests: As part of the pipeline, define steps to execute automated tests against the build. The results of these tests are crucial for assessing the quality of the integrated code.

Review Build Results: After the build completes, review the results, including test outcomes and any errors or warnings. Successful builds indicate that the changes can be safely merged, while failures require attention and correction.

Continuous Integration, as facilitated by Azure DevOps and Azure Pipelines, is indispensable in modern software development for maintaining high code quality, reducing integration issues, and speeding up the delivery of software updates. By automating the build and testing processes, CI allows development teams to focus on creating value and innovation, securely in the knowledge that their codebase remains stable and reliable. As part of the broader CI/CD pipeline, CI is a critical step towards achieving continuous delivery and deployment, empowering teams to release with confidence and efficiency.

Continuous Deployment (CD) extends CI by automatically deploying the code to a staging or production environment after the build stage, ensuring that the codebase is always in a deployable state.

Continuous Deployment (CD) is an advanced practice within the CI/CD pipeline, extending beyond Continuous Integration. While CI focuses on the integration and testing phases, CD automates the deployment process, ensuring that any code change passing through all stages of the production pipeline is released to customers automatically. This approach minimizes the manual steps involved in deploying software, thereby accelerating the delivery of features, fixes, and updates to users.

The Significance of Continuous Deployment

Continuous Deployment is crucial for organizations aiming to reduce the lead time for changes, enhance reliability, and improve the overall pace of innovation. By automating deployments, teams can:

Reduce Deployment Risks: Smaller, more frequent updates reduce the risk and complexity associated with deploying large batches of changes.

Improve Product Quality: Automated testing within the pipeline ensures that only high-quality code is deployed, while frequent releases allow for immediate feedback and quicker issue resolution.

Enhance Operational Efficiency: Minimizing manual intervention frees up teams to focus on more strategic tasks rather than routine deployment activities.

Implementing Continuous Deployment with Azure DevOps

Azure DevOps supports Continuous Deployment through Azure Pipelines, offering a seamless workflow from code repository to production. Here's an example of how to implement CD for a web application hosted in Azure App Services:

1. **Prerequisites**:
   - A web application configured for Continuous Integration in Azure Pipelines.
   - An Azure App Service instance for hosting the web application.

2. **Configure the Release Pipeline**:
   - In Azure DevOps, navigate to your project and select "Pipelines" > "Releases".
   - Create a new release pipeline, selecting the Azure App Service deployment template.
   - Link the artifact from your CI build pipeline.

3. **Define the Deployment Stage**:
   - Add a stage for deployment, naming it appropriately (e.g., "Production").
   - Specify the Azure subscription and the App Service name where the application will be deployed.
   - Configure any pre-deployment approvals if needed to control when deployments to production occur.

4. **Automate Deployment Trigger**:
   - Set the release pipeline to trigger automatically when a new artifact is available. This ensures that changes successfully passing through the CI pipeline are deployed without manual intervention.

5. **Add Post-deployment Actions** (Optional):

- ○ Configure actions such as running automated UI tests or sending notifications to stakeholders upon successful deployment.

6. **Monitor and Iterate**:
   - ○ Use Azure Monitor and Application Insights to track the application's performance and user feedback. Continuously refine your CD process based on insights gained.

```
trigger:
- main
pool:
vmImage: 'ubuntu-latest'
steps:
- task: NodeTool@0
inputs:
versionSpec: '10.x'
displayName: 'Install Node.js'
- script: |
npm install
npm build
displayName: 'npm install and build'
- task: AzureWebApp@1
inputs:
azureSubscription: '<Azure-Subscription-Service-Connection>'
appType: 'webAppLinux'
appName: '<App-Service-Name>'
package: '$(Build.ArtifactStagingDirectory)/**/*.zip'
runtimeStack: 'NODE|10.14'
```

Continuous Deployment in Azure DevOps simplifies and accelerates the delivery process, allowing teams to bring innovations to market faster while ensuring the reliability and stability of applications. By leveraging Azure Pipelines for CD, organizations can automate their deployment workflows, reduce manual errors, and ensure that their products are always in a state of readiness for release to customers.

This strategy not only enhances operational efficiency but also significantly improves the software delivery lifecycle, enabling a more agile, responsive approach to development.

Example YAML for an Azure App Service Deployment:

Azure DevOps: A Unified Suite for CI/CD

Azure DevOps provides an integrated set of features designed to support the development lifecycle, from planning and project management with Azure Boards to source control with Azure Repos and, most importantly, build and release services with Azure Pipelines.

Key Components for CI/CD in Azure DevOps

Azure Pipelines: Offers cloud-hosted pipelines for Linux, macOS, and Windows, allowing teams to build, test, and deploy any application, regardless of the platform or language. It supports containerization and Kubernetes deployments, integrates with Azure services, and offers extensions for third-party tools.

Azure Repos: Provides Git repositories for source control, offering all the distributed version control and source code management functionality of Git as well as adding its features.

Azure Artifacts: Allows teams to share packages such as npm, NuGet, and Maven from public and private sources and integrate package sharing into their CI/CD pipelines.

Implementing CI/CD with Azure DevOps

Setup Azure Pipelines: Start by configuring Azure Pipelines in your Azure DevOps project. Define your build pipeline, specifying the source repository (Azure Repos or external like GitHub), and select the appropriate template based on your project stack.

Define Build Tasks: Customize your pipeline by defining tasks for building your application, running tests (unit tests, integration tests), and generating artifacts. For instance, a .NET Core application might use tasks like **dotnet restore**, **dotnet build**, **dotnet test**, and **dotnet publish**.

Configure Deployment: Set up a release pipeline to deploy your artifacts to various environments. Use environment-specific configurations and approvals for staging and production deployments to ensure controlled rollouts.

Example YML for a Simple .NET Core Application:

```yaml
trigger:
- main
pool:
vmImage: 'ubuntu-latest'
steps:
- task: DotNetCoreCLI@2
inputs:
command: 'restore'
projects: '**/*.csproj'
- task: DotNetCoreCLI@2
inputs:
command: 'build'
arguments: '--configuration Release'
projects: '**/*.csproj'
- task: DotNetCoreCLI@2
inputs:
command: 'test'
arguments: '--configuration Release'
projects: '**/*Tests.csproj'
- task: DotNetCoreCLI@2
inputs:
command: 'publish'
publishWebProjects: true
arguments: '--configuration Release --output $(Build.ArtifactStagingDirectory)'
zipAfterPublish: true
- task: PublishBuildArtifacts@1
inputs:
pathtoPublish: '$(Build.ArtifactStagingDirectory)'
```

artifactName: 'myapp'

Monitor and Iterate: Utilize Azure DevOps reporting and monitoring tools to assess the success of your builds and deployments. Continuously refine your pipelines based on feedback and performance metrics.

Introduction to Azure DevOps Services:

Azure DevOps Services, offered by Microsoft, is an integrated suite of services that facilitate collaboration, automation, and integration across the software development lifecycle (SDLC). Aimed at improving team productivity and optimizing the software delivery process, Azure DevOps encapsulates a range of tools and services designed for project management, version control, build automation, testing, and deployment. This comprehensive overview introduces the core services of Azure DevOps, shedding light on how it empowers development teams to implement Continuous Integration (CI) and Continuous Deployment (CD) practices effectively.

Core Services of Azure DevOps

Azure DevOps Services encompasses several key components, each tailored to address specific needs within the SDLC:

Azure Boards: A project management tool that facilitates agile planning, tracking of work items, and visualization of work through dashboards and Kanban boards. It supports agile development practices, enabling teams to plan sprints, track progress, and manage backlogs efficiently.

Azure Repos: Offers version control capabilities using Git, providing a secure repository for source code management. It supports collaboration through pull requests and code reviews, enhancing code quality and facilitating team collaboration on code changes.

Azure Pipelines: A CI/CD service that automates the build, testing, and deployment phases, allowing teams to continuously integrate and deliver software updates. It supports a wide range of languages, platforms, and cloud environments, including Azure, AWS, and Google Cloud Platform.

Azure Test Plans: Provides a comprehensive suite of manual and exploratory testing tools that integrate with Azure Pipelines. It enables teams to plan, execute, and track testing activities, ensuring software quality and reliability.

Azure Artifacts: A package management service that allows teams to share packages such as Maven, npm, NuGet, and Python packages from public and private sources, seamlessly integrating package sharing into CI/CD pipelines.

Implementing CI/CD with Azure DevOps Services

Azure DevOps Services is particularly renowned for its robust support of CI/CD practices, streamlining the process of integrating new code changes and deploying software updates. Here's a simplified example of how Azure Pipelines can be used to implement CI/CD for a web application:

Continuous Integration (CI): Developers push code changes to Azure Repos. Azure Pipelines automatically triggers a build pipeline upon each commit, which:

- Compiles the code.
- Runs automated tests to verify changes.
- Generates artifacts ready for deployment.

Continuous Deployment (CD): Once the build pipeline succeeds and artifacts are created, Azure Pipelines triggers a release pipeline that deploys the application to various environments, such as staging and production, based on predefined conditions or manual approvals.

Example YAML for Azure Pipelines:

```
trigger:
- main
pool:
vmImage: 'ubuntu-latest'
```

```yaml
stages:
- stage: Build
jobs:
- job: BuildJob
steps:
- script: echo Compiling source code...
- script: echo Running tests...
- publish: $(System.DefaultWorkingDirectory)
artifact: MyApp
- stage: Deploy
condition: succeeded()
jobs:
- deployment: DeployJob
environment: 'production'
strategy:
runOnce:
deploy:
steps:
- script: echo Deploying application to production...
```

This YAML file defines a simple CI/CD pipeline with two stages: Build and Deploy. The Build stage compiles the code and runs tests, while the Deploy stage deploys the application to a production environment, contingent on the successful completion of the Build stage.

Azure DevOps Services offers a cohesive and comprehensive suite of tools that cater to the needs of development teams aiming to improve collaboration, streamline workflows, and accelerate the delivery of software projects. By embracing Azure DevOps, teams can leverage the power of CI/CD to ensure that their software is always in a releasable state, enhancing the agility and responsiveness of the software development process.

Implementing Continuous Integration:

Implementing Continuous Integration (CI) and Continuous Deployment (CD) is a cornerstone of modern software development practices, allowing teams to automate the process of integrating code changes and deploying applications to production environments. Azure DevOps provides a powerful platform for setting up CI/CD pipelines, streamlining these processes to enhance productivity and ensure the delivery of high-quality software.

Setting Up Continuous Integration (CI)

Continuous Integration automates the merging and testing of code changes. The goal is to identify integration errors as quickly as possible, maintain a high-quality codebase, and reduce the time to release new updates.

Example: Creating a CI Pipeline for a .NET Core Application

1. **Create a New Build Pipeline**: Start by creating a new build pipeline in Azure DevOps. Select your repository source (Azure Repos Git, GitHub, etc.), and choose the .NET Core template.
2. **Define Build Tasks**: Customize the pipeline by adding tasks for restoring dependencies, building the project, running tests, and publishing artifacts. Each task corresponds to a step in your CI process.

```
trigger:
- main
pool:
vmImage: 'ubuntu-latest'
steps:
- task: DotNetCoreCLI@2
inputs:
command: 'restore'
projects: '**/*.csproj'
- task: DotNetCoreCLI@2
```

```
inputs:
command: 'build'
projects: '**/*.csproj'
- task: DotNetCoreCLI@2
inputs:
command: 'test'
projects: '**/*Tests.csproj'
- task: DotNetCoreCLI@2
inputs:
command: 'publish'
publishWebProjects: true
arguments: '--configuration Release --output $(Build.ArtifactStagingDirectory)'
zipAfterPublish: true
- task: PublishBuildArtifacts@1
inputs:
pathtoPublish: '$(Build.ArtifactStagingDirectory)'
artifactName: 'webapp'
```

Configure Triggers: Set up triggers to automatically start the CI pipeline on code commits or pull requests to specified branches, ensuring new changes are integrated and tested promptly.

Setting Up Continuous Deployment (CD)

Continuous Deployment automates the deployment of applications to staging or production environments after the CI process. This ensures that your application can be deployed reliably at any time.

Example: Creating a CD Pipeline for Deployment to Azure App Service

1. **Create a New Release Pipeline**: In Azure DevOps, navigate to the Releases section under Pipelines. Create a new release pipeline and link it to the build pipeline's artifact.

2. **Define Deployment Stages**: Add stages for each environment (e.g., staging, production). You can configure pre-deployment

approvals for production deployments to ensure changes are reviewed before going live.

```yaml
stages:
- stage: DeployToStaging
jobs:
- deployment: DeployWebAppToStaging
environment: 'staging'
strategy:
runOnce:
deploy:
steps:
- task: AzureWebApp@1
inputs:
azureSubscription: '<YourSubscription>'
appType: 'webApp'
appName: '<YourAppName>-staging'
package: '$(Pipeline.Workspace)/webapp/*.zip'
- stage: DeployToProduction
condition: succeeded('DeployToStaging')
jobs:
- deployment: DeployWebAppToProduction
environment: 'production'
strategy:
runOnce:
deploy:
steps:
- task: AzureWebApp@1
inputs:
azureSubscription: '<YourSubscription>'
appType: 'webApp'
appName: '<YourAppName>'
package: '$(Pipeline.Workspace)/webapp/*.zip'
```

Automate Deployments: Configure the pipeline to automatically deploy to staging after a successful build. Use manual approvals or gates for production deployments to add an extra layer of validation.

By implementing CI/CD with Azure DevOps, development teams can automate the integration and deployment processes, enabling more frequent releases, improved application quality, and enhanced operational efficiency. The examples provided illustrate how Azure DevOps can be configured to support a streamlined workflow for a .NET Core application, from code commit through to deployment in Azure App Service. Adopting CI/CD practices with Azure DevOps not only accelerates the development cycle but also fosters a culture of continuous improvement and collaboration within teams.

Conclusion

Azure DevOps and its CI/CD capabilities enable teams to automate and streamline the building, testing, and deployment processes, significantly enhancing the development lifecycle's speed, efficiency, and reliability. By adopting Azure DevOps for CI/CD, organizations can achieve faster release cycles, improved product quality, and increased customer satisfaction. Through the effective implementation of CI/CD practices, teams are better positioned to respond to market changes, update applications swiftly in response to user feedback, and maintain high standards of code quality and security.

12

Chapter 8: Azure Architecture and Best Practices

Crafting solutions in Azure requires a thorough understanding of cloud architecture principles and the application of best practices to build reliable, scalable, secure, and cost-efficient systems. Azure's extensive suite of services and tools supports a wide range of architectures, from simple web applications to complex microservices and data processing pipelines.

Pillars of Azure Architecture

Security:

Prioritize security at every layer of your architecture, leveraging Azure's built-in security features like Azure Active Directory (AAD) for authentication, Network Security Groups (NSGs) for network isolation, and Azure Key Vault for managing secrets.

Security within Azure architecture is paramount, forming the foundation upon which safe, reliable, and trustworthy systems are built. Azure provides a comprehensive array of tools and features designed to bolster security at every level of your applications and infrastructure.

Key Security Considerations in Azure

Identity and Access Management (IAM): Central to securing your Azure resources is the management of identities and access permissions, ensuring that only authorized entities can access your resources.

Network Security: Protecting your network infrastructure from unauthorized access and potential threats is crucial for maintaining the integrity of your data and services.

Data Protection: Ensuring the confidentiality, integrity, and availability of your data is paramount, requiring strategies for encryption, backup, and secure data access.

Threat Protection and Monitoring: Continuously monitoring for and responding to security threats keeps your systems resilient against attacks.

Implementing Security Best Practices in Azure

Secure Authentication with Azure Active Directory (AAD)

Example: Implement Multi-Factor Authentication (MFA) for your Azure Active Directory users to significantly reduce the risk of unauthorized access due to compromised credentials.

Implementation: In the Azure portal, navigate to Azure Active Directory > Security > MFA > Getting started. Follow the steps to enable MFA for your organization.

Network Security with Network Security Groups (NSGs)

Example: Use NSGs to control inbound and outbound traffic to network interfaces (NIC), VMs, and subnets. This can effectively isolate segments of your network and protect sensitive systems from unauthorized access.

Implementation: Create an NSG and define inbound and outbound security rules that allow or deny traffic based on source and destination IP addresses, ports, and protocols. Associate the NSG with specific subnets or VM network interfaces.

az network nsg create --resource-group myResourceGroup --name myNSG

az network nsg rule create --resource-group myResourceGroup --nsg-name myNSG --name myNSGRule --priority 100 --source-address-prefixes '*' --destination-port-ranges 80 --access Allow --protocol Tcp --description "Allow HTTP traffic"

Data Encryption with Azure Key Vault

Example: Use Azure Key Vault to manage cryptographic keys and secrets used by cloud applications and services. Encrypt your data at rest using keys stored in Key Vault to enhance data security.

Implementation: Create a Key Vault and use it to encrypt/decrypt data in your application. Ensure that only authorized applications and users have access to the Key Vault.

az keyvault create --name <YourKeyVaultName> --resource-group <YourResourceGroupName> --location <YourLocation>

az keyvault key create --vault-name <YourKeyVaultName> --name <YourKeyName> --protection software

Enable Azure Defender for Integrated Threat Protection

Example: Activate Azure Defender to get advanced threat detection capabilities across your Azure services, including virtual machines, databases, and storage accounts.

Implementation: In the Azure portal, navigate to Azure Security Center > Pricing & settings. Select your subscription and turn on Azure Defender plans for the various Azure services.

Security is a critical pillar of Azure architecture, requiring a proactive and comprehensive approach to safeguard your resources. By implementing Azure's robust security features like Azure Active Directory, Network Security Groups, Azure Key Vault, and Azure Defender, you can create a secure foundation for your applications and data. These examples illustrate actionable steps you can take to enhance the security posture of your Azure solutions, emphasizing the importance of IAM, network security, data protection, and threat monitoring in building resilient cloud architectures.

Performance and Scalability:

Design for scalability from the outset, utilizing Azure services like Azure App Service for auto-scaling web applications and Azure SQL Database that automatically scales to meet demand.

Performance and scalability are fundamental pillars in Azure architecture, ensuring that applications not only run efficiently but also can gracefully handle growth in demand. Azure's vast array of services and features allows architects and developers to design systems that are both powerful and elastic, adapting to varying loads with minimal manual intervention.

Key Considerations for Performance and Scalability

Choosing the Right Services: Select Azure services that align with your performance requirements and scalability goals. For compute-intensive applications, consider Azure Kubernetes Service (AKS) or Azure Virtual Machines Scale Sets (VMSS). For data storage, options like Azure SQL Database and Azure Cosmos DB offer scalability and high performance.

Auto-scaling: Implement auto-scaling to adjust resources automatically based on demand, ensuring that your application maintains high performance without over-provisioning resources.

Caching: Use Azure Cache for Redis or Azure CDN to cache frequently accessed data and content, reducing latency and offloading backend services.

Optimized Data Storage and Access: Choose the appropriate data storage solution and access strategy to minimize latency and maximize throughput.

Implementing Best Practices with Examples

Auto-scaling with Azure Virtual Machine Scale Sets (VMSS)

Scenario: You have a web application experiencing variable loads throughout the day. To ensure consistent performance while optimizing costs, you deploy it using VMSS, configured to automatically scale.

Example:

```
az vmss create \
```

```
--resource-group myResourceGroup \
--name myScaleSet \
--image UbuntuLTS \
--upgrade-policy-mode automatic \
--admin-username azureuser \
--generate-ssh-keys \
--instance-count 2 \
--scale-in-policy NewestVM \
--custom-data cloud-init.txt \
--priority Spot \
--eviction-policy Delete \
--max-price -1
```

Here, a VMSS is created with a spot priority to reduce costs, starting with two instances and configured for automatic scaling and updates. The scale-in policy ensures that the newest VM is removed first during scale-in actions.

Enhancing Web Application Performance with Azure CDN

Scenario: Your global application serves static content, experiencing delays in load times for users far from the origin server. Implementing Azure CDN can drastically reduce load times by caching content at edge locations closer to users.

Example:

- Create a new CDN profile and endpoint in the Azure portal or via Azure CLI.
- Point the CDN to your application's static content origin.
- Configure caching rules as needed to optimize delivery.

Leveraging Azure Cache for Redis for Data Cachin

Scenario: An application frequently queries a database for read-only data, leading to unnecessary database load and latency. Implementing Azure Cache for Redis to cache this data improves response times and reduces database load.

Example:

```
IDatabase cache = Connection.GetDatabase();
// Try to get the data from the cache
string value = cache.StringGet("myKey");
if (value == null)
{
// Data not in cache, retrieve from database
value = GetDataFromDatabase();
// Store in cache for next time
cache.StringSet("myKey", value);
}
```

Optimizing Data Access in Azure Cosmos DB

Scenario: A globally distributed application requires fast read and write access to data across multiple regions. Azure Cosmos DB's global distribution features ensure data is available close to users, with multi-region writes for improved performance.

Example:

- Enable multi-region writes and geo-redundancy in your Cosmos DB account settings.
- Use the Azure portal or SDKs to configure regional preferences and conflict resolution policies, ensuring data consistency and availability.

Optimizing for performance and scalability is crucial in cloud architecture, enabling applications to serve users efficiently and cost-effectively under varying loads. Azure offers a wide range of services and features, from auto-scaling and global distribution to caching and data optimization, designed to build highly performant and scalable solutions. By following these best practices and leveraging Azure's capabilities, developers and architects can ensure their applications are ready to meet current and future demands.

Reliability and Availability:

Ensure high availability through redundancy and failover strategies, using services like Azure Availability Zones and leveraging geo-redundant storage options.

In the landscape of cloud computing, ensuring the reliability and availability of applications and services is fundamental. Azure's architecture is designed to support high availability and reliability, allowing businesses to deliver uninterrupted services to their users.

Understanding Reliability and Availability in Azure

Reliability in Azure architecture refers to the ability of an application or service to perform its intended function correctly and consistently over time. Availability, on the other hand, focuses on ensuring that services are accessible and operational when needed by users. Together, these pillars are crucial for maintaining user trust and satisfaction.

Key Strategies for Enhancing Reliability and Availability

Design for Failure: Assume that components can fail and design your architecture to minimize the impact of such failures.

Replication and Redundancy: Deploy resources across multiple regions or availability zones to protect against localized failures.

Load Balancing: Distribute traffic evenly across multiple instances or services to ensure optimal performance and uptime.

Monitoring and Alerts: Implement comprehensive monitoring to detect issues early and automate responses to potential failures.

Implementing Reliability and Availability Best Practices in Azure

Using Availability Zones for High Availability

Example: Deploy your application across multiple Availability Zones within an Azure region to protect against data center failures.

Implementation: When creating a Virtual Machine or another resource, select a region that supports Availability Zones and specify different zones for each resource instance.

```
az vm create --resource-group myResourceGroup --name myVM
--image UbuntuLTS --zone 1
az vm create --resource-group myResourceGroup --name myVM2
--image UbuntuLTS --zone 2
```

Load Balancing Across VM Instances

Example: Use Azure Load Balancer to distribute incoming traffic among multiple VM instances, ensuring that user requests are served even if one instance becomes unavailable.

Implementation: Create an Azure Load Balancer and configure it to distribute traffic to VM instances spread across different Availability Zones.

az network lb create --resource-group myResourceGroup --name myLoadBalancer --frontend-ip-name myFrontEndPool --backend-pool-name myBackEndPool --public-ip-address myPublicIP

Geo-Redundant Storage (GRS) for Data Durability

Example: Store your data in a Geo-Redundant Storage account to ensure it is replicated in a secondary region, protecting against regional outages.

Implementation: When creating an Azure Storage account, select the "Geo-redundant storage (GRS)" option for the redundancy level.

az storage account create --name mystorageaccount --resource-group myResourceGroup --location eastus --sku Standard_GRS

Application Gateway for High Availability and Autoscaling

Example: Use Azure Application Gateway with autoscaling enabled and configure it to span multiple Availability Zones, ensuring high availability for your web applications.

Implementation: Create an Application Gateway and enable autoscaling and multi-zone deployment during setup.

az network application-gateway create --name myAppGateway --resource-group myResourceGroup --location eastus --sku Standard_v2 --zones 1 2 3

Azure Cosmos DB for Globally Distributed Databases

Example: Utilize Azure Cosmos DB's multi-region replication to distribute your database globally, ensuring low latency access and high availability.

Implementation: When setting up your Azure Cosmos DB account, enable multi-region writes and select the regions that best match your users' locations.

az cosmosdb create --name myCosmosDB --resource-group myResourceGroup --locations regionName=eastus failoverPriority=0 isZoneRedundant=False --locations regionName=westus failoverPriority=1 isZoneRedundant=False --enable-multiple-write-locations true

Ensuring the reliability and availability of your Azure applications and services is crucial for maintaining user trust and business continuity. By leveraging Azure's comprehensive set of features designed for high availability, such as Availability Zones, Load Balancers, Geo-Redundant Storage, and globally distributed databases like Azure Cosmos DB, architects and developers can build resilient cloud solutions. These examples serve as a foundation for implementing best practices that enhance the reliability and availability of your Azure deployments, helping you deliver robust, uninterrupted services to your users.

Cost Optimization:

Monitor and manage costs by selecting the appropriate service tiers, using Azure Cost Management tools, and optimizing resource utilization.

Cost optimization is a fundamental aspect of cloud architecture, focusing on minimizing expenses while maximizing resource efficiency and performance. Azure provides a variety of tools and features designed to help architects and developers build cost-effective solutions. By adhering to cost optimization best practices, businesses can ensure their Azure deployments are both economical and powerful.

Understanding Cost Optimization in Azure

Cost optimization in Azure involves analyzing and adjusting your cloud spending to avoid unnecessary costs. It encompasses selecting the appropriate service types, sizes, and pricing models; monitoring and managing resource usage; and taking advantage of Azure's pricing and budgeting tools.

Key Strategies for Cost Optimization

Right-size Resources: Ensure that Azure services are sized according to your actual usage needs, avoiding over-provisioning.

Use Reserved Instances: Purchase Reserved Instances for services like Azure Virtual Machines (VMs) and Azure SQL Database to save money compared to pay-as-you-go pricing.

Leverage Autoscaling: Use autoscaling features to dynamically adjust resources in response to load, ensuring you only pay for what you need.

Clean Up Unused Resources: Regularly review and remove unused or temporary resources to cut unnecessary costs.

Implement Budgets and Alerts: Use Azure Cost Management and Billing to set budgets and alerts to monitor and control cloud spending.

Implementing Cost Optimization Best Practices with Examples

Right-sizing Azure VMs]

Example: Analyze the performance metrics of your VMs using Azure Monitor. If a VM is consistently underutilized, consider resizing it to a smaller instance type that matches its load.

Implementation:

```
az vm resize --resource-group myResourceGroup --name myVM --size Standard_B2s
```

This command resizes an existing VM to a smaller size that still meets performance requirements but costs less.

Reserved Instances for Long-term Savings

Example: For VMs running 24/7, such as those hosting critical applications, purchase Azure Reserved VM Instances to significantly reduce costs compared to pay-as-you-go pricing.

Implementation: Through the Azure portal, navigate to Reservations and choose to purchase a reservation for the VM size and region you require. Commit to a one or three-year term for the best savings.

Implementing Autoscaling for Azure App Services

Example: Use Azure App Service Plan's autoscale feature to automatically scale out/in based on demand, such as CPU usage or request rates.

Implementation: In the Azure portal, configure the Scale Out settings for your App Service Plan to automatically add or remove instances based on defined rules and metrics.

Cleaning Up Unused Resources with Azure Advisor

Example: Utilize Azure Advisor's cost recommendations to identify and remove unused resources, such as orphaned disk volumes or idle virtual network gateways.

Implementation: Review Azure Advisor's cost optimization recommendations regularly and take action to delete or downsize resources as suggested.

Setting Budgets and Alerts with Azure Cost Management

Example: Create a monthly budget for your Azure subscription and configure alerts to notify you when spending approaches or exceeds your budget.

Implementation: Use Azure Cost Management and Billing to define a budget based on your expected monthly costs. Set up alerts to email you at 50%, 75%, and 90% of budget utilization.

Cost optimization in Azure is an ongoing process that requires regular review and adjustment of resources and usage patterns. By implementing the strategies and examples provided, businesses can build and maintain efficient, cost-effective cloud solutions. Leveraging Azure's built-in tools like Azure Advisor, Azure Cost Management, and autoscaling features plays a crucial role in managing cloud expenditures, ensuring that Azure deployments remain within budget while meeting performance and operational requirements.

Operational Excellence:

Automate deployment and operations using Azure DevOps for CI/CD pipelines and Infrastructure as Code (IaC) practices with tools like Azure Resource Manager (ARM) templates or Terraform.

Operational Excellence in Azure architecture is about ensuring that systems are not only optimized for performance and cost but are also manageable, monitorable, and resilient to changes and failures. This pillar focuses on automating deployment, operations, and recovery processes to maintain a consistent, reliable service that meets business and customer needs. Below, we explore the strategies and practices underpinning operational excellence in Azure, supported by examples to illustrate how these can be implemented in practice.

Key Components of Operational Excellence

Automation: Automate repetitive tasks like deployments, scaling, and backups to reduce the potential for human error and free up time for innovation.

Monitoring and Logging: Implement comprehensive monitoring and logging to gain insights into application performance and system health, enabling proactive issue resolution.

Disaster Recovery and Backup: Ensure strategies are in place for data backup and disaster recovery to maintain business continuity in the face of failures.

Continuous Improvement: Adopt a culture of continuous improvement through regular reviews of operations and incident responses to learn and adapt.

Implementing Operational Excellence in Azure

Automating Deployments with Azure DevOps Pipelines

Example: Use Azure DevOps Pipelines to automate the build and deployment of a web application to Azure App Services, ensuring consistent and error-free deployments.

Implementation: Create a CI/CD pipeline in Azure DevOps that triggers a build whenever changes are committed to your Git repository. The pipeline should run tests, build the application, and deploy it to Azure App Services.

```
trigger:
- main
pool:
```

```
vmImage: 'ubuntu-latest'
steps:
- task: NodeTool@0
inputs:
versionSpec: '10.x'
- script: |
npm install
npm test
displayName: 'npm install and test'
- task: AzureWebApp@1
inputs:
azureSubscription: '<Azure-Subscription-Service-Connection>'
appType: 'webAppLinux'
appName: '<Your-App-Service-Name>'
runtimeStack: 'NODE|10.14'
package: '$(Build.ArtifactStagingDirectory)/**/*.zip'
```

Implementing Monitoring with Azure Monitor and Application Insights

Example: Configure Azure Monitor and Application Insights for your application to collect telemetry, performance metrics, and log data. Use this data to create dashboards, set up alerts, and diagnose issues.

Implementation: Integrate Application Insights into your application to start collecting telemetry. In the Azure portal, navigate to Azure Monitor to configure alerts based on metrics or log queries.

Disaster Recovery Strategy with Azure Site Recovery

Example: Use Azure Site Recovery to replicate VMs and critical workloads to another Azure region, ensuring that you can quickly fail-over in the event of a regional outage.

Implementation: Set up replication for your VMs through the Azure portal. Configure recovery plans that detail the order in which VMs are started during failover and any necessary scripts that need to run.

Continuously Improving Operations with Azure Advisor

Example: Utilize Azure Advisor to get personalized recommendations for optimizing your Azure resources across reliability, security, operational excellence, performance, and cost.

Implementation: Regularly review Azure Advisor recommendations in the Azure portal and implement suggested actions. Track improvements over time to measure the impact of changes.

Operational Excellence in Azure architecture is achieved by leveraging Azure's vast array of tools and services designed for automation, monitoring, disaster recovery, and continuous improvement. By embracing these practices, organizations can ensure their Azure solutions are not only optimized and reliable but also remain aligned with evolving business requirements. The examples provided offer a blueprint for integrating these principles into your Azure operations, laying the foundation for sustained operational success.

Best Practices with Examples

Secure Authentication and Authorization

Example: Use Azure Active Directory (AAD) for managing user identities and implementing secure access to your applications. Integrate AAD with your web applications for single sign-on (SSO) capabilities.

services.AddAuthentication(AzureADDefaults.AuthenticationScheme)

.AddAzureAD(options => Configuration.Bind("AzureAd", options));

Auto-scaling to Manage Load

Example: Configure auto-scaling rules for an Azure App Service to automatically scale out/in based on metrics like CPU utilization or request queue length.

- Navigate to your App Service in the Azure portal.
- Select "Scale out (App Service plan)" and define auto-scale rules based on metrics.

Implementing High Availability

Example: Deploy your application across multiple Azure regions and use Azure Traffic Manager to route traffic to the closest or most responsive region, enhancing availability and performance.

- Create instances of your application in multiple regions.
- Configure Azure Traffic Manager with a performance routing method.

Cost-Effective Storage Solutions

Example: Use Azure Blob Storage with lifecycle management policies to automatically transition older blobs to cooler storage tiers or delete them, optimizing storage costs.

```
{
"rules": [
{
"name": "moveToCoolStorage",
"enabled": true,
"type": "Lifecycle",
"definition": {
"filters": {
"blobTypes": ["blockBlob"],
"prefixMatch": ["logs/"]
},
"actions": {
"baseBlob": {
"tierToCool": { "daysAfterModificationGreaterThan": 30 }
}
}
}
}
]
}
```

Automation of Deployments and Infrastructure

Example: Use Azure DevOps Pipelines with ARM templates to automate the deployment of your infrastructure and application, ensuring consistent and repeatable setups.

```
trigger:
- main
stages:
- stage: Build
jobs:
- job: Build
steps:
- script: echo Build stage
- stage: Deploy
jobs:
- deployment: Deploy
environment: production
strategy:
runOnce:
deploy:
steps:
- script: echo Deploy stage
- task: AzureResourceManagerTemplateDeployment@3
inputs:
deploymentScope: 'Resource Group'
azureResourceManagerConnection: 'AzureConnection'
subscriptionId: 'xxxx-xxxx-xxxx-xxxx'
action: 'Create Or Update Resource Group'
resourceGroupName: 'MyResourceGroup'
location: 'West US'
templateLocation: 'Linked artifact'
csmFile: '$(Pipeline.Workspace)/drop/azuredeploy.json'
csmParametersFile:  '$(Pipeline.Workspace)/drop/azuredeploy.parameters.json'
```

Designing Scalable and Resilient Architectures:

Creating scalable and resilient architectures in Azure involves designing systems that can handle variable workloads efficiently and maintain functionality even in the face of failures or disruptions. This requires careful planning and the strategic use of Azure services designed to enhance scalability and resilience.

Key Considerations for Scalability and Resilience

Scalability:

The ability of a system to handle increases in load without compromising performance. In Azure, scalability can be achieved both vertically (by increasing the size of resources) and horizontally (by increasing the number of resources).

In the realm of cloud computing, scalability is a cornerstone of designing effective architectures. It allows applications to accommodate growth in users, data, or computing power seamlessly and efficiently. Azure offers a comprehensive set of services and features designed to support scalable architectures, enabling systems to adapt to fluctuating demands without compromising performance or incurring unnecessary costs.

Understanding Scalability in Azure

Scalability can be categorized into two types: vertical (scaling up/down) and horizontal (scaling out/in). Vertical scaling involves increasing the capacity of existing resources (e.g., upgrading to a larger VM size), while horizontal scaling adds or removes resources to match demand (e.g., increasing the number of VM instances).

Key Considerations for Scalability

Elasticity: The ability to automatically scale resources based on demand ensures that applications can handle peaks efficiently without manual intervention.

Distributed Systems: Designing applications as distributed systems across multiple computing resources can enhance scalability by distributing loads and reducing points of failure.

Stateless Components: Building stateless application components ensures that any instance of the application can serve any request, simplifying horizontal scaling.

Examples of Implementing Scalability in Azure

Auto-scaling with Azure App Service

Azure App Service supports both vertical and horizontal scaling. For web applications experiencing variable traffic, enabling auto-scale can dynamically adjust the number of instances serving the application.

Example: Configuring auto-scale based on CPU usage for a web app.

Implementation:

- Navigate to your App Service in the Azure portal.
- Select "Scale out (App Service plan)" > "Enable autoscale".
- Create an autoscale rule, e.g., "Increase instance count by 1 when CPU % > 70".

Utilizing Azure Kubernetes Service (AKS) for Scalable Container Orchestration

AKS facilitates easy deployment and management of containerized applications, with built-in support for horizontal scaling.

Example: Automatically scaling out AKS pods based on CPU usage.

Implementation:

- Deploy your application on AKS and define resource requests and limits for your pods.
- Enable the Horizontal Pod Autoscaler (HPA) by running:

```
kubectl autoscale deployment <your-deployment> --cpu-percent=50 --min=1 --max=10
```

The HPA automatically adjusts the number of pods in a deployment based on observed CPU utilization.

Azure Cosmos DB for Scalable NoSQL Data

Azure Cosmos DB is a globally distributed database service that offers horizontal scaling across geographic regions.

Example: Distributing database operations across multiple regions to balance loads and reduce latency.

Implementation:

- When creating a Cosmos DB account, enable "Multi-region Writes" to allow data to be written and read from multiple regions.
- Use the Azure portal or Azure CLI to add regions to your Cosmos DB account, enhancing the database's scalability and availability.

Scalability is critical to the success of cloud-based applications, ensuring they can grow and adapt to changes in demand. By leveraging Azure's scalable services and following best practices for design, such as embracing elasticity, designing distributed systems, and building stateless components, developers can create scalable and efficient architectures. These examples showcase just a few ways in which Azure facilitates scalability, offering a path toward building resilient and adaptable cloud solutions.

Resilience:

The capability of a system to continue operating despite failures or disruptions. Resilience in Azure architectures can be enhanced through redundancy, failover strategies, and the use of managed services with built-in high availability features.

Resilience in cloud architecture refers to the ability of a system to withstand and recover from failures, ensuring continued operation and minimizing impact on users. In Azure, designing for resilience involves strategic planning around redundancy, failover mechanisms, data replication, and disaster recovery strategies. This approach not only safeguards against potential service disruptions but also ensures that applications remain available and data is preserved. Below, we explore the key considerations for building resilient architectures in Azure, supported by examples that illustrate these concepts in action.

Key Considerations for Resilience

Redundancy and Replication: Ensuring that critical components and data are duplicated across geographically dispersed locations to protect against regional outages.

Failover Strategies: Implementing automatic failover mechanisms to seamlessly switch to backup systems or services in the event of a failure.

Disaster Recovery Planning: Establishing a comprehensive disaster recovery plan that includes regular backups, data recovery procedures, and clearly defined roles and responsibilities.

Monitoring and Alerting: Continuously monitoring the health of services and implementing alerting mechanisms to quickly identify and respond to issues.

Examples of Implementing Resilience in Azure

Geo-Redundant Storage (GRS) for Data Durability

Azure provides Geo-Redundant Storage (GRS) as a way to replicate data across multiple regions, ensuring that your data remains accessible even if a primary region becomes unavailable.

Example: Configuring a storage account to use GRS for critical data storage.

Implementation: When creating or updating a storage account in the Azure portal or via Azure CLI, select "Geo-redundant storage" as the account's redundancy option.

Availability Zones for High Availability

Availability Zones in Azure offer a way to protect applications and data from datacenter failures by distributing resources across multiple, physically separated zones within a region.

Example: Deploying VMs or other critical services across Availability Zones.

Implementation:

- Ensure your resources are created in a region that supports Availability Zones.
- Specify the zone for each resource during creation, either through the Azure portal, Azure CLI, or ARM templates.

az vm create --resource-group myResourceGroup --name myVM --image UbuntuLTS --zone 1

Azure Site Recovery for Disaster Recovery

Azure Site Recovery provides a disaster recovery solution for Azure VMs, on-premises servers, and virtual machines hosted in other clouds, allowing services to be restored in a secondary location if the primary site fails.

Example: Implementing disaster recovery for an Azure VM application.

Implementation:

- Configure Azure Site Recovery through the Recovery Services vault in the Azure portal.
- Set up replication for the VMs involved in your application to a secondary region.
- Regularly test failover to the secondary site to ensure that your disaster recovery process is effective and that services can be quickly restored.

Application Gateway with Auto-Failover Groups

Using Azure Application Gateway in conjunction with auto-failover groups can enhance the resilience of web applications by automatically rerouting traffic in the event of a failure.

Example: Setting up an auto-failover group for a multi-region web application deployment.

Implementation:

- Deploy Application Gateway instances in multiple regions, each fronting the regional deployment of your web application.
- Configure an auto-failover group using Azure Traffic Manager to monitor the health of your application endpoints and automatically direct traffic to the healthy region.

Building resilience into your Azure architecture is essential for maintaining service continuity, protecting data, and ensuring a positive user experience, even in the face of system failures or disasters. By leveraging Azure's capabilities for redundancy, replication, failover, and disaster recovery, architects and developers can design systems that are robust and capable of withstanding various failure scenarios. These examples provide a foundation for implementing resilience strategies in Azure, emphasizing the importance of planning, testing, and continuous monitoring in achieving operational resilience.

Best Practices for Designing Scalable and Resilient Architectures

Leverage Azure Auto-scaling Features

Example: Use Azure App Service Auto-scaling to automatically scale out web app instances based on demand.

Implementation: Configure auto-scaling rules in the Azure portal for your App Service, specifying a metric (e.g., CPU usage) and thresholds that trigger scale actions.

Deploy Across Multiple Availability Zones

Example: Deploy critical components of your application across multiple Availability Zones within an Azure region to ensure high availability.

Implementation: When creating resources such as VMs or databases, select a region that supports Availability Zones and distribute your resources across these zones.

az vm create --resource-group myResourceGroup --name myVM1 --image UbuntuLTS --zone 1 az vm create --resource-group myResourceGroup --name myVM2 --image UbuntuLTS --zone 2

Implement Load Balancing and Traffic Management

Example: Use Azure Load Balancer and Azure Traffic Manager to distribute incoming traffic across multiple instances and regions, respectively.

Implementation: Set up an Azure Load Balancer to distribute traffic among VMs within a region, and use Azure Traffic Manager to route users to the closest or most responsive region based on their geographic location.

Utilize Cosmos DB for Globally Distributed Data

Example: Store application data in Azure Cosmos DB, leveraging its global distribution capabilities to ensure low-latency access and high availability across regions.

Implementation: Create an Azure Cosmos DB account, enable multi-region writes, and configure the regions to which your data should be replicated.

Incorporate Data Replication and Backup Strategies

Example: Use Azure SQL Database with active geo-replication to replicate databases across regions, and configure Azure Backup for automated backups.

Implementation: Enable Active Geo-Replication for your Azure SQL Database through the Azure portal, specifying a secondary region. Set up Azure Backup with a Recovery Services vault to schedule regular backups of your data.

Monitoring and Diagnostics for Scalability and Resilience

Implement Comprehensive Monitoring: Use Azure Monitor and Application Insights to collect and analyze metrics, logs, and telemetry data, enabling proactive scaling and quick response to issues.

Regular Testing and Validation: Periodically test your failover and disaster recovery procedures to ensure that your scalability and resilience strategies are effective and that your team is prepared to respond to incidents.

Designing scalable and resilient architectures in Azure requires a strategic approach that leverages Azure's powerful scalability features, distributes resources for high availability, and ensures data is replicated and backed up across regions. By following the best practices outlined and implementing the provided examples, you can create Azure solutions that not only meet current demands but are also prepared to handle future growth and potential disruptions. This approach not only enhances the reliability and performance of your applications but also ensures a seamless experience for your users, regardless of load or unforeseen challenges.

Best Practices for Cost Management and Optimization:

Effective cost management and optimization are critical for maximizing the value of your investments in Azure. As organizations migrate and scale their services in the cloud, maintaining control over costs becomes increasingly important. Azure provides tools and features designed to help users monitor, manage, and optimize their spending. Implementing best practices for cost management ensures that you are only paying for the resources you need and use.

Establish Cost Management and Monitoring

Use Azure Cost Management + Billing: Azure Cost Management + Billing offers a comprehensive view of your Azure spending. It provides analysis tools, budgets, and recommendations to help reduce unnecessary spending.

Example: Setting up a monthly budget and alerts for your Azure subscription to monitor spending trends and receive notifications when spending reaches predefined thresholds.

Implementation:

- Navigate to the Azure portal, select "Cost Management + Billing" > "Budgets" and create a new budget.

- Define the monthly budget based on your expected spending and configure alerts to notify you via email when spending reaches 50%, 75%, and 100% of the budget.

Optimize Resource Utilization

Right-size Underutilized Resources: Regularly review performance metrics and usage patterns to identify underutilized resources. Adjust the size or tier of these resources to better match your actual needs.

Example: Downscaling an over-provisioned Azure SQL Database that consistently shows low CPU and IO usage.

Implementation:

- Use Azure Advisor to identify performance recommendations for Azure SQL Database.
- Adjust the database's pricing tier in the Azure portal based on the Advisor's recommendations.
- **Leverage Reserved Instances**: Purchase Reserved Instances for virtual machines and other services like Azure SQL Database to save costs over pay-as-you-go pricing for predictable workloads.

  Example: Purchasing a 1-year Reserved Instance for a VM used for a long-term project.

  Implementation:
    - Estimate your long-term usage with the Azure Pricing Calculator.
    - Purchase the Reserved Instance through the Azure portal, selecting the appropriate VM size and term.

Use Azure's Autoscaling Capabilities

Implement Autoscaling: Use Azure Autoscale to dynamically adjust the number of instances or resources based on load, ensuring you're not paying for idle capacity during off-peak times.

Example: Configuring autoscaling for an Azure App Service to scale out to more instances during peak hours and scale in during off-peak hours.

Implementation:

- In the Azure portal, navigate to your App Service > "Scale out (App Service plan)" > "Enable autoscale" and define scale conditions based on metrics like CPU percentage.

Clean Up Unused Resources

Regularly Review and Remove Unused or Temporary Resources: Identify and delete resources that are no longer needed to avoid unnecessary charges.

Example: Using Azure tags to identify resources associated with a completed project and deleting them.

Implementation:

- Tag resources with project-specific identifiers.
- Use Azure Resource Graph Explorer to query resources by tag and review them for deletion.

Effective cost management in Azure is an ongoing process that involves monitoring usage, optimizing resource allocations, and eliminating waste. By implementing these best practices, organizations can achieve significant cost savings while ensuring that their Azure environments are optimized for their specific needs. Tools like Azure Cost Management + Billing, Azure Advisor, and Azure Autoscale play pivotal roles in this process, offering insights and automation to help maintain cost efficiency.

Conclusion

Adhering to Azure architecture principles and best practices is essential for building effective, secure, and cost-efficient solutions in the cloud. By leveraging Azure's comprehensive suite of services and tools, developers and architects can design architectures that scale with demand, withstand failures, and align with business objectives. The examples provided offer a glimpse into the practical application of these principles, serving as a foundation for developing robust solutions in Azure. As Azure continues to evolve, staying informed about the latest best practices and features will ensure that your architectures remain resilient, performant, and secure. Top of Form

13

Chapter 9: Data Analytics and AI in Azure

Azure offers a robust ecosystem for data analytics and artificial intelligence (AI), providing tools and services that enable businesses to extract insights from data and build intelligent solutions. From data ingestion and storage to analytics and machine learning model deployment, Azure's comprehensive suite caters to a wide array of data-driven requirements.

<u>Azure Services for Data Analytics</u>

Azure Data Lake Storage:

An enterprise-wide hyper-scale repository for big data analytics workloads, enabling you to store data of any size, type, and ingestion speed in one single place for operational and exploratory analytics.

Azure Data Lake Storage (ADLS) is a highly scalable and secure data lake that allows you to store and analyze large volumes of data in its native format. ADLS is built on Azure Blob Storage, providing enhanced capabilities specifically designed for big data analytics. This includes fine-tuned control over access permissions, the ability to handle high-throughput analytics workloads, and integration with a wide array of analytics services. Below, we delve into the specifics of

ADLS and its role in Azure's data analytics offerings, complemented by practical examples.

Key Features of Azure Data Lake Storage

Hierarchical Namespace: ADLS introduces a hierarchical file system atop Azure Blob Storage, simplifying big data management. This allows for efficient data organization and access, mimicking the traditional directory structures found in file systems.

Scalability: Designed for enterprise big data analytics, ADLS can store and serve trillions of files, scaling to petabytes of data without compromising performance.

Security and Compliance: ADLS offers robust security features, including encryption at rest and in transit, fine-grained access control via POSIX-like ACLs, and integration with Azure Active Directory for authentication and authorization.

Optimized for Performance: Supports high-throughput and low-latency data access, making it ideal for big data analytics workloads. It's optimized to work seamlessly with big data analytics services like Azure Databricks, Azure HDInsight, and Azure Synapse Analytics.

Practical Examples of Azure Data Lake Storage

1. Storing IoT Sensor Data

- **Scenario**: A manufacturing company collects terabytes of sensor data from its equipment daily. The data is used for predictive maintenance, operational optimization, and historical analysis.
- **Implementation**: Data from IoT devices is ingested in real-time using Azure Event Hubs and stored in Azure Data Lake Storage. The hierarchical namespace feature allows organizing data by device, date, and sensor type. Azure Databricks processes this data nightly, running predictive maintenance algorithms and aggregating metrics for dashboard visualization.

2. Big Data Analytics with Azure Databricks

- **Scenario**: A retail company wants to analyze customer behavior and sales data to optimize product placements and promotions.
- **Implementation**: Raw sales and customer interaction data are stored in ADLS, using the hierarchical file system to organize data by store, date, and event type. Azure Databricks notebooks are used to perform data exploration, generate insights, and build machine learning models for customer segmentation and sales prediction. The results are then visualized in Power BI for strategic decision-making.

3. Historical Data Archiving for Compliance

- **Scenario**: A financial institution needs to archive transactional data for regulatory compliance, requiring secure, long-term storage that can be easily queried when needed.
- **Implementation**: Transactional data is archived in Azure Data Lake Storage, leveraging the scalability and security features of ADLS for compliance with financial regulations. Data is organized hierarchically by year, month, and transaction type. Azure Synapse Analytics is used for on-demand querying and reporting during audits, with data access controlled through fine-grained permissions.

Azure Data Lake Storage is a foundational component of Azure's data analytics ecosystem, offering a secure, scalable, and performance-optimized storage solution for big data analytics workloads. By leveraging ADLS in conjunction with Azure's analytics services, organizations can unlock valuable insights from their data, driving innovation and informed decision-making. The examples provided illustrate how ADLS serves as a versatile storage platform, capable of supporting a wide range of analytics scenarios from IoT data processing to compliance archiving and big data analytics.

Azure Synapse Analytics:

Integrates big data and data warehousing, offering a limitless analytics service that brings together enterprise data warehousing and Big Data analytics.

Azure Synapse Analytics stands as a pivotal service within Azure's analytics landscape, offering a unified analytics platform that seamlessly combines big data and data warehousing. It enables businesses to query data on their terms, at scale, across data warehouses and big data analytics systems. With Azure Synapse Analytics, organizations can ingest, prepare, manage, and serve data for immediate business intelligence and machine learning needs.

Key Features of Azure Synapse Analytics

Integrated Analytics: Azure Synapse brings together big data and data warehousing, breaking down silos to process and analyze data more efficiently.

On-demand Querying: Offers on-demand or provisioned resources, allowing you to query data across all your data sources, including relational, non-relational, and data lakes, using either serverless or dedicated options.

Deep Integration: Seamlessly integrates with other Azure services like Power BI for visualization, Azure Machine Learning for advanced analytics, and Azure Data Lake Storage for secure and scalable data storage.

Security and Compliance: Provides advanced security and privacy features, including dynamic data masking, automated threat detection, and fine-grained access control.

Practical Examples of Azure Synapse Analytics

1. Real-time Analytics Dashboard

- **Scenario**: A retail company wants to create a real-time dashboard to monitor sales performance across various regions and adjust marketing strategies accordingly.

- **Implementation**: Data from point-of-sale systems is ingested into Azure Data Lake Storage, where it's stored in a raw format. Azure Synapse Analytics is then used to process and analyze this data in real-time, leveraging the on-demand query capability to join sales data with inventory and customer data stored in relational databases. The processed data is visualized in Power BI, providing business leaders with real-time insights into sales performance.

2. Predictive Maintenance for Manufacturing

- **Scenario**: A manufacturing company aims to implement a predictive maintenance system to anticipate equipment failures before they occur, based on historical sensor data.
- **Implementation**: Sensor data collected from manufacturing equipment is stored in Azure Data Lake Storage. Azure Synapse Analytics processes this data, applying machine learning models developed with Azure Machine Learning to predict equipment failures. The results are visualized in Power BI dashboards, enabling maintenance teams to proactively address potential issues.

3. Customer Data Platform

- **Scenario**: A marketing department wishes to create a 360-degree view of customer interactions across multiple channels to tailor marketing campaigns more effectively.
- **Implementation**: Customer interaction data from various channels, including web, mobile, and in-store purchases, is ingested into Azure Data Lake Storage. Azure Synapse Analytics is used to aggregate and analyze this data, creating comprehensive customer profiles. By integrating with Azure Machine Learning, personalized marketing campaigns are developed based on

customer behavior and preferences. The insights are shared with marketing teams via Power BI dashboards.

Azure Synapse Analytics provides a powerful, integrated analytics solution that simplifies how businesses analyze their data across various sources. By offering both on-demand and provisioned query capabilities, deep integration with other Azure services, and robust security features, Synapse enables organizations to unlock actionable insights from their data. The examples provided showcase just a few ways organizations can leverage Azure Synapse Analytics to drive business intelligence, predictive analytics, and personalized customer experiences, making it an indispensable tool in the modern data analytics toolkit.

Azure Databricks:

An Apache Spark-based analytics platform optimized for Azure, providing collaborative notebooks, integrated workflows, and a scalable infrastructure for big data analytics and machine learning.

Azure Databricks is a fast, easy-to-use, and collaborative Apache Spark-based analytics platform optimized for Azure. It provides a unified environment for data engineering, data science, machine learning, and analytics, enabling teams to work collaboratively with data in a secure and scalable manner. Azure Databricks integrates seamlessly with Azure services, facilitating a wide range of analytics and AI solutions.

Key Features of Azure Databricks

Collaborative Workspaces: Offers collaborative notebooks that allow data scientists, data engineers, and business analysts to work together in real-time, sharing insights and models across the team.

Optimized for Azure: Deeply integrated with Azure services like Azure Data Lake Storage, Azure Synapse Analytics, and Azure Cosmos DB, providing a seamless analytics experience.

Performance and Scalability: Built on Apache Spark, it delivers high performance for big data processing and can scale automatically to accommodate workloads of any size.

Machine Learning Support: Includes MLflow, an open-source platform for managing the complete machine learning lifecycle, simplifying model training, tracking, and deployment.

Practical Examples of Azure Databricks

1. Real-Time Stream Processing

- **Scenario**: A logistics company wants to monitor and analyze IoT sensor data from its fleet of trucks in real-time to optimize routes and maintenance schedules.
- **Implementation**: IoT sensor data is ingested through Azure Event Hubs into Azure Databricks. Using Databricks' structured streaming capabilities, the data is processed in real-time to identify patterns, such as increased engine temperature or deviations from planned routes. The insights are then visualized in Power BI and can trigger alerts for immediate action.

2. Advanced Analytics for Customer Insights

- **Scenario**: An e-commerce platform seeks to enhance its recommendation engine by analyzing customer behavior, purchase history, and product interactions.
- **Implementation**: Customer data is stored in Azure Data Lake Storage and processed using Azure Databricks. Collaborative notebooks are utilized by data scientists to develop and refine machine learning models for personalized product recommendations. The models are trained using Databricks' scalable Spark clusters and integrated into the e-commerce platform for real-time recommendations.

3. Genomic Data Analysis

- **Scenario**: A biotech company needs to process and analyze genomic data to accelerate its drug discovery process.
- **Implementation**: Genomic data, stored in Azure Data Lake Storage, is analyzed using Azure Databricks. Data engineers use Databricks to preprocess the data, while data scientists develop algorithms to identify genetic markers associated with specific diseases. The analysis leverages Databricks' ability to handle large-scale data processing and machine learning to uncover potential targets for drug development.

Azure Databricks provides a powerful platform for a wide array of data analytics and AI tasks, from real-time stream processing to advanced analytics and machine learning model development. Its integration with Azure services, combined with the performance of Apache Spark and collaborative features, makes it an essential tool for teams looking to extract deep insights from their data. The examples provided demonstrate just a fraction of Azure Databricks' potential applications, showcasing its versatility and capacity to drive innovation and decision-making through data analytics.

Azure HDInsight:

A fully managed cloud service for open-source analytics frameworks such as Hadoop, Spark, Hive, LLAP, Kafka, and more, making it easier to process and analyze large volumes of data.

Azure HDInsight is a fully-managed cloud service that makes it easier, faster, and more cost-effective to process massive amounts of data. It provides open-source analytics frameworks such as Apache Hadoop, Spark, HBase, Kafka, and Storm, optimized for the cloud. The flexibility of Azure HDInsight enables a wide range of big data analytics and processing scenarios, from ETL (Extract, Transform, Load) tasks to real-time analytics and machine learning applications.

Key Features of Azure HDInsight

Open-Source Frameworks: Offers fully-managed Apache Hadoop clusters and other popular big data frameworks, allowing you to use familiar tools and technologies in a cloud environment.

Scalability and Flexibility: Easily scale your clusters up or down based on your workload requirements, and pay only for what you use.

Integration: Seamlessly integrates with Azure services like Azure Blob Storage and Azure Data Lake Storage, providing a comprehensive data platform solution.

Security and Compliance: Ensures data is protected with enterprise-grade security features, including encryption, access control, and monitoring.

Practical Examples of Azure HDInsight

1. **Real-Time Log Analytics with Apache Kafka and Spark**

- **Scenario**: A web application generates large volumes of log data that need to be analyzed in real-time to monitor user activities and system health.
- **Implementation**: Use Azure HDInsight to create Apache Kafka clusters for ingesting streaming log data. Then, process and analyze these data streams with Apache Spark clusters in HDInsight to identify trends, anomalies, or potential issues in real-time. The processed data can be stored in Azure Data Lake Storage for long-term analysis or visualized using tools like Power BI for immediate insights.

2. **ETL Processing with Apache Hadoop**

- **Scenario**: A company needs to perform ETL operations on large datasets to prepare data for analytics and reporting.
- **Implementation**: Deploy Azure HDInsight with Apache Hadoop to leverage Hadoop's MapReduce programming model for efficient ETL processing. Raw data stored in Azure Blob

Storage or Azure Data Lake Storage can be processed and transformed into structured formats suitable for analysis. The results can be moved to Azure Synapse Analytics for further analysis and reporting.

3. Interactive Data Exploration with Apache Spark

- **Scenario**: Data scientists require a platform for interactive data exploration and machine learning model development.
- **Implementation**: Utilize Azure HDInsight with Apache Spark for its in-memory processing capabilities, which facilitate fast queries and data exploration. Spark's MLlib library supports machine learning model development directly on the cluster. Azure HDInsight's integration with Jupyter notebooks allows data scientists to interactively query data, visualize results, and build predictive models. Results can be stored back in Azure Data Lake Storage or passed to Azure Machine Learning for operationalization.

4. Large-Scale Batch Processing with Apache Hadoop

- **Scenario**: Periodic batch processing of terabytes of data for insights and trend analysis.
- **Implementation**: Implement Azure HDInsight with Apache Hadoop for resilient, distributed computing and storage. Use Hadoop's distributed file system (HDFS) for storage and its powerful MapReduce framework for parallel processing of batch jobs. This setup is ideal for processing large datasets overnight or at scheduled intervals, outputting results to Azure Data Lake Storage for subsequent analysis or reporting in Power BI.

Azure HDInsight provides a flexible, scalable platform for a wide range of big data analytics scenarios, supporting both real-time and batch processing workloads. By leveraging managed clusters of open-source analytics frameworks, organizations can focus on extracting insights and creating value from their data rather than managing infrastructure. The integration with other Azure services enhances HDInsight's capabilities, offering a holistic approach to big data processing and analytics in the cloud. Through the examples provided, it's evident how Azure HDInsight serves as a powerful tool in the modern data analytics toolkit, enabling businesses to tackle complex data challenges at scale.

Azure Services for Artificial Intelligence

Azure Cognitive Services:

A collection of APIs, SDKs, and services available to developers to make their applications more intelligent, engaging, and discoverable. It includes capabilities like vision, speech, language, decision, and web search.

Azure Cognitive Services represents a collection of cloud-based services and APIs that empower developers to incorporate intelligent features into their applications without needing deep knowledge of AI or data science. These services enable applications to see, hear, speak, understand, and even begin to reason. By harnessing the power of Azure Cognitive Services, developers can create more engaging and intelligent solutions across a wide range of domains, including web and mobile applications, IoT devices, and beyond.

Key Capabilities of Azure Cognitive Services

Vision: Services such as Computer Vision and Custom Vision allow applications to interpret the content of images and videos. Features include image classification, facial recognition, and object detection.

Speech: Services like Speech to Text, Text to Speech, and Speaker Recognition enable applications to convert spoken language into text, synthesize text into speech, and identify speakers from their voice.

Language: Text Analytics, Language Understanding (LUIS), and Translator Text provide capabilities for applications to process and analyze text, understand user intents, and translate text between languages.

Decision: Services such as Personalizer and Anomaly Detector help applications make intelligent decisions, personalize user experiences, and identify unusual patterns or anomalies.

Practical Examples of Azure Cognitive Services

1. Enhancing Customer Support with Chatbots

- **Scenario**: A company wants to improve its customer support by implementing an intelligent chatbot that can handle common inquiries and escalate more complex issues to human agents.
- **Implementation**: Use the Azure Bot Service in conjunction with the Language Understanding (LUIS) service to build and deploy an intelligent chatbot. LUIS enables the chatbot to understand user queries in natural language, providing relevant responses or actions. The bot can be integrated into websites, apps, and messaging platforms like Microsoft Teams or Slack.

2. Content Moderation for User-Generated Content

- **Scenario**: A social media platform needs to automatically moderate user-generated content, filtering out inappropriate images, videos, or text.
- **Implementation**: Utilize the Content Moderator service to scan images, videos, and text submitted by users. The service can detect adult or racy content, potentially offensive language, and even check text against a custom list of banned terms. Content that fails moderation can be flagged for review or automatically blocked from posting.

3. Multilingual Support for Global Applications

- **Scenario**: An e-commerce website seeks to provide product descriptions and support in multiple languages to serve a global customer base.
- **Implementation**: Implement the Translator Text API to dynamically translate product descriptions, reviews, and support content into multiple languages. This enables customers to interact with the website in their preferred language, enhancing the user experience and broadening the website's reach.

4. Personalized Recommendations

- **Scenario**: An online streaming service wants to provide personalized content recommendations to its users based on their viewing history and preferences.
- **Implementation**: Use the Personalizer service to rank and suggest content to users. Personalizer learns from user interactions and feedback to continuously improve the relevance of its recommendations, encouraging higher engagement and satisfaction.

Azure Cognitive Services democratizes artificial intelligence, making it accessible to developers of all skill levels to add AI capabilities to their applications. Through a simple API call, applications can harness powerful AI features, enhancing user experiences and enabling smarter, more context-aware interactions. The examples provided showcase the breadth of possibilities with Cognitive Services, from improving customer support with intelligent chatbots to personalizing user experiences with dynamic content recommendations. As these services continue to evolve, the potential for creating innovative and intelligent solutions in Azure becomes virtually limitless.

Azure Machine Learning:

A fully managed cloud service that enables you to easily build, deploy, and share predictive analytics solutions. It offers a studio that provides a drag-and-drop interface to create machine learning workflows.

Azure Machine Learning (Azure ML) is a cloud-based service that allows data scientists, developers, and researchers to efficiently build, train, and deploy machine learning (ML) models. Offering a wide range of tools and capabilities, Azure ML accelerates the process of turning data into actionable insights and predictive models.

Core Features of Azure Machine Learning:

Automated Machine Learning (AutoML): Automatically identifies the best ML models from a range of algorithms based on the provided dataset, significantly reducing the time and expertise required to develop models.

ML Pipelines: Facilitates the creation and management of end-to-end ML workflows, enabling scalable and reproducible model training and deployment processes.

Integrated Development Environment (IDE): Supports ML model development in familiar environments like Jupyter notebooks, Visual Studio Code, or the Azure Machine Learning studio for drag-and-drop experiment creation.

Model Deployment and Management: Provides tools for deploying ML models as web services in the cloud, on-premises, or at the edge, complete with monitoring and version control for models in production.

Examples of Implementing Azure Machine Learning

1. Predictive Maintenance for Manufacturing Equipment

- **Scenario**: A manufacturing company seeks to leverage historical sensor data to predict equipment failures, reducing downtime and maintenance costs.
- **Implementation**: Use Azure ML's AutoML feature to automatically select the best performing model based on the historical sensor data. Create ML pipelines to preprocess data, train the selected model, and evaluate its performance. Once satisfied, deploy the model as a web service using Azure ML for real-time

inference, allowing the system to predict potential equipment failures and alert maintenance teams proactively.

2. Customer Churn Prediction for Subscription Services

- **Scenario**: A subscription-based service wants to identify customers at risk of churning, enabling targeted interventions to improve retention.
- **Implementation**: Data scientists use Azure ML to develop and train a classification model on customer usage data, demographics, and subscription history to predict churn likelihood. The model is then deployed as a web service, which the customer service team integrates into their CRM system to receive real-time predictions and implement retention strategies for at-risk customers.

3. Real-time Fraud Detection in Financial Transactions

- **Scenario**: A financial institution aims to enhance its fraud detection system by incorporating machine learning to identify fraudulent transactions as they occur.
- **Implementation**: Leveraging Azure ML, develop an anomaly detection model using historical transaction data. Deploy this model using Azure ML's real-time inferencing capabilities, allowing the system to analyze transactions in real-time and flag potential fraud for review. ML pipelines automate the retraining of the model with new transaction data, ensuring the model adapts to evolving fraud patterns.

4. Personalized Recommendations in Retail

- **Scenario**: An online retailer wants to offer personalized product recommendations to customers based on their browsing and purchase history.
- **Implementation**: Utilize Azure ML to build a recommendation system using collaborative filtering or content-based filtering techniques. Train the model with user interaction data and product information, then deploy it as a web service. Integrate the recommendation service with the retailer's website to dynamically generate personalized product recommendations for each customer, enhancing the shopping experience and increasing sales.

Azure Machine Learning democratizes the creation and deployment of machine learning models, offering a comprehensive platform that spans from data preparation to model deployment and management. Through its intuitive tools and scalable infrastructure, Azure ML empowers organizations to harness the power of AI, transforming data into predictive insights that drive decision-making and innovation. The examples provided illustrate the versatility of Azure ML in addressing real-world challenges across industries, showcasing its potential to revolutionize how businesses leverage data and machine learning.

Practical Examples

1. Sentiment Analysis with Azure Cognitive Services

- **Scenario**: A company wants to analyze customer feedback from social media in real-time to gauge sentiment trends.
- **Implementation**: Use the Text Analytics API from Azure Cognitive Services to assess sentiment. Data can be ingested using Azure Event Hubs, processed and analyzed for sentiment, and then stored in Azure Cosmos DB or visualized in a Power BI dashboard.

2. Real-time Data Analytics with Azure Synapse Analytics

- **Scenario**: An e-commerce platform requires real-time analytics on sales data to adjust marketing strategies swiftly.
- **Implementation**: Stream sales data using Azure Event Hubs into Azure Synapse Analytics. Use Synapse SQL pool to query data in real-time and generate insights, which can then drive dynamic content on the e-commerce platform or trigger marketing actions.

3. Predictive Maintenance with Azure Machine Learning

- **Scenario**: A manufacturing company wants to predict when equipment will fail so maintenance can be performed just in time to prevent unplanned downtime.
- **Implementation**: Collect sensor data from equipment and store it in Azure Data Lake Storage. Use Azure Databricks to pre-process the data, then build and train machine learning models with Azure Machine Learning. Deploy the model as a web service and integrate it with the company's maintenance scheduling system to predict and notify when maintenance is required.

4. Real-time Fraud Detection

- **Scenario**: A financial institution needs to detect fraudulent transactions in real-time to prevent financial losses.
- **Implementation**: Transactions are streamed through Azure Event Hubs. Azure Databricks processes the transactions and uses a machine learning model hosted on Azure Machine Learning to score transactions for fraud likelihood. Alerts for potentially fraudulent transactions are then pushed to an operations dashboard or directly to a case management system.

Leveraging Azure Data Lake and Data Factory:

In the realm of Azure's data analytics and AI services, Azure Data Lake and Azure Data Factory play pivotal roles in storing vast amounts of data and orchestrating data movement and transformation, respectively. Together, these services provide a robust infrastructure for building scalable data analytics solutions, enabling businesses to extract valuable insights from their data.

Azure Data Lake

Azure Data Lake Storage (ADLS) is a highly scalable and secure data lake that allows for the storage of structured and unstructured data at any scale. It is built on top of Azure Blob Storage, providing a hierarchical file system and fine-grained control over access permissions, making it ideal for big data analytics workloads.

Key Features:

Hierarchical Namespace: Simplifies data management and access by organizing data into a familiar directory structure.

Massive Scalability: Supports petabytes of data, accommodating the storage needs of even the largest datasets.

Integration with Analytics Services: Seamlessly integrates with services like Azure Databricks, Azure HDInsight, and Azure Synapse Analytics for comprehensive data processing and analysis.

Example: Data Lake as a Foundation for Advanced Analytics

A healthcare organization collects vast amounts of patient data, including medical records, sensor data from wearable devices, and genomic data. By storing this data in Azure Data Lake, the organization can use Azure Databricks to run large-scale analytics and machine learning models to predict patient health outcomes, identify effective treatments, and improve patient care.

Azure Data Factory

Azure Data Factory (ADF) is a cloud-based data integration service that allows you to create, schedule, and orchestrate data pipelines for moving and transforming data between different sources and destinations.

Key Features:

Data Integration Pipelines: Create complex ETL (Extract, Transform, Load) processes that can ingest data from various sources, transform it using compute services like Azure HDInsight or Azure Databricks, and load it into a data store for analysis.

Code-free Transformation: Offers a visual interface for building data transformation workflows, simplifying the development process.

Built-in Connectors: Provides a wide range of connectors for popular data sources and destinations, facilitating easy integration.

Example: Automating ETL Workflows for Business Intelligence

A retail company collects sales data across multiple online and offline channels. Using Azure Data Factory, the company creates a data pipeline to ingest sales data from these channels into Azure Data Lake for storage. The pipeline includes data transformation steps implemented using Azure Databricks to clean and normalize the data. Finally, the transformed data is loaded into Azure Synapse Analytics, where it is used to generate real-time business intelligence dashboards and reports.

Leveraging Azure Data Lake and Data Factory Together

Combining Azure Data Lake and Azure Data Factory enables organizations to build a comprehensive data analytics platform. Data Lake provides the scalable storage solution necessary for accumulating vast datasets, while Data Factory orchestrates the movement and transformation of that data, preparing it for analysis.

Integrated Example: Real-time Analytics for IoT Devices

An energy company monitors electricity usage through IoT devices installed in homes. Data from these devices is ingested in real-time into Azure Data Lake using Azure Event Hubs. Azure Data Factory periodically triggers data transformation jobs in Azure Databricks to analyze usage patterns, detect anomalies, and predict peak demand periods. Insights derived from this analysis are then made available to customers through a web application, helping them optimize their energy consumption.

Azure Data Lake and Azure Data Factory are essential components of Azure's data analytics and AI ecosystem, providing the infrastructure needed to store, process, and transform large volumes of data. By leveraging these services, organizations can implement sophisticated data analytics solutions that drive decision-making and create value from their data assets. The examples provided illustrate the versatility and power of Azure Data Lake and Azure Data Factory in supporting diverse analytics and AI applications.

Building AI Solutions with Azure Machine Learning:

Azure offers a rich ecosystem for developing artificial intelligence (AI) solutions, notably through Azure Machine Learning and Azure Cognitive Services. These services provide a comprehensive platform for data scientists and developers to build, train, and deploy AI models and incorporate intelligent features into applications with minimal effort. Azure Machine Learning empowers users to create custom machine learning models tailored to specific needs, while Azure Cognitive Services offers pre-built models for common AI tasks like vision, speech, language, and decision-making.

Azure Machine Learning

Azure Machine Learning is a cloud-based service for creating and managing machine learning solutions. It provides tools for every stage of the machine learning lifecycle, including model training, deployment, and management, making it easier for data scientists and developers to bring their AI projects to fruition.

Key Features:

Automated Machine Learning:

Automatically identify the best machine learning algorithms and hyperparameters for your data.

Automated Machine Learning (AutoML) in Azure Machine Learning is a game-changing feature that significantly simplifies the process of building and deploying machine learning models. By automating the selection of algorithms and hyperparameter tuning, AutoML enables data scientists and developers to focus more on problem-solving and less on the time-consuming tasks traditionally associated with model development.

Key Features of Automated Machine Learning

Efficiency and Accessibility: AutoML democratizes machine learning by making model development more accessible to non-experts and more efficient for experienced data scientists.

Algorithm Selection and Hyperparameter Tuning: Automatically identifies the best machine learning algorithms and hyperparameters for your data, reducing the trial-and-error aspect of model development.

Feature Engineering: Provides automatic feature scaling, normalization, and generation of time-series features, among other preprocessing capabilities, to enhance model performance.

Practical Examples of Automated Machine Learning

1. **Customer Churn Prediction**

- **Scenario**: A telecommunications company wants to predict which customers are likely to churn so they can take proactive measures to retain them.
- **Implementation with AutoML:**
  - **Data Preparation**: The company compiles customer data, including demographics, service usage, billing history, and previous churn status.
  - **AutoML Configuration**: Using Azure Machine Learning, the company sets up an AutoML experiment, specifying churn prediction as the target variable and selecting classification as the task type.

- **Model Training and Evaluation**: AutoML automatically experiments with various algorithms and hyperparameters, training multiple models and evaluating their performance. The best-performing model is identified based on accuracy, F1 score, or another relevant metric.
- **Deployment**: The selected model is deployed as a web service in Azure, enabling real-time predictions and integration with the company's customer relationship management (CRM) system.

2. Sales Forecasting for Retail Inventory Management

- **Scenario**: A retail chain seeks to improve inventory management by forecasting future sales at the product and store levels.
- **Implementation with AutoML**:
  - **Data Preparation**: Historical sales data, including product features, store information, promotions, and external factors like holidays, are gathered.
  - **AutoML Configuration**: In Azure Machine Learning, an AutoML experiment is created with sales forecasting as the objective. The task is defined as time-series forecasting to account for temporal dependencies.
  - **Model Training and Evaluation**: AutoML explores various time-series forecasting models, automatically engineering features like lag values and rolling windows. The best model is selected based on metrics like root mean squared error (RMSE).
  - **Deployment**: The model is deployed to Azure Kubernetes Service (AKS) for scalable, real-time forecasting, assisting in inventory decisions across the retail chain.

Automated Machine Learning in Azure Machine Learning revolutionizes how organizations approach machine learning model development. By automating critical steps in the model-building process, AutoML not only accelerates the development cycle but also enables the creation of more accurate and efficient models. Whether predicting customer churn, forecasting sales, or tackling other predictive challenges, AutoML provides a powerful toolset that democratizes machine learning, making advanced analytics accessible to a broader range of professionals. The examples highlighted demonstrate the practical application and benefits of leveraging AutoML within Azure's AI ecosystem.

ML Pipelines:

Create reproducible workflows for training and deploying models.

Machine Learning (ML) Pipelines in Azure Machine Learning represent a critical advancement in structuring and automating the workflows involved in the data science lifecycle. By defining a series of interconnected steps that cover data preparation, model training, model evaluation, and deployment, ML pipelines facilitate the creation, management, and reuse of robust machine learning workflows. These pipelines not only enhance productivity and collaboration among data science teams but also ensure that machine learning processes are reproducible and scalable.

Key Features of ML Pipelines

Reusability and Modularity: Pipelines allow data scientists to break down the machine learning process into discrete, reusable components, promoting modularity and simplification of complex workflows.

Automated Workflows: Automate the entire data science workflow, from data preprocessing and feature engineering to model training and evaluation, streamlining the model development process.

Scalability: Easily scale out computational resources to handle large datasets and complex computations, leveraging Azure's cloud infrastructure.

Version Control and Experiment Tracking: Maintain version control of data, models, and pipeline definitions, and track experiments to improve model accuracy and performance over time.

Practical Examples of ML Pipelines

1. Automated Data Preprocessing and Model Training Pipeline

- **Scenario**: A financial institution wants to automate the preprocessing of loan application data and the training of a model to predict loan default risk.
- **Implementation**:
    - **Data Ingestion Step**: The first step in the pipeline ingests raw loan application data from Azure Data Lake Storage.
    - **Data Preprocessing Step**: This step cleans the data, handles missing values, and encodes categorical variables. The processed data is stored in an intermediate location for use in subsequent steps.
    - **Model Training Step**: The clean data feeds into a model training step, where multiple classification algorithms are evaluated using Azure Machine Learning's AutoML feature.
    - **Model Evaluation Step**: A final step evaluates the trained models against a validation dataset, selecting the model with the best performance based on predefined metrics.

The pipeline is defined and executed within Azure Machine Learning, and once the process is automated, it can be triggered on a schedule or in response to data updates.

2. Continuous Model Retraining and Deployment Pipeline

- **Scenario**: An e-commerce company aims to maintain a high-performing product recommendation model by continuously retraining it with new user interaction data.

- **Implementation:**
  - **Data Collection Step:** Periodically collect new user interaction data from the company's website and store it in Azure Blob Storage.
  - **Model Retraining Step:** Use a pipeline that automatically retrains the recommendation model with the new data on a weekly basis. The pipeline preprocesses the new data, combines it with historical data, and re-trains the model using Azure Machine Learning.
  - **Model Evaluation and Deployment Step:** After training, the model's performance is evaluated. If the new model outperforms the current production model based on specific metrics, the pipeline automatically deploys the updated model to Azure Kubernetes Service (AKS) for serving recommendations.

This pipeline ensures that the recommendation model adapts to changing user preferences and behaviors over time, maintaining its relevance and accuracy.

ML Pipelines in Azure Machine Learning significantly streamline the process of developing, deploying, and managing machine learning models. By encapsulating the data science workflow into a series of definable, scalable, and reusable steps, ML pipelines facilitate more efficient experimentation, collaboration, and operationalization of machine learning models. The examples provided illustrate the power of ML pipelines in automating data preprocessing, model training, evaluation, and deployment tasks, showcasing their potential to enhance productivity and model performance in various AI-driven applications.Top of Form

Model Deployment and Management:

Deploy models as web services on Azure Container Instances, Azure Kubernetes Service, or IoT Edge devices, and monitor their performance and health.

Model deployment and management are crucial stages in the machine learning lifecycle, marking the transition from development to production. Azure Machine Learning and Azure Cognitive Services provide robust capabilities for deploying machine learning models as scalable and secure web services or to edge devices, and for managing these models throughout their lifecycle.

Model Deployment in Azure

Deployment in Azure involves packaging your machine learning model into a container, such as a Docker container, and then deploying that container to a cloud service where it can be consumed as a web service. Azure supports various deployment targets, including Azure Container Instances (ACI), Azure Kubernetes Service (AKS), and Azure IoT Edge, among others, offering flexibility based on your needs for scalability, management, and edge computing.

Web Service Deployment: Models can be deployed as RESTful web services to ACI for low-scale, CPU-based workloads or to AKS for high-scale production workloads requiring autoscaling, fast response times, and GPU support.

Edge Deployment: Azure Machine Learning also supports deploying models to edge devices using Azure IoT Edge, enabling low-latency predictions and offline scenarios.

Model Management in Azure

Once a model is deployed, Azure Machine Learning provides tools for monitoring its performance, collecting data on predictions, and managing model versions. Model management is essential for maintaining the reliability and accuracy of your AI solutions over time.

Model Monitoring and Data Collection: Azure Machine Learning allows you to monitor the health and performance of your deployed models and collect data on predictions made by the model.

Model Versioning: Azure Machine Learning supports versioning of models, enabling you to track and manage different versions of your models over time.

Continuous Integration and Deployment (CI/CD): Azure DevOps integration enables automated model retraining and deployment workflows, facilitating continuous improvement of models based on new data.

Practical Examples

1. Deploying a Predictive Maintenance Model to AKS

- **Scenario**: A manufacturing company has developed a machine learning model to predict when equipment will require maintenance. The model needs to be deployed to handle a high volume of requests from various manufacturing sites.
- **Implementation**:
    - The model is registered in Azure Machine Learning, with each iteration versioned for tracking.
    - A Docker image is created containing the model and scoring script.
    - The image is deployed to Azure Kubernetes Service (AKS) for high availability and autoscaling. An endpoint is created for applications to consume the model.
    - Azure Application Insights is enabled for monitoring the performance and usage of the model.

2. Edge Deployment of an Anomaly Detection Model

- **Scenario**: An energy company wants to deploy an anomaly detection model to wind turbines to identify potential failures in real-time, even in locations with intermittent internet connectivity.
- **Implementation**:
    - The anomaly detection model is trained and registered in Azure Machine Learning.
    - The model is packaged into a Docker container optimized for edge computing.

- ○ Using Azure IoT Edge, the model is deployed to edge devices located on the wind turbines, allowing for real-time data processing and anomaly detection on the device.
- ○ Predictions and telemetry are synced to the cloud when connectivity is available, and model updates can be pushed to the edge devices remotely.

Deploying and managing machine learning models in Azure using Azure Machine Learning and Cognitive Services provides a comprehensive framework for bringing AI solutions to production. By leveraging Azure's deployment targets and management tools, organizations can ensure their models are scalable, secure, and maintained efficiently. The examples provided illustrate the flexibility and power of Azure in supporting both cloud and edge AI scenarios, enabling businesses to deploy intelligent solutions that drive value and innovation.

Example: Predictive Maintenance for Manufacturing Equipment

A manufacturing company wants to predict when equipment might fail to schedule maintenance proactively. Using Azure Machine Learning, they build a predictive model using historical sensor data from the equipment. The model is trained to identify patterns that precede failures and is deployed as a web service. The company then integrates this service with their operational systems to receive maintenance alerts, reducing downtime and maintenance costs.

Azure Cognitive Services

Azure Cognitive Services provides a suite of pre-built AI models that developers can use to add intelligent features to applications without deep AI expertise. These services cover a wide range of AI capabilities, enabling applications to see, hear, speak, understand, and interpret user needs through natural methods of communication.

Key Features:

Vision APIs:

Analyze content in images and videos for scenarios like facial recognition, object detection, and optical character recognition (OCR).

Azure Cognitive Services offers a suite of Vision APIs designed to enable applications to interpret the world visually, just as humans do. These APIs harness advanced machine learning models to analyze images and videos for various purposes, including identifying objects, detecting faces, recognizing text, and more. By integrating Vision APIs into applications, developers can create more interactive and intelligent solutions without the need for extensive machine learning expertise.

Capabilities of Vision APIs

Computer Vision: Analyzes content in images and videos to provide information about visual features and objects. It can extract metadata, identify objects, generate captions, and recognize printed and handwritten text.

Face API: Detects human faces in images and provides attributes such as emotion, age, gender, and facial landmarks. It also supports face verification, identification, and grouping.

Custom Vision: Allows you to build and train custom image classification and object detection models tailored to your specific needs, using your own labeled images.

Form Recognizer: Extracts text, key/value pairs, and tables from documents, forms, and receipts, turning them into usable data.

Practical Examples of Vision APIs

1. Retail Inventory Management with Custom Vision

- **Scenario**: A retail company wants to automate inventory management by identifying products on shelves using CCTV camera feeds.
- **Implementation**:
    - The company trains a Custom Vision model with images of their products on shelves, labeled by product type and location.

- The trained model is deployed as an endpoint and integrated with their inventory management system.
- CCTV camera feeds are analyzed in near real-time using the Custom Vision model to detect products on shelves. The inventory management system is updated accordingly, providing insights into stock levels, product placement, and restocking needs.

2. Automated Document Processing with Form Recognizer

- **Scenario**: A financial institution processes thousands of loan applications monthly, requiring significant manual effort to extract data from various forms.
- **Implementation**:
  - The institution uses Form Recognizer to automate the extraction of data from loan application forms.
  - Loan application forms are scanned, and the images are submitted to the Form Recognizer API.
  - Form Recognizer extracts data fields such as applicant name, income, loan amount, and more, converting them into structured data.
  - The structured data is then automatically fed into the loan processing system, streamlining the application review process.

3. Enhancing Social Media Platforms with Computer Vision

- **Scenario**: A social media platform wants to enhance user engagement by automatically generating captions for user-uploaded images.
- **Implementation**:
  - The platform integrates the Computer Vision API to analyze images uploaded by users.

- For each image, the Computer Vision API generates a description or caption based on the content identified in the image.
- The generated captions are presented to users as suggestions when they upload images, enriching the content creation process and enhancing user engagement.

4. Security Enhancement with Face API

- **Scenario**: An organization seeks to enhance security at its facilities by implementing facial recognition-based access control.
- **Implementation**:
  - Security cameras at entry points are connected to a system that uses the Face API to recognize individuals' faces.
  - The Face API is trained with images of employees and authorized visitors, enabling it to verify identities in real-time.
  - When an individual approaches an entry point, the Face API checks their face against the trained model. Access is granted if a match is found, ensuring that only authorized individuals can enter secure areas.

Azure Cognitive Services' Vision APIs provide powerful tools for incorporating visual understanding into applications, making it possible to process and analyze images and videos in sophisticated ways. By leveraging these pre-built models, developers can add rich functionality to their applications, from automating inventory management and document processing to enhancing user experiences on social media platforms and improving security systems. The examples highlighted demonstrate the breadth of possibilities enabled by Vision APIs, showcasing how they can be applied to solve real-world challenges across various industries.

Speech APIs:

Convert speech to text, synthesize text to speech, and identify speakers.

Azure Cognitive Services' Speech APIs empower applications with sophisticated speech capabilities, enabling them to understand and generate spoken language. These APIs leverage advanced neural network models to provide a wide range of speech services, including speech to text, text to speech, speech translation, and speaker recognition. By integrating Speech APIs into applications, developers can create more natural, intuitive user interfaces and enhance accessibility.

Capabilities of Speech APIs

Speech to Text: Converts spoken language into text in real-time, supporting various languages and dialects. It can be used for voice commands, speech transcription, and more.

Text to Speech: Synthesizes natural-sounding speech from text using neural voice technologies, offering a range of voices and languages.

Speech Translation: Provides real-time speech translation, enabling spoken language to be translated and output as synthesized speech or text.

Speaker Recognition: Identifies and verifies individual speakers based on their voice characteristics, supporting use cases like personalized user experiences and voice-based authentication.

Practical Examples of Speech APIs

1. Voice-Enabled Customer Service Bot

- **Scenario**: A company wants to enhance its customer service experience by introducing a voice-enabled virtual assistant that can understand customer inquiries and provide spoken responses.
- **Implementation**:
    - The virtual assistant uses the Speech to Text API to transcribe customer queries spoken into a phone or computer microphone.
    - The transcribed text is processed to understand the customer's intent, and an appropriate response is generated.

○ The Text to Speech API is then used to convert the response into natural-sounding speech, providing customers with a conversational and interactive experience.

2. Real-Time Meeting Transcription and Translation

- **Scenario**: An international organization conducts meetings with participants who speak different languages and requires real-time transcription and translation to ensure effective communication.
- **Implementation**:
  - ○ During the meeting, participants' speech is captured and sent to the Speech to Text API for transcription.
  - ○ The transcribed text is processed by the Speech Translation API to translate the content into multiple languages simultaneously.
  - ○ The translated text can be displayed as subtitles in real-time, or the synthesized speech in the target language can be played back to participants, facilitating seamless multilingual communication.

3. Accessible Educational Content Creation

- **Scenario**: An educational platform aims to make its online courses more accessible by providing audio versions of text-based content for students with visual impairments or those who prefer auditory learning.
- **Implementation**:
  - ○ Course materials, including lecture notes and reading assignments, are converted into speech using the Text to Speech API, producing natural-sounding audio files.

- A selection of neural voices ensures that the synthesized speech is engaging and easy to listen to, enhancing the learning experience for students.

4. Secure Authentication with Speaker Recognition

- **Scenario**: A financial services app wants to implement an additional layer of security for user authentication by recognizing individuals based on their voice.
- **Implementation**:
  - During the account setup, users are prompted to enroll their voice by recording specific phrases, which are processed by the Speaker Recognition API to create a voice signature.
  - For subsequent logins or sensitive transactions, users verify their identity by speaking into their device's microphone. The Speaker Recognition API compares the spoken audio against the enrolled voice signature, granting access only if a match is confirmed.

Azure Cognitive Services' Speech APIs offer powerful tools for incorporating speech capabilities into applications, making interactions more natural and accessible. From voice-enabled customer service bots and real-time transcription services to creating accessible educational content and implementing voice-based authentication, the Speech APIs enable a wide array of use cases across different domains. The examples provided showcase the versatility of Speech APIs in enhancing application functionality and user experience, demonstrating their potential to transform how we interact with technology.

Language APIs:

Understand sentiment, extract key phrases, detect language, and translate text.

Azure Cognitive Services' Language APIs offer a suite of machine learning and AI capabilities designed to understand, interpret, and generate human language. These APIs enable applications to process natural language, analyze sentiments, extract key phrases, translate text across languages, and more, making them invaluable tools for creating intelligent, user-centric solutions.

Capabilities of Language APIs

Text Analytics: Provides features such as sentiment analysis, key phrase extraction, named entity recognition, and language detection to understand the context and meaning of text.

Translator Text: Offers real-time text translation capabilities, supporting over 60 languages, enabling the development of applications that can communicate across language barriers.

Language Understanding (LUIS): Allows for the creation of custom natural language understanding models that can interpret user intentions from text inputs, facilitating the development of conversational AI applications.

QnA Maker: Enables the creation of a knowledge base from your content, which can then be used to answer user questions in a natural, conversational manner.

Practical Examples of Language APIs

1. Multilingual Customer Support Platform

- **Scenario**: A global e-commerce company wants to offer customer support in multiple languages without hiring language-specific support teams.
- **Implementation**:
  - Customer queries submitted via the company's support portal are first analyzed by the Text Analytics API to detect the language.
  - Queries are then translated into English using the Translator Text API for internal processing and response drafting.

- Responses drafted in English are translated back into the customer's language using the Translator Text API before being sent, ensuring clear and effective communication.

2. Social Media Sentiment Analysis Dashboard

- **Scenario**: A brand wishes to monitor social media for mentions and understand public sentiment toward its products in real-time.
- **Implementation**:
  - Social media posts mentioning the brand are collected and processed using the Text Analytics API to analyze sentiment and extract key phrases.
  - The analyzed data is visualized on a dashboard, showing positive, neutral, and negative sentiment trends, as well as commonly mentioned aspects of the products, helping the marketing team to gauge public perception and react accordingly.

3. Conversational Bot for Booking Appointments

- **Scenario**: A healthcare provider wants to streamline the appointment booking process by allowing patients to book appointments through a conversational interface.
- **Implementation**:
  - The provider uses the Language Understanding (LUIS) service to develop a model that can understand patient intentions from natural language inputs, such as "I need a doctor's appointment next Tuesday."
  - A chatbot, integrated with LUIS, interprets user queries to identify the intent (booking an appointment) and entities (date and time).

- The chatbot responds conversationally to guide the user through the booking process or provide information, improving accessibility and user experience.

4. Knowledge Base for Customer Self-Service

- **Scenario**: A software company wants to improve its customer service by providing users with a self-service portal where they can find answers to common questions.
- **Implementation**:
    - The company uses QnA Maker to create a knowledge base from their existing documentation, FAQs, and support forums.
    - Users input their questions into the self-service portal, and QnA Maker processes these questions to return the most relevant answers, enabling users to find solutions quickly without direct support intervention.

Azure Cognitive Services' Language APIs equip developers with sophisticated tools to build applications that can understand, interpret, and interact with users in natural language, bridging communication gaps and enhancing user experiences. Whether it's through sentiment analysis, language translation, natural language understanding, or question answering, these APIs offer diverse capabilities to address a wide range of language-related challenges in application development. The examples provided showcase the potential of Language APIs to revolutionize how applications engage with users, making them more accessible, informative, and engaging.

Decision APIs:

Personalize user experiences and detect anomalies in data.

Azure Cognitive Services' Decision APIs provide a suite of capabilities designed to help applications make smarter decisions, automate content moderation, personalize user experiences, and detect anomalies. These APIs use advanced machine learning algorithms to process and analyze data, supporting decision-making processes with greater accuracy and efficiency.

Capabilities of Decision APIs

Personalizer: Leverages reinforcement learning to provide personalized content and recommendations to users based on their past interactions and preferences.

Content Moderator: Helps automate the process of checking text, images, and videos for potentially offensive, undesirable, or risky content, making it easier to maintain community standards and comply with regulations.

Anomaly Detector: Enables applications to detect unusual patterns or rare events in data that could indicate issues, fraud, or other significant concerns.

Practical Examples of Decision APIs

1. Personalized News Feed with Personalizer

- **Scenario**: An online news portal wants to increase user engagement by tailoring the news feed to individual user preferences and behaviors.
- **Implementation**:
    - The portal integrates the Personalizer API to rank news articles based on the likelihood of a user's interest. It considers user interaction history, such as articles read, liked, or shared, as well as contextual information like time of day or device type.
    - As users interact with the personalized news feed, feedback is sent back to the Personalizer API, continuously improving the personalization model.
    - Users receive a dynamically generated news feed that aligns with their interests, increasing engagement and time spent on the portal.

2. Moderating User-Generated Content with Content Moderator

- **Scenario**: A social media platform seeks to automatically moderate user-generated content to prevent the spread of inappropriate or harmful material.
- **Implementation**:
  - The platform uses the Content Moderator API to scan images, text, and videos uploaded by users for explicit content, hate speech, and other policy violations.
  - Content identified as potentially violating community guidelines is flagged for review by human moderators or automatically removed, depending on the confidence level of the assessment.
  - This automated moderation process helps maintain a safe and welcoming environment for the community while reducing the burden on human moderators.

3. Real-Time Fraud Detection with Anomaly Detector

- **Scenario**: A financial services company aims to enhance its fraud detection system by identifying unusual transaction patterns that may indicate fraudulent activity.
- **Implementation**:
  - Transaction data is continuously analyzed using the Anomaly Detector API, which looks for deviations from normal patterns, such as unusually large transactions, rapid succession of transactions, or transactions in atypical locations.
  - When the Anomaly Detector API identifies a potential anomaly, an alert is generated, triggering further investigation or automatic blocking of suspicious transactions.

- This real-time detection system helps protect customers from fraud while minimizing false positives that could disrupt legitimate transactions.

Azure Cognitive Services' Decision APIs empower applications to make informed decisions, automate content moderation, personalize experiences, and detect anomalies with ease. By leveraging advanced machine learning models, these APIs enhance the intelligence of applications, making them more responsive to user needs and capable of identifying and reacting to significant events. The examples provided demonstrate the versatility of Decision APIs in addressing diverse challenges across various industries, showcasing their potential to transform how applications interact with users and data. Whether optimizing user experiences, maintaining community standards, or safeguarding against fraud, Azure's Decision APIs offer powerful tools for building more intelligent, autonomous solutions.

Example: Enhancing Customer Service with a Virtual Agent

A retail company implements a virtual agent to handle customer inquiries. The agent uses the Language Understanding (LUIS) service from Azure Cognitive Services to understand customer intents expressed in natural language. It also utilizes the Text Analytics API to determine sentiment, helping to prioritize and tailor responses to customer mood. This virtual agent is integrated into the company's website and mobile app, providing 24/7 customer support and freeing human agents to focus on more complex queries.

Combining Azure Machine Learning and Cognitive Services

Integrating custom models from Azure Machine Learning with pre-built models from Azure Cognitive Services can address a broader spectrum of AI scenarios, combining the flexibility of custom solutions with the convenience of ready-made models.

Integrated Example: Real-Time Social Media Monitoring

A marketing firm develops a solution to monitor and analyze social media posts about their clients in real-time. They use Azure Machine

Learning to train custom sentiment analysis models that understand industry-specific jargon and contexts. This custom model is combined with the pre-built text analytics and language detection models from Azure Cognitive Services to process posts across different languages and platforms. Insights extracted from this analysis help their clients to gauge public sentiment, identify trends, and respond to customer feedback promptly.

Azure Machine Learning and Azure Cognitive Services together provide a robust framework for building AI solutions, from custom model development to integrating intelligent capabilities into applications. Whether you're predicting future trends with machine learning or enhancing applications with pre-built AI models, Azure's AI services offer the tools and scalability to meet a wide array of business needs. The examples provided illustrate just a few of the many possibilities for leveraging Azure to create impactful AI solutions.

Conclusion

Data analytics and AI in Azure provide powerful capabilities to process, analyze, and extract meaningful insights from vast amounts of data, as well as to create intelligent applications that enhance business processes and customer experiences. By leveraging Azure's comprehensive data analytics and AI services, organizations can unlock new opportunities, drive innovation, and maintain competitive advantage in today's data-driven world. The examples provided illustrate just a fraction of the possibilities, demonstrating how Azure can be utilized to address real-world challenges through data analytics and artificial intelligence.

14

Chapter 10: Case Studies of Azure in Action

Part IV: Real-World Scenarios and Case Studies

Azure's comprehensive suite of services for data analytics and AI has been pivotal in transforming various industries by providing scalable, efficient, and innovative solutions. These technologies have been leveraged in numerous real-world applications, demonstrating Azure's versatility and power.

Healthcare: Personalized Patient Care

Scenario: A leading healthcare provider sought to improve patient outcomes through personalized care plans. The challenge was to analyze vast amounts of patient data, including medical records, lab results, and wearable device data, to identify tailored treatment options.

Solution: The healthcare provider used Azure Databricks for big data analytics, processing the patient data to identify patterns and insights. Azure Machine Learning was then employed to develop predictive models that could forecast patient risks and recommend personalized care plans. By integrating these insights into their patient management system, the provider was able to offer customized care plans that led to improved patient outcomes and satisfaction.

Outcome: Enhanced patient care through personalized treatment plans, leading to better health outcomes and increased patient engagement.

Retail: Optimizing Inventory Management

Scenario: A global retail chain faced challenges in managing inventory levels across its vast network of stores, leading to stockouts and overstock situations that affected sales and operational efficiency.

Solution: The retailer implemented Azure Synapse Analytics to aggregate and analyze sales, inventory, and supply chain data across all stores in real time. Azure Machine Learning was used to develop forecasting models that predicted inventory demand more accurately. The insights generated allowed the retailer to optimize inventory levels, reducing stockouts and overstock.

Outcome: Improved inventory management, resulting in increased sales, reduced operational costs, and enhanced customer satisfaction.

Financial Services: Fraud Detection

Scenario: A financial institution needed to enhance its fraud detection capabilities to protect its customers from fraudulent transactions without introducing friction to the customer experience.

Solution: Azure Cognitive Services and Azure Machine Learning were deployed to develop an advanced fraud detection system. The system used real-time analytics and machine learning models to score transactions based on the likelihood of fraud. High-risk transactions were flagged for review, while maintaining a seamless experience for legitimate transactions.

Outcome: Significant reduction in fraudulent transactions, enhanced security for customers, and maintained user experience without unnecessary friction.

Manufacturing: Predictive Maintenance

Scenario: A manufacturing company aimed to reduce downtime and maintenance costs by predicting equipment failures before they occurred.

Solution: The company leveraged Azure IoT Hub to collect real-time data from sensors on their equipment. Azure Databricks processed the sensor data, and predictive models built with Azure Machine Learning analyzed the data to predict equipment failures. Alerts were generated for proactive maintenance actions.

Outcome: Decreased equipment downtime, reduced maintenance costs, and increased operational efficiency through predictive maintenance.

Energy: Optimizing Renewable Energy Production

Scenario: An energy company wanted to optimize the performance of its renewable energy sources, particularly wind farms, to maximize energy production and reduce waste.

Solution: The company used Azure HDInsight to process and analyze weather data, sensor data from wind turbines, and historical energy production data. Azure Machine Learning models predicted energy production levels based on weather conditions and turbine status, enabling the company to adjust operations for optimal energy production.

Outcome: Increased efficiency and output of renewable energy sources, contributing to sustainability goals and operational cost savings.

Case Study 1: Migrating Legacy Systems to Azure:

The migration of legacy systems to cloud platforms like Azure represents a significant step for organizations seeking to modernize their infrastructure, improve efficiency, and leverage advanced data analytics and AI capabilities. This case study focuses on a financial institution that embarked on a journey to migrate its legacy banking system to Azure, highlighting the challenges, solutions, and outcomes of this transformation.

Background

A mid-sized financial institution, facing operational inefficiencies, security vulnerabilities, and escalating costs associated with its aging on-premises legacy banking system, decided to migrate to Azure. The primary goals were to enhance operational efficiency, improve customer experience, and leverage Azure's analytics and AI services for better decision-making.

Challenges

- **Data Migration**: Migrating vast amounts of sensitive financial data securely without disrupting ongoing operations was a major concern.
- **System Complexity**: The legacy system had evolved over decades, resulting in a complex web of interdependent components that were poorly documented.
- **Regulatory Compliance**: As a financial institution, maintaining compliance with industry regulations during and after the migration was paramount.
- **Skill Gaps**: The existing IT team lacked experience with cloud technologies, posing a challenge for the migration and subsequent management of the Azure environment.

Solution

The financial institution approached the migration in phases, starting with a comprehensive assessment of its existing infrastructure, applications, and data.

- **Infrastructure as a Service (IaaS)**: Initial migration efforts focused on lifting and shifting the existing applications and databases to Azure Virtual Machines, ensuring minimal changes to the applications while benefiting from the scalability and security of Azure.
- **Data Modernization**: Critical data was migrated to Azure SQL Database and Azure Data Lake Storage, benefiting from high

availability, built-in security features, and scalability. Azure Data Factory was used to automate data pipelines, ensuring seamless data flows between systems.

- **Application Modernization**: Key components of the banking system were gradually refactored into microservices, leveraging Azure Kubernetes Service (AKS) for orchestration, which improved system flexibility and scalability.

- **Analytics and AI Integration**: With the data securely housed in Azure, the institution utilized Azure Synapse Analytics for real-time business intelligence and Azure Machine Learning for predictive analytics, enhancing decision-making processes.

- **Compliance and Security**: Azure's comprehensive compliance offerings and security features, such as Azure Policy and Azure Security Center, were leveraged to ensure that the migrated system adhered to financial industry regulations.

- **Training and Upskilling**: The institution invested in training programs for its IT staff, facilitated by Microsoft and Azure-certified partners, to bridge skill gaps in cloud technology.

Outcomes

- **Operational Efficiency**: The migration to Azure resulted in significant improvements in system performance, reliability, and scalability, reducing downtime and operational costs.

- **Enhanced Customer Experience**: The modernized banking system offered faster transaction processing, improved online banking services, and personalized customer interactions through AI-driven insights.

- **Innovation and Agility**: With a modern cloud infrastructure, the financial institution could rapidly deploy new features and services, responding more effectively to market demands and competitive pressures.

- **Data-Driven Decision Making**: Leveraging Azure's analytics and AI services, the institution gained deeper insights into customer behavior, operational risks, and market opportunities, informing strategic decisions.

Migrating legacy systems to Azure offers a pathway to digital transformation, enabling organizations to overcome the limitations of outdated infrastructure and embrace the benefits of cloud computing. This case study illustrates how a financial institution successfully navigated the complexities of such a migration, transforming its operations, enhancing customer service, and positioning itself for future growth and innovation. Through careful planning, phased implementation, and a focus on upskilling, organizations can achieve a seamless transition to Azure, unlocking new capabilities and opportunities.

Case Study 2: Building a Scalable E-commerce Platform:

In the rapidly evolving e-commerce sector, scalability and reliability are paramount for meeting fluctuating demands and ensuring a seamless customer experience. This case study explores how an e-commerce company successfully leveraged Azure to build a scalable, resilient, and efficient online shopping platform, capable of adapting to varying loads and providing personalized customer experiences.

Background

A mid-sized e-commerce company, facing growth limitations due to its on-premises infrastructure, sought to migrate to a cloud platform that could scale dynamically in response to traffic spikes, especially during sales events. The company aimed to enhance the shopping experience through personalized recommendations and ensure high availability, even under peak loads.

Solution Overview

The company selected Azure as its cloud platform, leveraging a range of services to construct a scalable, data-driven e-commerce platform.

- **Azure Kubernetes Service (AKS)**: Deployed the e-commerce application on AKS, ensuring scalability and manageability. AKS allowed for automatic scaling of the application based on demand, improving resource utilization and response times.
- **Azure Cosmos DB**: Chosen for its global distribution, horizontal scaling, and low latency capabilities, Azure Cosmos DB served as the database for storing product catalogs and user data, supporting fast, responsive user experiences.
- **Azure Cognitive Services**: Utilized for building personalized product recommendations. The company integrated Azure Cognitive Services to analyze user behavior and preferences, enabling tailored recommendations that enhanced the shopping experience.
- **Azure Search**: Implemented to provide powerful search capabilities within the platform, making it easier for customers to find products through a rich, intuitive search experience.
- **Azure Front Door**: Used to ensure global high availability and content delivery optimization, Azure Front Door routed user requests to the nearest AKS cluster, reducing latency and improving load times.
- **Azure DevOps**: Adopted for CI/CD pipelines, enabling streamlined deployment processes and faster delivery of new features and updates.

Implementation Process

1. **Application Modernization**: The company refactored its monolithic application into microservices, containerized the services, and deployed them on AKS for better scalability and resilience.
2. **Database Migration**: Migrated product catalogs and user profiles to Azure Cosmos DB, leveraging its global distribution to ensure data was close to users, reducing access times.

3. **Personalization Implementation**: Integrated Azure Cognitive Services to analyze user interactions and feedback, developing machine learning models that provided personalized product recommendations.

4. **Search Optimization**: Implemented Azure Search for enhanced search capabilities, incorporating features like faceted search, auto-complete, and synonyms to improve product discovery.

5. **Global Distribution**: Configured Azure Front Door to distribute traffic across AKS clusters in different regions, ensuring the platform remained highly available and responsive worldwide.

6. **DevOps Integration**: Established Azure DevOps pipelines for continuous integration and deployment, automating the build, test, and deployment processes to accelerate feature releases and updates.

Outcomes

The migration to Azure resulted in a scalable, resilient e-commerce platform that could dynamically adapt to changing demands. The use of AKS and Azure Cosmos DB ensured that the platform could handle traffic spikes without degradation in performance. Personalized recommendations powered by Azure Cognitive Services significantly improved customer engagement and sales. Global distribution through Azure Front Door enhanced user experience with reduced latency. Lastly, Azure DevOps facilitated a more agile development process, enabling the company to innovate rapidly.

This case study exemplifies how Azure can transform e-commerce platforms, providing the scalability, performance, and capabilities needed to meet modern consumer expectations. By leveraging Azure's comprehensive suite of services, the company not only optimized its infrastructure for peak performance but also unlocked new opportunities for growth and customer engagement.

Case Study 3: Implementing IoT Solutions with Azure:

The Internet of Things (IoT) has become a transformative force across industries, enabling businesses to gain unprecedented insights into their operations, enhance efficiency, and create new value streams. This case study explores how a manufacturing company leveraged Azure IoT Hub to implement a comprehensive IoT solution, enhancing its operational efficiency and predictive maintenance capabilities.

Background

A manufacturing company specializing in high-precision equipment faced challenges in monitoring the health of its machinery across multiple factories. The goal was to implement an IoT solution that could collect real-time data from various sensors installed on the equipment, analyze this data to predict maintenance needs, and reduce downtime.

Solution Overview

The company chose Azure IoT Hub as the backbone of its IoT solution, capitalizing on its robust features for device management, secure communication, and data ingestion. The solution architecture also incorporated other Azure services for data processing, storage, and analytics.

- **Azure IoT Hub**: Served as the central hub for bi-directional communication between the company's devices and the Azure cloud, ensuring secure, reliable messaging at scale.
- **Azure Stream Analytics**: Processed real-time data streams from IoT Hub, applying analytics to identify patterns indicative of potential equipment failures.
- **Azure Machine Learning**: Used to develop predictive maintenance models. Historical sensor data was analyzed to train models that could predict equipment failures before they occurred.
- **Azure Data Lake Storage**: Stored large volumes of sensor data, providing a scalable data repository for analytics and machine learning.

- **Power BI**: Integrated for visualizing real-time data and predictive analytics, enabling operational teams to monitor equipment health and receive alerts on potential issues.

Implementation Process

1. **Sensor Integration and Device Provisioning**: Sensors were installed on machinery to collect various operational metrics. Each device was registered with Azure IoT Hub, which managed device identities and facilitated secure communication.
2. **Real-Time Data Ingestion and Analysis**: Sensor data was continuously streamed to Azure IoT Hub and then to Azure Stream Analytics. Stream Analytics processed the data in real-time, applying logic to detect anomalies that could indicate equipment issues.
3. **Predictive Maintenance Modeling**: Historical sensor data was used to train predictive maintenance models in Azure Machine Learning. These models analyzed incoming data to predict potential failures, allowing for proactive maintenance scheduling.
4. **Data Storage and Reporting**: Sensor data and analysis outcomes were stored in Azure Data Lake Storage, providing a historical data archive for deeper analytics. Power BI dashboards visualized this data, offering insights into equipment health, operational efficiency, and maintenance needs.
5. **Operational Integration**: Predictive maintenance alerts generated by the solution were integrated into the company's maintenance scheduling system, enabling automated scheduling of maintenance activities based on predictive insights.

Outcomes

The implementation of the Azure IoT solution transformed the company's approach to equipment maintenance and operational monitoring. Key outcomes included:

- **Reduced Equipment Downtime**: Predictive maintenance capabilities allowed the company to address equipment issues before failures occurred, significantly reducing unplanned downtime.
- **Enhanced Operational Efficiency**: Real-time monitoring and analytics enabled more efficient use of machinery, optimizing production schedules and reducing maintenance costs.
- **Data-Driven Decision Making**: The integration of Power BI provided decision-makers with actionable insights into operational performance, supporting informed strategic decisions.

This case study demonstrates the power of Azure IoT Hub and complementary Azure services in enabling effective IoT solutions. By leveraging Azure for IoT, the manufacturing company not only improved its operational efficiency and maintenance processes but also laid the foundation for ongoing innovation and optimization. Through the strategic use of IoT technologies, businesses can transform their operations, uncover new opportunities, and drive significant value.

Conclusion

These case studies illustrate the transformative potential of Azure's data analytics and AI services across various sectors. By leveraging Azure, organizations can harness the power of their data, gain actionable insights, and implement intelligent solutions that drive efficiency, innovation, and competitive advantage. Azure's scalable, flexible, and secure platform continues to be a key enabler of digital transformation, empowering businesses to tackle complex challenges and achieve their strategic objectives.

15

Chapter 11: Preparing for Azure Certifications

Azure certifications are highly regarded in the tech industry, validating skills and knowledge in cloud services ranging from foundational understanding to advanced solutions and architecture. Preparing for these certifications requires a structured approach to learning Azure's vast array of services and capabilities.

Understanding Azure Certification Paths

Azure offers a variety of certification paths to cater to different professional roles, including Azure Fundamentals, Azure Administrator, Azure Developer, Azure Solutions Architect, and more specialized roles like Azure AI Engineer or Azure Data Scientist. Each certification requires passing one or more exams that assess specific Azure-related skills.

Preparation Strategies

Choose the Right Certification: Start by identifying the certification that aligns with your career goals and current skill level. For beginners, the Azure Fundamentals certification (AZ-900) is a recommended starting point.

Leverage Microsoft Learn: Microsoft Learn provides free, interactive learning paths tailored to various Azure certifications. These modules combine theoretical knowledge with practical exercises, offering a comprehensive preparation resource.

Example: Preparing for the AZ-104 Azure Administrator certification, you can follow the "Azure Administrator" learning path on Microsoft Learn, which covers managing Azure identities, governance, storage, compute, and virtual networks.

1. **Official Certification Guides**: Purchase or borrow the official certification guides published by Microsoft Press. These guides are structured around the exam objectives and provide in-depth coverage of the topics.
   - **Example**: The "Exam Ref AZ-303 Microsoft Azure Architect Technologies" book is an essential resource for candidates preparing for the Azure Solutions Architect certification.

2. **Hands-On Practice**: Build practical experience by implementing real-world scenarios in your Azure account. Azure offers a free account with $200 credit for the first 30 days, allowing you to experiment with different services.
   - **Example**: Gain hands-on experience with Azure virtual machines, Azure Functions, and Azure SQL Database by setting up a basic web application architecture within your Azure free account.

3. **Practice Tests**: Use practice exams to familiarize yourself with the format of the actual certification exam and to identify areas where further study is needed.
   - **Example**: Utilize the official Microsoft practice tests available through Pearson VUE or third-party practice exams from providers like Whizlabs for the AZ-204 Developing Solutions for Microsoft Azure exam.

4. **Study Groups and Forums**: Join study groups or online forums to connect with others preparing for the same certification. Sharing knowledge and experiences can provide additional insights and motivation.

   ○ **Example**: Participate in the Azure certification study group on LinkedIn or the Microsoft Tech Community forums, where you can ask questions, share study resources, and find study partners.

5. **Instructor-Led Training**: Consider enrolling in instructor-led training courses offered by Microsoft Learning Partners if you prefer a structured classroom setting or need more personalized guidance.

   ○ **Example**: Attend an instructor-led training course for the AZ-500 Azure Security Technologies certification, covering topics like identity and security, platform protection, security operations, and data and applications security.

Overview of Azure Certifications:

Azure certifications validate the skills and knowledge professionals have regarding Microsoft Azure's cloud services, ranging from foundational to advanced levels. These certifications are designed to align with various job roles in the cloud computing industry, including administration, development, security, data science, AI, and solutions architecture. Each certification pathway is structured to ensure that individuals are proficient in specific aspects of Azure.

Azure Fundamentals (AZ-900)

- **Target Audience**: Beginners to Azure, individuals looking to validate foundational cloud knowledge.
- **Skills Covered**: Basic understanding of cloud services, core Azure services, security, privacy, compliance, and trust, as well as Azure pricing and support.

- **Example Use Case**: Ideal for individuals new to cloud computing or those in non-technical roles such as sales, marketing, or management who require a basic understanding of Azure services.

Azure Administrator Associate (AZ-104)

- **Target Audience**: Azure administrators who manage cloud services related to computing, storage, network, and security.
- **Skills Covered**: Managing Azure identities and governance, implementing and managing storage solutions, deploying and managing Azure compute resources, configuring and managing virtual networks, and monitoring and backing up Azure resources.
- **Example Use Case**: Suitable for IT professionals responsible for the day-to-day management of Azure cloud services and infrastructure.

Azure Developer Associate (AZ-204)

- **Target Audience**: Developers designing, building, testing, and maintaining cloud applications and services on Microsoft Azure.
- **Skills Covered**: Developing Azure compute solutions, Azure Functions, web apps, managing Azure storage, implementing Azure security, monitoring, troubleshooting, and optimizing Azure solutions.
- **Example Use Case**: Developers working on building scalable and reliable cloud applications using Azure services.

Azure Solutions Architect Expert (AZ-303 & AZ-304)

- **Target Audience**: Solutions architects who have advanced experience and knowledge across various aspects of IT operations, including networking, virtualization, identity, security, business continuity, disaster recovery, data platforms, and governance.

- **Skills Covered**: Implementing and designing infrastructure solutions in Azure, configuring and deploying virtual machines, designing an Azure data solution, and determining workload requirements.
- **Example Use Case**: Experienced IT professionals who design cloud and hybrid solutions that run on Microsoft Azure, including aspects like compute, network, storage, and security.

Azure AI Engineer Associate (AI-102)

- **Target Audience**: Professionals specializing in the use of cognitive services, machine learning, and knowledge mining to architect and implement Microsoft AI solutions.
- **Skills Covered**: Planning and managing an Azure Cognitive Services solution, implementing computer vision solutions, natural language processing, conversational AI, and deploying AI solutions.
- **Example Use Case**: Individuals looking to develop AI solutions that leverage Azure Cognitive Services, Azure Machine Learning, and related AI technologies on Azure.

Azure Data Scientist Associate (DP-100)

- **Target Audience**: Data scientists and professionals applying machine learning and AI to implement and run machine learning workloads on Azure.
- **Skills Covered**: Setting up an Azure Machine Learning workspace, running experiments and training models, optimizing and managing models, and deploying machine learning solutions.

- **Example Use Case**: Data scientists who prepare data for training, perform feature engineering, create and validate machine learning models, and deploy automated, predictive APIs.

Preparation Pathways

For each certification, Microsoft provides a combination of free online learning paths on Microsoft Learn, instructor-led training courses, and hands-on labs. Additionally, practicing with real Azure environments and utilizing practice exams can greatly aid in understanding the material and passing the certification exams.

Azure certifications offer a structured path for professionals to validate their cloud expertise in various roles within the Azure ecosystem. From foundational knowledge to specialized areas like AI and data science, these certifications can significantly enhance an individual's employability and career progression in the rapidly evolving cloud computing industry.

Study Tips and Resources:

Achieving an Azure certification requires dedication, structured study, and the use of effective resources. This comprehensive guide provides study tips and outlines essential resources to help candidates efficiently prepare for Azure certification exams. Whether you're new to Azure or looking to advance your skills, these strategies and tools will support your certification journey.

Study Tips for Azure Certifications

1. **Understand the Exam Objectives**: Begin by reviewing the exam guide available on the official Microsoft Certification page. Understanding the scope, topics, and objectives of the exam is crucial for effective study planning.
2. **Create a Study Plan**: Allocate regular study times and set realistic goals based on your current knowledge and the exam date.

Breaking down the exam objectives into manageable topics can help organize your study sessions more effectively.

3. **Hands-On Practice**: Azure is primarily about practical application. Utilize the Azure free account to experiment with services covered in the exam. For example, if preparing for the Azure Administrator exam (AZ-104), practice creating and managing Azure virtual networks, VMs, and storage accounts.

4. **Leverage Microsoft Learn**: Microsoft Learn offers free, interactive learning paths aligned with Azure certification exams. These modules combine explanations, hands-on exercises, and knowledge checks. For instance, the "Azure Fundamentals" learning path is an excellent start for the AZ-900 exam candidates.

5. **Incorporate Various Study Resources**: Don't rely solely on one type of resource. Use a combination of official documentation, books, online courses, and practice tests. For example, the "Exam Ref series" by Microsoft Press provides detailed coverage of exam objectives.

6. **Join Study Groups and Forums**: Engaging with a community of learners can provide support, clarify doubts, and offer insights from different perspectives. Reddit and the Microsoft Tech Community have active Azure certification forums.

7. **Regularly Review and Test Your Knowledge**: Use practice tests to familiarize yourself with the exam format and identify areas needing improvement. Companies like MeasureUp and Whizlabs offer reputable practice exams for various Azure certifications.

Essential Resources for Azure Certifications

- **Microsoft Learn**: A comprehensive, free resource offering learning paths specifically designed for Azure certifications. Each path is structured around specific roles and certifications, like Azure Developer or Azure Solutions Architect.

- **Azure Documentation**: Official Azure documentation is an invaluable resource for understanding concepts, features, and best practices.
- **Online Courses and Tutorials**: Platforms such as Pluralsight, Udemy, and Coursera offer courses tailored to Azure certification exams. For example, Udemy frequently has updated courses on the latest Azure exam versions.
- **Books and Guides**: The "Exam Ref" books by Microsoft Press are tailored to each certification exam and provide in-depth coverage of the exam objectives. They're an excellent resource for deeper study.
- **Practice Tests**: Practice exams simulate the actual certification test environment, helping you gauge your readiness. MeasureUp is the official provider of practice tests for Microsoft certifications.
- **Community and Study Groups**: Platforms like LinkedIn, Reddit, and the Microsoft Tech Community offer forums and groups where you can ask questions, exchange study tips, and find study partners.

Example Study Resource Combination for AZ-104: Azure Administrator

Microsoft Learn Path: "Azure Administrator" for foundational concepts and exercises.

Azure Documentation: Deep dives into specific services like Azure Active Directory, Azure Backup, and Azure Monitor.

Udemy Course: "AZ-104: Microsoft Azure Administrator - Full Course" for video-based learning and additional practical scenarios.

Exam Ref AZ-104 Microsoft Azure Administrator: For comprehensive reading and understanding of complex topics.

MeasureUp Practice Test: To assess readiness and identify areas needing improvement before taking the official exam.

Preparing for Azure certifications demands a well-structured approach, utilizing a variety of learning resources and practical experiences. By following these study tips and leveraging the recommended resources, candidates can significantly enhance their understanding of Azure services and improve their chances of achieving certification. Remember, the journey to Azure certification is not just about passing an exam but building a solid foundation in cloud technologies that will support your professional growth.

Mock Exam Questions and Answers:

Mock exams are an essential part of preparing for Azure certifications. They not only familiarize you with the format and style of the actual exam but also help identify areas where further study is needed.

Azure Fundamentals (AZ-900)

Question 1: Which Azure service would you recommend for storing large amounts of unstructured data that is accessible from anywhere in the world?

1. Azure SQL Database
   B. Azure Virtual Machines
   C. Azure Blob Storage
   D. Azure Cosmos DB

Answer: C. Azure Blob Storage

Explanation: Azure Blob Storage is designed for storing large amounts of unstructured data, such as text or binary data, making it ideal for scenarios like storing documents, media files, backups, and logs. It is accessible from anywhere in the world over HTTP or HTTPS.

Azure Administrator (AZ-104)

Question 2: You need to ensure that an Azure Virtual Network named VNet1 can communicate securely with an on-premises network via a site-to-site VPN. Which Azure resource should you deploy?

1. Azure ExpressRoute
   B. Azure Virtual Network Gateway
   C. Azure Application Gateway
   D. Azure Traffic Manager

Answer: B. Azure Virtual Network Gateway

Explanation: The Azure Virtual Network Gateway is used to send encrypted traffic between an Azure virtual network and an on-premises location over the internet, making it the correct choice for setting up a site-to-site VPN.

Azure Developer (AZ-204)

Question 3: You are developing a .NET Core application that needs to read from and write to an Azure SQL Database. Which Azure service provides a managed identity that can be used for authenticating to the database without storing credentials in the application?

1. Azure Key Vault
   B. Azure Active Directory (Azure AD)
   C. Azure Managed Identity
   D. Azure App Service

Answer: C. Azure Managed Identity

Explanation: Azure Managed Identity provides Azure services with an automatically managed identity in Azure AD. You can use this identity to authenticate to any service that supports Azure AD authentication, including Azure SQL Database, without credentials embedded in your code.

Azure Solutions Architect (AZ-303 & AZ-304)

Question 4: You are designing a solution that includes a set of web apps and background processing tasks. The solution must be highly available and stateless. Which Azure service should you use to host the background processing tasks?

1. Azure Functions
   B. Azure Kubernetes Service (AKS)
   C. Azure Virtual Machines
   D. Azure Batch

Answer: A. Azure Functions

Explanation: Azure Functions is ideal for hosting stateless, highly available background processing tasks. It allows you to run small pieces of code (functions) in response to events, and it's serverless, meaning it scales automatically and you only pay for the compute time you consume.

Practicing with mock exam questions is a vital step in preparing for Azure certifications. It not only tests your knowledge but also builds confidence and helps reduce exam anxiety. The questions and answers provided here cover a range of Azure certifications and key topics likely to be encountered on the exams. Along with other study materials and hands-on practice, these mock questions can significantly aid in your exam preparation journey, enhancing your chances of success.

Conclusion

Preparing for Azure certifications demands a combination of theoretical learning, hands-on practice, and assessment through practice tests. By following a structured preparation strategy and leveraging the wide array of resources available, candidates can significantly increase their chances of passing Azure certification exams. Achieving an Azure certification not only validates your cloud skills but also enhances your professional credibility and career opportunities in the rapidly growing field of cloud computing.

16

APPENDICES

Appendix A: Azure Resources and Tools:

In the context of Azure certifications and general cloud computing education, having a consolidated list of Azure resources and tools can significantly enhance one's learning journey. This appendix aims to provide an overview of essential Azure resources and tools that are beneficial for students, professionals, and organizations looking to deepen their Azure knowledge and skills. Whether you're preparing for an Azure certification or looking to implement Azure solutions, these resources serve as a cornerstone for your cloud computing endeavors.

Azure Documentation

- **Overview**: The official Azure documentation (https://docs.microsoft.com/azure/) offers in-depth articles, tutorials, and quickstarts covering every Azure service. It is an indispensable resource for understanding specific Azure features, configurations, and best practices.
- **Example Usage**: Utilize the Azure documentation to explore the capabilities of Azure Virtual Machines, including setup, management, and scaling.

Microsoft Learn

- **Overview**: Microsoft Learn (https://docs.microsoft.com/en-us/learn/azure/) provides free, interactive learning paths and modules tailored to various roles and technologies within the Azure ecosystem. It's designed to help users build practical skills through guided learning and hands-on exercises.
- **Example Usage**: Follow the learning path for the Azure Fundamentals certification (AZ-900) to grasp the basics of cloud services, core Azure services, security, privacy, compliance, and trust.

Azure CLI and PowerShell

- **Overview**: The Azure Command-Line Interface (CLI) and PowerShell module are tools for managing Azure resources directly from the command line or through scripts, offering a flexible way to automate tasks.
- **Example Usage**: Create and manage Azure resources, such as virtual networks or storage accounts, using Azure CLI commands or PowerShell cmdlets to automate deployment processes.

Azure Portal

- **Overview**: The Azure Portal (https://portal.azure.com) is a web-based user interface for managing Azure subscriptions and services. It allows users to create, configure, and monitor Azure resources through a graphical interface.
- **Example Usage**: Deploy a new Azure App Service directly from the Azure Portal and configure its settings through the user interface.

Azure Free Account

- **Overview**: Azure offers a free account (https://azure.com/free) for new users, which includes $200 of Azure credits for the first 30 days and limited access to certain free services for 12 months, enabling hands-on practice without initial investment.
- **Example Usage**: Sign up for an Azure free account to experiment with creating and configuring Azure services like Azure SQL Database or Azure Functions.

Azure DevOps

- **Overview**: Azure DevOps (https://azure.com/devops) provides a suite of development tools for CI/CD, agile planning, repos, and artifact management, facilitating efficient software development and deployment in the cloud.
- **Example Usage**: Use Azure Pipelines within Azure DevOps to create and automate a CI/CD pipeline for deploying web applications to Azure App Service.

Visual Studio Code

- **Overview**: Visual Studio Code (VS Code) is a free, open-source code editor that supports development in multiple languages and has extensions for working with Azure services directly within the IDE.
- **Example Usage**: Install the Azure Functions extension in VS Code to develop, test, and deploy serverless Azure Functions locally.

Azure Marketplace

- **Overview**: The Azure Marketplace (https://azuremarketplace.microsoft.com/) is an online store offering thousands of

IT software, services, and solutions, including third-party applications and Azure Managed Applications.

- **Example Usage**: Browse and deploy pre-configured software solutions like WordPress or Drupal to Azure directly from the Azure Marketplace.

This appendix provides a snapshot of the wealth of resources and tools available for mastering Azure services and preparing for Azure certifications. By leveraging these resources, individuals and organizations can accelerate their Azure learning curve, stay updated with the latest Azure features, and effectively implement cloud solutions tailored to their needs.

Appendix B: Glossary of Azure Terms:

The cloud computing landscape, particularly within Microsoft Azure, is replete with specific terminology that can be complex for newcomers and even for experienced professionals. This appendix aims to demystify Azure-related terms, providing clear definitions for a selection of essential concepts and services within the Azure ecosystem. This glossary serves as a quick reference to enhance understanding and communication when working with Azure.

Azure Active Directory (Azure AD)

- **Definition**: A cloud-based identity and access management service that enables your employees to sign in and access resources.

Azure Blob Storage

- **Definition**: Microsoft's object storage solution for the cloud, designed to store large amounts of unstructured data, such as text or binary data.

Azure Cosmos DB

- **Definition**: A globally distributed, multi-model database service designed for high availability, low latency, and scalable applications.

Azure Functions

- **Definition**: A serverless compute service that enables you to run event-triggered code without having to explicitly provision or manage infrastructure.

Azure Kubernetes Service (AKS)

- **Definition**: A managed container orchestration service based on Kubernetes, making it easier to deploy, manage, and scale containerized applications.

Azure Machine Learning

- **Definition**: A cloud service for training, deploying, automating, and managing machine learning models.

Azure Resource Manager (ARM)

- **Definition**: A deployment and management service that provides a management layer enabling you to create, update, and delete resources in your Azure account.

Azure SQL Database

- **Definition**: A fully managed relational database service that offers SQL Server engine compatibility, built-in intelligence, and scalability.

Azure Virtual Machines (VMs)

- **Definition**: One of several types of on-demand, scalable computing resources offered by Azure, allowing users to deploy and manage VMs in the cloud.

Azure Virtual Network (VNet)

- **Definition**: A logically isolated network within Azure that enables Azure resources to securely communicate with each other, the internet, and on-premises networks.

Cognitive Services

- **Definition**: A collection of APIs, SDKs, and services available to developers to make their applications more intelligent and engaging by incorporating AI capabilities.

Container Instances

- **Definition**: Azure Container Instances (ACI) offers the fastest and simplest way to run a container in Azure, without having to manage any virtual machines or adopt additional services.

Event Hubs

- **Definition**: A big data streaming platform and event ingestion service, capable of receiving and processing millions of events per second.

Logic Apps

- **Definition**: A cloud service that helps you schedule, automate, and orchestrate tasks, business processes, and workflows when you need to integrate apps, data, systems, and services across enterprises or organizations.

Power BI

- **Definition**: A business analytics service by Microsoft that provides interactive visualizations and business intelligence capabilities with an interface simple enough for end users to create their own reports and dashboards.

Subscription

- **Definition**: A container for billing, management, and access control of resources in Azure. It holds the details of all your resources like virtual machines, databases, etc.

Appendix C: Further Reading and Resources:

To deepen your understanding of Azure and stay updated with the latest developments in cloud computing, a well-curated list of further reading and resources is invaluable. This appendix provides a selection of books, websites, blogs, and community forums that offer insightful information on Azure services, best practices, and innovative solutions. Whether you're preparing for Azure certifications or looking to implement Azure solutions, these resources can enhance your knowledge and skills.

Books

1. **"Azure for Architects"** by Ritesh Modi: This book offers a comprehensive guide to designing and implementing scalable and secure applications on Azure, covering a wide range of Azure services.
2. **"Pro Azure Governance and Security"** by Peter De Tender, David Rendon: A deep dive into the governance and security aspects of Azure, crucial for deploying secure and compliant Azure solutions.
3. **"Exam Ref series by Microsoft Press"**: Tailored to specific Azure certification exams, the Exam Ref books provide thorough coverage of the exam objectives, practical scenarios, and best practices for exam preparation.

Websites

1. **Azure Architecture Center** (https://docs.microsoft.com/en-us/azure/architecture/): Provides best practices, patterns, and guidance on building end-to-end solutions on Azure.
2. **Azure Updates** (https://azure.microsoft.com/en-us/updates/): The official source for the latest updates and news regarding Azure services and features.
3. **Microsoft Azure Blog** (https://azure.microsoft.com/en-us/blog/): Offers insights, announcements, and tutorials from Azure engineers and the cloud computing community.

Online Courses and Learning Platforms

1. **Microsoft Learn** (https://docs.microsoft.com/en-us/learn/azure/): Free, interactive learning paths and modules tailored to various Azure roles and technologies.
2. **Pluralsight** (https://www.pluralsight.com/): Offers a wide range of video courses on Azure topics, from fundamentals to advanced concepts, taught by industry experts.

3. **Udemy** (https://www.udemy.com/): Hosts affordable courses on Azure certifications and specific Azure services, suitable for learners at all levels.

Community Forums and Groups

1. **Microsoft Tech Community** (https://techcommunity.micro-soft.com/): A platform for connecting with peers and Azure experts, discussing best practices, and sharing knowledge.
2. **Stack Overflow** (https://stackoverflow.com/): A widely-used Q&A site where you can find answers to technical questions on Azure and contribute your own expertise.
3. **Reddit** (https://www.reddit.com/r/AZURE/): The Azure sub-reddit is a place for news, tips, and discussions on Azure services and solutions.

Blogs

1. **Azure Greg** (https://gregorsuttie.com/): Gregor Suttie, an Azure MVP, shares tutorials, study guides, and personal insights on Azure technologies.
2. **Thomas Maurer's Blog** (https://www.thomasmaurer.ch/): Focuses on Azure, cloud computing, and Microsoft technologies, providing valuable tips and walkthroughs.

YouTube Channels

1. **Microsoft Azure** (https://www.youtube.com/user/windowsazure): The official Azure YouTube channel, featuring tutorials, product overviews, and technical sessions from Azure experts.
2. **Azure Friday** (https://www.youtube.com/playlist?list=PLLasX02E8BPCNCK8Thcxu-Y-XcBUbhFWC):

Scott Hanselman hosts a series of informative and casual conversations with the engineers who build Azure services.

This collection of further reading and resources offers a comprehensive toolkit for anyone looking to master Azure. By exploring these materials, you can build a strong foundation in cloud computing, keep abreast of the latest Azure developments, and gain insights into practical implementations of Azure solutions. Whether you're a beginner or an experienced professional, these resources can support your journey toward becoming an Azure expert.

Conclusion

This glossary of Azure terms is not exhaustive but includes fundamental concepts and services that are crucial for anyone working with or learning about Azure. Familiarity with these terms will aid in navigating Azure's comprehensive suite of services and features more effectively.